CAN WE LIVE HERE?

CAN WE
LIVE HERE?

SARAH ALDERSON

BLINK
bringing you closer

Published by Blink Publishing
107-109 The Plaza,
535 King's Road,
Chelsea Harbour,
London, SW10 0SZ

www.blinkpublishing.co.uk
facebook.com/blinkpublishing
twitter.com/blinkpublishing

978-1-910536-11-7

A CIP catalogue of this book is available from the British Library.

Design by Blink Publishing
Printed and bound by Clays Ltd, St Ives Plc

1 3 5 7 9 10 8 6 4 2

Extract from *Why Be Happy When You Could Be Normal?* by Jeanette Winterson
reprinted by permission of Peters Fraser & Dunlop (www.petersfraserdunlop.com)
on behalf of Jeanette Winterson

Extract from *The Left Hand of Darkness* by Ursula Le Guin, reprinted by permission
of Little Brown Book Group Ltd

Papers used by Blink Publishing are natural, recyclable products made from
wood grown in sustainable forests. The manufacturing processes conform to the
environmental regulations of the country of origin.

Every reasonable effort has been made to trace copyright holders of material
reproduced in this book, but if any have been inadvertently overlooked the
publishers would be glad to hear from them.

Blink Publishing is an imprint of the Bonnier Publishing Group
www.bonnierpublishing.co.uk

For John and Alula

'It is good to have an end to journey toward;
but it is the journey that matters, in the end.'

Ursula Le Guin

CONTENTS

INTRODUCTION
9

PART I: THE BEFORE PART
13

PART 2: THE TRAVELLING PART
45

PART 3: THE LIVING PART
139

THE AFTER PART
283

ACKNOWLEDGEMENTS
287

INTRODUCTION

It all began on a plane back from Mexico. A Thompson charter plane, to be precise, complete with broken seats, a defunct media system, a half-naked drunk Brit kicking my seat while hollering for more Dos Equis and our screaming toddler kicking John in the nuts while hollering for Upsy Daisy.

I contemplated throwing open the emergency exit and sky-diving 37,000 feet. It was at that point, as I thought about going back to work the following Monday, that I wondered what the hell we were doing. Why were we saving every penny and every scrap of leave to go on a two-week holiday once a year? Why were we spending most waking moments juggling childcare, work, house-work and paying bills? Why couldn't we have stayed in Mexico like so many expats we'd met there, running businesses? If they could do it, why couldn't we?

'We don't speak Spanish,' John answered, which did slightly put a dampener on things.

But not too much of a dampener. We do like a challenge, after all. I went out and bought Tim Ferris's book *The 4-Hour Work Week* and fell in love with the concept of never working again. Or for just four hours a week, which seemed triflingly little – about as much time as I spent watching *Corrie*. And even though I was a tad, shall we say, *sceptical*, about the reality of only working 4 hours a week and still earning enough to keep myself in wine and chocolate, I silenced my very loud inner sceptic by cutting out her tongue. It sounded like a plan to me. And a great one at that! Go Tim!

I then read a book that totally changed my life: *Fuck It: The Ultimate Spiritual Way,* and I decided from that point on to say *Fuck It* to everything. Job? *Fuck It.* Scared of not having an income? *Fuck It.* Possibility of getting amoebic dysentery in India with a child in tow? *Fuck It.*

I stole some Post-its from work (and a Sharpie... *Fuck It!*) and together John and I wrote down our vision for the life we were trying to create. Our list included: better education for Alula, hot sun, sea, outdoors, no more commute, possibility of starting a business, freedom from nine-to-five, opportunity to do things we love, pursuit of outrageous potential (this had been in John's wedding vows) and more time for Alula.

We stuck the Post-its to our bedroom wall and I then decorated a board with pictures of turreted chateaux, tropical beaches and luxury villas... possibly a glittery unicorn or two made it on there as well.

It took us ten months from that point in early 2009 to make it out the door and onto the plane with just two rucksacks between us, a confused toddler in a pink tutu, and hearts bursting with an almost ketamine-level paralysing mix of excitement and fear.

At that point I had absolutely no clue how I was going to make money or survive financially. I mean, John was fine – he had transferable, useful skills and talents as a designer – but I had no skills whatsoever at all (no exaggeration here: I have a first in Italian Studies, which is about as useful as mudguards on a tortoise. I can order wine, pizza and ice cream, and swear like a banshee in Italian almost as well as I can in English (which is very well indeed), but that is about it).

Swimming one day in Beckenham public swimming baths, five months before leaving, I turned my attention to money-making ideas (being a feminist I was determined to contribute an equal share). Realising I couldn't just say '*Fuck It*' to the issue of no income, however much I wished I could, I came up with a list of people who were rich, to see if I could somehow emulate their success. Stephenie Meyer, who wrote the *Twilight* series of books, sprang instantly to mind. She'd become a gazillionaire, all for writing about sparkly vampires. Hah! I shall do the same, I thought. Except without the sparkly vampires. Four lengths later I had the kernel of a story idea. Being naive, I never bothered to Google how much most authors earn or I might never have touched pen to paper.

That night, in a state of blissful ignorance, I went home and, on a borrowed laptop from work, I began writing the story that would become *Hunting Lila*, my very first novel. Four months later I finished it. The day before we left on our round-the-world trip I sent it off to a dozen literary agents. About a month later, when I was on the beach in Goa, I received by email two offers of representation. I signed with my wonderful agent that week and within a month she had got me a two-book deal with Simon & Schuster.

Five years on and I'm on my seventh young adult book. Last year another big publisher asked if I wanted to write adult novels for them. (It turns out that I do, in fact, have a talent after all! I have a wild imagination and am very good at writing steamy sex scenes... my parents are so, so proud.)

Not happy with just writing books and a blog about our journey I decided that I wanted to write movies too, as that seemed to be where the real money was, so I read a few how-to books and then started doing that too. And somehow, through luck or just perseverance, I managed to get myself a film agent. So now, as well as churning out the books, I'm also paid, *paid* (it still boggles my mind), to write screenplays.

When I tell people my story, their jaws hit the floor. Hell, my own jaw resides there these days too. I'd never taken a creative writing course in my life. When I was eighteen, my English teacher told me not to bother reading English at university. *Hah to you with knobs on. Literally, in the case of my adult writing.*

As I said, we left the UK five years ago. We travelled the world. We lived in Bali for four of those years. Our daughter Alula (or, Lula as she likes to be known now, believing that Alula was her hippy Bali name and Lula is more suited to English climes) speaks with a transatlantic accent and calls pavements sidewalks. She mixes Bahasa Indonesian into her sentences, knows the life cycle of a rice paddy and prays to the Hindu god Ganesha (so do I, mind).

We've just left Bali and arrived back in the UK, a place I vowed I would never return to three seconds after stepping off the plane in India – our very first stop. But it isn't the end of our adventure, it's just the intermission. *Can We Live Here? Part Two* is just about to begin.

PART I: **THE BEFORE PART**

SEPTEMBER 2009

NIGHTMARES

Last night, I dreamed I was racing around a giant supermarket. It had towering, empty, white shelves. We were in India. I was searching desperately for something. I can't remember what now. But I do remember that I was projectile-vomiting all over the shelves.

The night before that, I dreamed – and this is a little weirder – that I was tied to a giant wooden cross (like the one from the *Jesus Christ Superstar* musical) and thrown into a swimming pool, face down.

The night before that... no... I'm not going to go there. Suffice to say that it was dark. And so graphic that the weirdos who occupy the darkest corners of the internet would probably look at me askance if I described it out loud. Which makes it sound like it was sexual – it wasn't (for me at any rate, though I'm sure for said weirdos it probably would be). It was more, shall we say, *scatological*, in nature.

I do what I always do with my hallucinogenic dreams: I turn to John and ask him to decipher them using his knowledge of pop psychology and his even greater knowledge of my neuroses.

Even he struggles to keep his face neutral at the symbolism of me drowning while being tied to a giant cross. He tells me that it's obvious: the fears I'm prodding down during the day are rearing up at night, bursting into my dreams like rabid, hungry beasts.

But I don't get it – *fear*? Why is fear hiding out in my subconscious? The first week after I slammed my resignation letter down on my CEO's desk, the smile that was splitting my face was so wide I was in danger of needing stitches to my cheeks. I wasn't afraid. I was euphoric! But now the euphoria has started to fade. Which sucks because I can't get it back. You can only resign once from the same job, after all.

So I start blaming the voice of authority in my head for seeding the fear. Occasionally I hear it mumbling loudly, in a voice that sounds a little like my bank manager's, that I'm 'insane to give up a well-paid job in the middle of a recession'. I'll be typing something and the voice will start ordering me to shuffle over to my boss on bended knees and beg for my resignation letter to be shredded.

Luckily, before I can do this, the voice of the 16-year-old who normally rules the airwaves in my head (and convinces me that I'm not too old to shop at Topshop) is like, 'whatever, shuttup!' to the authority voice and she's shouting louder and has a wicked eyeball roll, so I'm listening to her.

Anyway, I don't need a job for the next year because the bank is nice (and fabulously gullible) and think we're getting a new bathroom, so we have more money in our account right now than we've probably ever had or will likely ever have again (I budgeted for a marble-topped, gold-tapped bathroom that would make a Saudi Prince's eyes pop with jealousy). Hurrah!

I have thus declared to John that when we combine the bathroom slush fund with the money in the bump account (money we saved for a second child that we're now definitely *not* having … because why, God, why would anyone do this twice?) we will have enough to see us through on our journey.

'We will be living cheaply in South East Asia on rice and beans,' I tell John when he looks doubtfully at the sums I've scribbled on the back of a crumpled, tea-stained bank statement. He suggests we couchsurf – this thing where you sleep on strangers' sofas – to help stretch our meagre budget further.

I smile and nod and tell him that sounds like a great idea, though in my head I'm thinking, 'Um, *you* can couchsurf'. Alula and I meanwhile will be checking into a hotel. One with a mini-bar and room service and little testers and sewing kits that I can steal, and an actual bed, not a couch, to sleep on.

OCTOBER 2009

EXPLAINING THE WORLD TO A TODDLER

'So, Lula, do you know what we're doing next year?'

It's a stupid question because for Alula next year could just as well be in five minutes' time. She thinks her birthday is every single day of the year, that Christmas is next week and that Claude, her favourite person in the whole world, is coming to stay in her pink house at the weekend, when she is 18.

'We're going travelling,' she answers.

She says 'travelling' with the gravitas of Captain Scott discussing his plan to take a little walk on a snowy Antarctic afternoon. Yet I am fairly sure she knows not what this means. So I attempt to explain several concepts at once in a way that a three year old with a princess obsession can understand. I have to break it to her that:

1) Her world map puzzle (age 3+) is not a direct representation of the globe. Which is in reality neither flat nor made up of interlocking pieces.

2) As such, we won't therefore be seeing kangaroos half the size of Australia or a Golden Gate Bridge that stretches 300 kilometres out to sea.

3) Travelling means leaving behind most of her toys and books, including Marcel Mouse and her fairy wings, *but* there is room for her pink flower princess dress, so she mustn't panic.

4) Molly the cat won't fit in her Upsy Daisy backpack.

I wonder at what point when we're away she'll turn to us and say: 'Can we go home now?'

In Mexico it took about a week. When we went camping in Somerset last May it took her about an hour. To be fair, it took me 15 minutes.

At least, though, she doesn't understand the concept of time. So when we say: 'Not for seven more months darling,' she'll probably think that that means on her birthday this coming Friday, just before Father Christmas arrives with a sack-load of presents and the day after Claude moves into her pink Wendy House.

NOVEMBER 2009

HOW TO PACK UP AN ENTIRE HOUSE IN THE MANNER OF A TATE INSTALLATION

Tomorrow we are having people around for dinner. Our friend Claude will be having his in Lula's pink Wendy house if she gets her way. He will be wearing a prince outfit, she a bridal veil made of her christening blanket and a Rambo-style hairband.

Explaining to her that Claude already has a girlfriend and wants to eat at the grown-ups' table is the least of my worries right now though. The house is so full of boxes it's like the Amazon warehouse and I'm not sure we can find the table in among them all, in which case Claude will be the only one eating.

Packing up is quite a task. My friend is moving house and I ask her how she is managing to stay away from the Valium and keep sane. She looks at me blankly and then tells me they're getting in packers. I stare at her amazed that there is such a thing (I've never moved house before) and for about five seconds I can breathe again.

Then I realise that packers are for when you are *moving* house and not when you are squeezing excess furniture into your spare garage among all your mother's rotting junk, and have no new house to put your belongings into. We are essentially trying to shove a whole house, minus a few bits of furniture, into one rucksack. Surprisingly, it won't all fit.

The hallway has become my dumping ground for things I may possibly want to take but can't quite make up my mind on, like: flip-flops, out-of-date sun cream, flash cards (someone's going to have to take over where the preschool will leave off) and a pile of books so high it's skyscrapering the wardrobe. And we're not even leaving for another 18 weeks. When I work that ou I start to hyperventilate again and miss letters off words when typing.

I stare lovingly at our Philippe Starck kitchen stools for half an hour. Then at the railway sleeper coffee table that we found in a shop in Brighton. It feels like I'm renouncing middle-classness in one fell swoop.

I go upstairs and kneel before my wardrobe. I have to put my head between my knees. I decide I must give every piece and all my shoes a turn before I pack everything away and entomb it in our loft – a bit like I used to do with my teddy bears at bedtime when I was a kid, rotating them on a nightly basis so none of them would feel left out.

How will I be able to whittle it all down though? What will I do with my excessively large collection of nail polish? I look up and see the three-metre squared canvas on the wall that John and I made by covering our naked selves in paint and rolling all over it. (If you look closely, those two orbs – that's my butt. Who the hell is going to want that on their wall? Possibly the Tate. I will call and check.) Then I remember I have Molly the cat to rehouse and must get on with figuring that out.

You can see where my priorities lie.

JOHN CAN'T TAKE HIS VINYL COLLECTION WITH US

There is a wall of records in John's study. Roughly 5,000 in total. They make up the third person in our marriage but I have long since come to love them, a bit like Keira Knightley does in that movie *The Duchess* when that other woman who shacks up in her house sleeps with her husband.

In a remarkably similar set-up, John spends most of his nights with his vinyl collection, but, just like Keira, I've learned to not be jealous. They make him happy and, when he puts on a good disco classic, they make me happy too. Once, someone asked him what he would save first in a fire – his records or me – and he actually paused. He paused before answering, 'You. Quickly.'

I have no doubt that he has counted each and every one of his records and that if he had more time they would be sorted by alphabetical order and cross-referenced by genre. He has also already sourced a shipping quote, on the off-chance that we do decide we are moving to Australia or Bali or America. I wind him up by asking what he'll do if the ship sinks or if it gets captured by Somalian pirates. I want to know how much he'd pay in ransom. He doesn't answer but we both know that it would undoubtedly be way more than he'd pay for me.

I go stare at the wall of records, like a mountaineer contemplating the north face of the Eiger. I look at the loft planks John has bought. He is intending to pack all this vinyl into boxes and then put it up in the loft.

Good luck with that, I think. Never have I been so pleased to have the bad-back excuse. Sorry, darling. I so want to help you but I just can't chance it, herniated disc and all.

John and I have very different approaches to packing and cleaning – to living, in fact. He does detail. I do not. He does perfection, ponderously. I do imperfection, fast. Somewhere there is a middle ground but we struggle to find it. I guess all marriages are a compromise.

To illustrate this in the context of the house clearance currently going on, yesterday we decided to tackle the garage across the way – the one that is full of my mother's junk. The one that should have a sign over it reading: Abandon all hope, ye who enter here.

I decided the best way to deal with it was to not look in any of the boxes currently stuffed in there but to just shove them in the car and take them to the dump. My mum will probably never even remember what she stored in here… I hope.

John's approach, which I gawped at open-mouthed, was to sort through each box, putting everything into *Freecycle, recycle, eBay* and *dump* piles and then sweep out the garage. I'm literally dumb-struck. I would never have even thought about doing that. The effort. The point! But the result is amazing. We could almost set up home in the garage once he is done. It is perfect. Ready to accept the offerings of furniture and household goods that I have boxed up ready to go.

Then John looks at the boxes I have sealed up. They are the card-board equivalent of badly preserved mummies, ones embalmed by a drunk priest, perhaps – parcel tape wrapped around and around them in ever increasing desperation, vainly trying to contain con-tents that are clearly the wrong size and shape for the box.

'Dude,' I say to John. 'They're just going into the garage, who cares?'

'I hope it's not my stuff,' he comments as he eyes them suspi-ciously.

'As if I'd dare,' I mumble.

IS THIS ALL JUST ONE BIG AVOIDANCE STRATEGY?

When I was 17 I made my boyfriend at the time kiss me. He had pustular tonsillitis. I ended up in an isolation unit on an IV drip.

But I did get out of taking my mock A-level exams.

I use this as an example of how far I will go to avoid doing things I don't like doing… like running (I wonder whether herniating a disc in my back was a deliberate act to avoid ever having to run again, but then I remember that the same boyfriend I had at 17 was responsible for herniating it, so scratch that). Other things I avoid doing: emptying the bin, answering the phone, checking my bank balance, parallel parking, exercising, shopping in Bromley.

Today I am wondering whether – like snogging someone with pustular tonsillitis – packing up our house and travelling around the world is another extreme reaction to doing things I don't like doing. In this instance, looking for a new job and chairing the Residents' Association, which got foisted on me last year because the average age of all the other neighbours is 112.

Maybe, I'm just involved in some massive avoidance strategy for dealing with things that suck. Wow. It has taken me twelve years, a tonsillectomy, queuing for 50 hours in the Halifax to draw cheques for the communal gardener, as well as several thousand pounds in airfares to reach this epiphany.

I prod the epiphany for holes and can't find any. My first reaction when having to deal with anything unpleasant (like scavenging through the job pages of *The Guardian*, answering questions on Henry VIII's reformation and neighbours asking me for my opinion on the buddleia) is to run. Which is ironic because I just said I don't like running. You know what I mean.

My best friend Vic lives in Grand Cayman. It's in the Caribbean – think *Pirates of the Caribbean* but with lots of accountants instead of pirates. She, her lovely husband and her gorgeous baby upped sticks and moved there last year. They have a boat, a swimming pool and, did I mention, a boat? (Which they had no clue how to sail – I love that about them.)

Admittedly, there is no shopping on the island unless you're after duty-free bling or some rum cake. Not much in the way of entertainment either – unless you like paying over \$100 and taking tea at the Ritz – and, on the downside, they have to contend with the odd hurricane and the fact that the island is populated by accountants and lawyers. But on the upside they do have near year-round sunshine and a boat (did I mention the boat?) that you can sail to Stingray City and Starfish Alley.

When I went out there for their wedding, being on that boat deck was the closest I've ever come to feeling like a Bond girl.

I ask Vic if she has plans to come back to England and she wrinkles her nose at me. It looks doubtful. She mentions the British Virgin Islands or the US or Canada as a possible next stop. I feel inspired and I realise that even if this whole project of ours is an avoidance strategy and I'm just trying to escape things I don't like doing, does it actually matter?

Isn't that a sane thing to do? Wouldn't it be *in*sane to keep on doing things I don't like?

STARBUCKS IS DEFINITELY TO BLAME

A decaf skinny extra-hot tall white caffe mocha – hold the cream – for £2.70.

The man at Starbucks' nostrils flare – but he doesn't bat an eyelid because he is used to my coffee requirements by now. But the thing is, neither do I. Not so much as a flicker. And I really should be batting an eyelid. If I added up how much I spend on coffee, in Pret a Manger, and on Walkers crisps and Minstrels from the vending machine at work – hell, the amount I spend on Percy Pigs weekly – it would likely plug the national debt.

It hit me how much I fritter on stuff I don't actually need (decaf coffee – the point? And from Starbucks – I'm appalled at myself) just yesterday when I was talking to a friend and rhapsodising about an amazing body moisturiser I've recently discovered. She asked how much it cost. Eighteen pounds, I told her. She laughed and told me that was crazy expensive.

It's hardly Crème de la Mer, I thought, but then it hit me. She was right. Spending £18 on moisturiser is crazy. Spending £2.70 on coffee that doesn't even taste of coffee or zing you with a caffeine hit of happiness is crazy.

Keeping M&S afloat however… definitely not crazy. A world without Percy Pigs and M&S knickers is a more troubling vision even than the one painted by Cormac McCarthy in *The Road*.

In the light of this rude but timely financial awakening, I am making it a point to notice the price of things. I haven't yet got to the point of stopping actually buying things – let's not get ahead of ourselves, people. One thing at a time. It's like AA. It will be a 12-step process and only by the 12th step will I actually be able to keep walking on past the pink gelatinous farmyard animals.

I have just done a quick sum and realised that I'm spending approximately £1,000 a year on Starbucks coffee that doesn't taste of coffee, Percy Pigs and Walkers crisps. I wish now that I'd saved that money. Not only would I be approximately ten pounds thinner, I would also be way richer, and we could use that extra money to fund another month in India. Or buy poker chips in Vegas. Or pay for nights in hotels with actual beds and room service and mini-bars while John couchsurfs.

Huh. I sigh at the realisation that that's not going to happen now because I frittered away the money on sugar hits and making the shareholders of big corporations happy.

I'm so depressed at my shortsightedness that I need a packet of Percy Pigs just to get over it.

LULA THE CLIMATE-CHANGE PROTESTER

John and I are standing, frozen, clutching a box roughly the size of a small dining table between us. The box is also roughly the same size as a Winnie the Pooh plastic aeroplane that makes taking-off sounds and engine-in-trouble sounds and lets you store your hair-clips and teddies and Mummy's keys and loose change in it.

We have been caught red-handed by Lula. She is standing between us and we are poised for the monumental outburst that is about to happen any second now, because in moving the box we have inadvertently started it jingling.

Lula's look of horror is replaced by an ear-piercing scream: 'Why are you putting my plane in a box?'

John and I exchange a glance. The kind of glance that two people who've been caught by a serial killer would exchange if said serial killer then asked them to decide who got chopped into pieces first.

'Why didn't you take the batteries out?' John hisses at me.

I shrug. 'Because you need a screwdriver and that was way too much effort.'

He shakes his head at me in disgust while Lula attempts to launch herself on top of the box like a climate-change protester onto the head of a riot policeman.

'Sweetheart, darling,' I say. 'It's just going on a little trip. To the garage.'

'But I want my plane!' There are tears now, coming thick and fast. 'Why is it in a box?'

'Because, remember what we're doing next year?' I say.

She sobs. 'We're going travelling.'

'That's right. So the plane has to go into the box and then into the garage for storage.'

'But why?'

'Because we're renting out the house.'

'But why?'

'Because,' I sigh, 'we need someone else to pay the bills and mortgage when we're away.'

'But why?'

'So that we can afford to buy you hairclips and food and clothes – and stickers!' I say, suddenly inspired, thinking that I've surely hit on a winning argument for her three-year-old ears.

She considers it for a moment. 'But I want my plane!' she yells.

By now the box is in the hallway where John has dumped it. Lula starts tugging frantically at the brown parcel tape circumventing the box, trying to break into it to rescue her plane. She is wearing her ballet outfit and tutu so it looks quite comical. I have to bodily remove her with promises that by the time we get back from ballet Daddy will have taken the plane out of the box.

I push her out the door towards the car and hiss up the stairs at John to make sure he's moved the box into the garage before we get back from ballet. Out of sight, out of mind. She won't remember it in an hour, I desperately hope.

When we get back an hour later though we haven't even swung into the drive and Lula is already wondering out loud whether Daddy has gotten her plane out of the box.

Damn, I think, well at least he'll have moved the box so I can just tell her that he can get it later. ('Later' being a point in time that will forever be two minutes away.)

We enter the hallway. Has he moved the box?

What do you reckon?

GIVING UP STEAK NIGHT WEDNESDAYS

'When I look at a cow I just want to eat it.'

'When I look at a cow I see a cow,' John says, looking at me weirdly.

'But when I look at a vegetable patch I just see dirt,' I continue, ignoring him. 'I think this means I am a carnivore. Nature made me this way.' I shrug. 'I can't fight nature.'

The conversation has come about because of the recent Stern Review and Paul McCartney and their combined vegetarian effort to save the world. In theory, I agree. In theory, I agree that they should make cows that don't fart. They can splice genes and clone animals yet they can't make a cow that doesn't fart. Why not? I don't think they're trying hard enough.

'It's not just the farting,' John says to me.

Yeah, whatever, I think. (Actually, I think I say that out loud.) 'What will we do in India?' I muse. 'We shouldn't eat meat there, apparently.' Richard, John's brother, who lives in India, says we'll see the butchers' shops and become vegetarian on the spot.

They will have to be pretty fly-blown, those carcasses though, to make me not want to eat them, I think to myself. Something worse even than a scene from *Saw VI*. I love steak. I love burgers. I love meat. Rich is a vegetarian – the meat counter at Waitrose is repellent to him – so our standards are vastly different. Also in India a lot of people are Hindu and cows are holy and you can't eat them; can't even look at them and think tasty thoughts, I imagine. I am quite distressed by all this – not least because this will mean the cessation of Steak Night Wednesdays, a weekly tradition in our house.

Due to a miscommunication between John and myself though, tonight is a Wednesday, and we have had to forego steak and make do with a vegetable stir-fry. I'm now so hungry I could eat my own arm. But John's arm is tastier. I actually just took a bite out of it. See, I am a carnivore.

'We'll have to give up meat,' I moan, already mourning its loss. 'We'll have to be vegetarian – at least until we get to Australia.'

'But this whole trip is about trying new things and breaking away from our comfort zones,' John says. 'I'm going to do yoga. I've never done it before.'

I wrinkle my nose. Yoga. I used to do that until giving birth to Alula herniated my spine in several places. I think hard for a moment. 'I'm going to do Buddhism,' I tell John.

He raises an eyebrow at me.

Even I have to laugh.

JUMPING OFF CLIFFS WHILE DRINKING GALICIAN HOMEMADE HOOCH

'You're not stepping off the escalator, Sarah.'

'I'm not?'

'No, you're jumping off a cliff.'

'Oh.' That doesn't sound like something I want to be doing. But I don't want the panic to show on my face so I reach for my glass and laugh loudly while swigging back the contents in two gulps.

I'm having lunch (wine, wine, some more wine followed by some Galician hooch that is making my eyes water) with my ex-boss. He's like the oracle. When he talks, I listen. When he used to chuck things at my head, I ducked. Now the only things he's chucking at me are metaphors I can't unravel.

It started with me explaining to him about our grand plan to go travelling and how, to stop panicking at the thought I was committing career suicide, I keep reminding myself that I could always step back onto the career escalator if I wanted to. (After three months of him chucking things at my head he'd promoted me from being his PA to a project management role and from there I'd climbed the ladder to senior management.)

But now he's just told me that I'm not stepping off an escalator, I'm jumping off a cliff.

I'm not sure I like this. It doesn't sound too safe. Or sane. I prefer the escalator metaphor. No one has killed themselves jumping off an escalator, that I know of (I'm scared to Google it and find out).

More importantly it's far easier to step back onto an escalator. Not so a cliff. That would involve climbing, if I even survived the fall onto sharpened rocks below in the first place. But maybe he has a point. Somewhere in the fog that is my brain, I'm sure he has a point. Thing is, I can't actually figure out what it is because I have managed to drink holes the size of China through my mind.

As well as feeling faintly nauseous and head-spinny, I also come away from lunch feeling inspired and filled with self-belief. The kind of self-belief that only alcohol can fuel, but I know it will soon wear off.

However, in the cold and sober light of my office that afternoon, I recall that by saying I was jumping off a cliff he meant there was no way I'd want to come back to London to a similar job, that opportunities would arise and I'd end up somewhere completely different, doing something completely different.

Things are up and down at the moment and it's exhausting me.

One day I'm completely fanatical about how everything is going to be amazing and wonderful. I look at John and rave at him about how brilliant it is and how we will find some hidden talent and we will make enough money to live on the beach in a gorgeous house in a bohemian dream (the vision goes all blurry at the point where I have to think about what I'm actually doing to earn money). Then the next day I'm in the depths of despair, turning to John every five minutes for reassurance that everything is going to be OK, that we aren't crazy and doing the stupidest thing ever.

Is jumping off a cliff really a good idea? Should we at least attach a bungee cord first?

I AM TAUGHT A LESSON BY LIFE

If I had a bullet and a gun right now I'd kill myself.
Ahhhhhhhhhhhhhhhhhhhhhhhhhh I'm definitely going to kill myself.

I am sending texts to my work-husband. People are walking between the tables like prison guards at The Maze and I'm half-expecting a baton to come crashing down on my illicitly texting hand.

I'm at some sort of un-conference, which is sort of like a conference that the organisers don't want to call a conference because they want to seem cool, but by calling it an un-conference they're just proving how desperately uncool they actually are. Anyway, I think they could have better marketed it as an alternative to a fume-filled car.

It's kind of ironic that this mental torture is happening in Amnesty International's HQ. I want to start screaming about human rights violations but then I turn and see the pictures on the wall of refugees and starving children, and guilt swallows my temper tantrum. I decide to focus instead… on what my feedback comments are going to be.

At 1.01pm I can be found propping up the bar in the nearby Barley Mow pub where I have fled so fast that the other people at the un-conference are probably still rising from their seats to join the queue for limp sandwiches while I am already pouring a cold beer down my throat.

I contemplate staying here all afternoon making friends with Negra Modelo but then a woman with a voice like she's been dragged over hot coals whilst smoking fifty B&H all at once sits next to me and orders a double Baileys.

I see the future and decide to be brave and return.

Refreshed from my pint and a quick spin around the shops, I bounce back into the room where people are still eating the soggy sandwiches. My bounce quickly flattens out.

The afternoon session trudges by, though they cut the last hour – something I feel I can take some credit for: having an un-poker face can work wonders. Without saying a word I have curdled the atmosphere to such a degree that four grown adults feel the only cure is to bring proceedings to a premature close. Bliss – there is now time for a quick file-and-varnish at Nails Inc. Don't tell my boss.

Yesterday, I muse, I was waxing lyrical about how great work was and how I was having second thoughts about leaving. Well now, life – that great, wise teacher – has ripped the rose-tinted contact lenses from my eyes and reminded me that there's quite a lot I don't enjoy in my day-to-day working life.

Today has once and for all cured me of my fear of jumping off the cliff. I am now running full-tilt towards the precipice.

MONKEY-BEATING AND RABIES

'Note that rabid animals may pose a risk.'

Quite why I have decided to read the health risks and annoyances section of the *Lonely Planet* guide to India is unclear; given that we've already resigned and forked out several thousand pounds on tickets, it's all a little too late. I should just have skipped straight to the photos of Goan beaches. But now, with words like 'encephalitis' teasing me with their erotic Japanese allusions, I have to keep reading.

After the diarrhoea comes a list of diseases so terrifying I have to check I'm still reading a travel guide and not a sci-fi horror novella. It goes like this – Japanese encephalitis (causes brain damage), meningitis (can kill), hepatitis (I skip this as I have had the shot), malaria, thrush, fungal infections, respiratory infections, swine flu, avian flu and there, in block letters: RABIES.

I don't care so much for me, but what if Alula decides to pet a monkey? Or refuses to take her malaria pill? We can't even get her to take a teaspoon of Calpol when cunningly mixed in a bucket of chocolate butter icing. How will we get an anti-malarial down her gullet? Maybe in the manner of giving deworming tablets to dogs? We will have to clamp her mouth shut and stroke her throat in downwards motions. Suppositories won't work, will they, given the likelihood of Delhi belly?

I re-read the health warnings again, hoping my first alarmed speed-read has made me miss vital information like 'this last occurred in 1976 so don't worry about it' or 'beer will provide adequate immunisation'. But no, the words haven't changed.

'Honey,' I say to John. 'I'm having second thoughts. Again.'

'Too late,' he says and continues packing away his vinyl.

I return to the *Lonely Planet* and start to analyse every sentence. The very fact they've included fungal infections and thrush arouses my suspicions and I nod happily to myself having figured it all out. They're blatantly covering all bases! The fact the *Lonely Planet* has only just stopped short of including strep throat, period pains and ingrown toenails makes it clear that they're thinking bases, coverings and litigations by ambulance chasers. (The *LP* didn't tell us about the monkeys – *sue them!*)

I flick the page to see whether they're listing things like appendicitis too. But that just takes me to the list of annoyances – corrupt policemen, wandering hands, pickpockets, violent robbery. Not much different from taking the tube in London then.

So, feeling a bit better about it all, I start a list of things to pack: rehydration sachets, Calpol, anti-malarials, Percy Pigs and, last but not least, a scalpel. The last three to be used in conjunction… we used to do this with pills for our dog.

DECEMBER 2009

WHICH COSTS MORE: CILLIT BANG OR A TIGER?
'They're moving into our house so you can buy me Percy Pigs.'

I love Lula's mind, her reductive view of the world. I wish life really was that simple. I wish I could spend £1,300 a month on Percy Pigs but that wouldn't simplify things, it would only complicate them – I'd be unable to squeeze my obese frame through the doorway to fend off the bailiffs.

The reason she thinks the rent is keeping her in Percy Pigs is because I have failed to explain the concept of a mortgage to her.

Because I couldn't explain it to myself let alone to a child.

I'm now pondering how to start explaining the concept of money to her before she thinks I can buy her a tiger or something. She knows it doesn't grow on trees because that's my standard response when she asks why she can't buy everything pink in Sainsbury's, including Cillit Bang. But that's where her knowledge stops.

'Mummy, when we go travelling we are going to have so, so, so much fun.'

'Yes, darling, we are going to have lots of fun.' (I try not to think about the rabies or malaria.)

Oh God, I think to myself. Now what am I going to do? In an attempt to make Lula feel better about leaving behind all her friends and toys, I have been spinning her various scenarios involving buckets, spades, beaches, platypuses, tigers, elephants, buried treasure, fairy palaces, real princesses, Mickey Mouse and kangaroos. No wonder she's finding it hard to get to sleep tonight. I did this because I wanted to prepare her for diarrhoea and feeling ill. I figured if she was really excited about the princesses and the kangaroos she'd not demand to go home when she gets 'farty poppy tummy'.

The plan sounded good in my head but now she's so excited I'm not sure our trip can possibly ever live up to her expectations

'Mummy, when we go to the moon we'll have so much fun.'

'Yes, we will – wait… did you say moon?'

'Yes.'

'Er, we're not going to the moon, my love.'

'Why not?' she asks.

'Because it's India we're going to, and because we'd need a spaceship to go to the moon and we only have a Honda.'

'Can we get a spaceship?' she asks.

'No, it would cost a lot of money.'

She frowns at me like I've told her we can't buy any more chocolate buttons. And I wonder why I didn't explain the concept of money back when we bought her that Fisher Price till. It would have been a whole lot easier.

BURROWING THROUGH SHIT

Opposite me are six men in suits. They are grey and weary and joyless. Having said that, I am pretty joyless too right now. I wish they would stop holding these conferences on high floors. It's just tempting fate. Either I'm going to jump or I'm going to push someone. Though, as it's a voluntary sector conference, I'd have to navigate around way too many soapboxes to make it to the window and I'm too lazy for that.

After the first three syllables spoken by the keynote speaker, my brain, of its own accord, switches off like when they stick a knife in the cerebral cortex of a Terminator T-800 model to stop it rampaging. I know that my work-husband Andrew is bored too because out of the corner of my eye I can see he is mauling his pen like a hungry cocker spaniel chewing on a bone. This is a dead giveaway that he is either thinking or bored. In this case I opt for bored because there's nothing to be thinking about other than how to make it to the windows, and he has just reached for his stash of Rennie and popped one, which means he is bored *and* frustrated. Join the club. I wish he had something stronger I could pop.

I gaze out of the window and see the tower of the Truman brewery and sigh audibly. Four days suddenly seems like a very, very long time. As in, about as far away as the Paleozoic era looking backwards. It feels like we'll have colonised the moons of Jupiter before I get to hand over my work security pass.

In truth, I am feeling very ambivalent about four days' time, because in four days' time life as I know it ends. Maybe I'm institutionalised – like the guy from *The Shawshank Redemption* who gets paroled and finds freedom all too much, so hangs himself. At least I'll have a soapbox to stand on if I choose to do the same.

I wasn't this freaked out before childbirth. I was so ready for that. So ready, in fact, that at eight-months pregnant I was sharpening the knife and preparing to give myself a C-section, so done was I with waiting. This, however, this stepping into the realms of the unemployed and possibly insane, this I'm not ready for at all. I have no idea how I'm going to feel on Friday when I wake and realise that I don't have to go to work – that place where I've spent most of my time for the past eight years and which has occupied way too much of my brain space.

Mostly, I'm scared about who I'll be after Friday. I will be me, of course, but I'll be a different me. I will not have a title for one thing.

I am starting to understand why Princess Di fought to keep her title in the divorce. One grows very fond of such things. If I'm not Head of Projects, what will I be? I try to list all the other things I am known as, to make myself feel less of a nobody: Mummy mo (to the bean), sugarplum (to a select few), lardarse (to my brother – this doesn't make me feel better, strangely), blossom (to my dad). Once I was called a MILF by a random stranger … that does make me feel better.

Where am I going with this? I know this is classic psychotherapy material. I must rid myself of ego and all that, but one thing at a time. I need to rid myself of my security pass first and that's going to be a big enough challenge.

Then I wonder what other things might change after Friday, other than my bank balance, my alarm-setting and my freedom from conferences that make me want to leap from high buildings. I wonder whether certain character traits I possess might disappear along with my business cards. For example, what will happen to my perennial impatience, intolerance of stupidity, cynicism, sarcasm, brusqueness and flaring nostrils? Will they vanish too? Yeah. Not likely.

I'll keep you posted.

POVERTY AND BURSTING A BIG PINK BUBBLE

'I want a magazine!' Alula demands as soon as we swish through the doors of Sainsbury's.

I push the trolley past the CBeebies magazines with their cello-phaned child-magnet landfill toys.

'I want a lemon,' she says next, pointing at the melons.

'I want Moreganix!' she says whilst trying to grab six pink packets of Organix in her arms as we wheel past.

'I want buttons.'

'Yeah, well I want to win the lottery and Ryan Gosling to build me a house with a wrap-around veranda, and I'd love a free Ocado delivery every day. Sometimes life just doesn't work out the way we want it to,' I say wearily.

'It's not fair.'

'Well, life's not fair, my sweet.'

'But I *want* buttons.'

'I want a child who doesn't say "I want" all the time and who actually bothers to say please. And if you stand up once more in the trolley we're going to walk out of this supermarket with nothing. We'll put the Moreganix right back. In fact, we'll put everything back. And you'll never eat another chocolate button ever again, ever, so help me God.'

'NOOOOOOOOOO!!!!'

When we're in the car and Lula is eating her Moreganix contentedly I say to her, 'You know, you've really got to stop asking for things all the time. This incessant "I want, I want" is just so spoilt.'

'No, it's not.'

'Er, actually, yes it is.'

It's pantomime season in the car.

'Oh no it isn't.'

I hate panto. 'You know, really, you're a very lucky girl.'

'Why?'

'Because you have a pink bedroom and a mummy who buys you Organix and rents you *Sleeping Beauty* on-demand and a daddy who reads you bedtime stories and puts up with you jumping on him every morning, and there are a lot of children out there who don't even have enough to eat, let alone free rein at the DVD store. Some don't even have mummies and daddies.'

Have I gone too far? As soon as I say the words I regret it.

Alula stops munching her Morganix. 'Why don't they have mummies and daddies?' she asks in wonderment.

I think about HIV and AIDS and malaria and the fact that almost 99 per cent of maternal deaths happen in developing countries and think perhaps that's all a bit much for a three-year-old to comprehend. We haven't done death yet. How do you explain why some people are born rich and some are born poor? Why some are born in countries that give you decent healthcare and to households with three televisions, while other children are born and live in slums and are given no opportunities to do anything – let alone choose which overpriced organic corn snacks they want. I can't even explain to her why daddy doesn't have boobies or why she can't open every window of her advent calendar at once. These are BIG topics. About capitalism, inequality, corrupt pharmaceutical companies and governments, injustice, sexism and death. I struggle to understand the lack of fairness in the world myself.

'Well, because, like I said, life isn't fair,' I begin, reversing out of my parking space. 'When we're in India you'll see that.'

Sometimes I think we've bitten off more than we can chew. But if it comes down to staying and reinforcing her world view that food grows magically in Sainsbury's, and is paid for by a piece of plastic that mummy happens to keep in her wallet, or vagabonding the world and showing her a less pink view of it, I think we're doing the right thing.

THE MORNING AFTER

There's a smile splitting my face in two at 7.30am despite my epic hangover. Let's analyse why…

1. I don't have to get up for work.

Don't look for number two. There is no two. I don't have to get up for work *ever* again. *Shhhhh*, don't interrupt my joy with questions like: *'For ever? Or just for the next year?'* In this world, in this pre-lit dawn, I'm going with for ever.

I lie there contemplating this astonishing truth. I was poised for terror, panic, crippling, paralyzing, I'm-being-chased-by-a-serial-killer-zombie fear. It takes me a few seconds to scan my mind space, like a person who's just been shot trying to figure out which parts of their body are still functioning. Then it comes to me. That strange, startling, blinding feeling is euphoria. I am, I realise, more intensely happy than I've been in, ooooh, a pretty damn long time. Let's go with the 'forever' word again.

Birth of first child? Wedding day? Err. Maybe this happy. But probably not.

I lie there cocooned in a mountain of giant pillows that Lula has piled over me to keep the monsters at bay, pondering this alien feeling. Then I throw off the monster barriers and, without really thinking about what I'm doing, walk to my wardrobe and start ripping through it, yanking all the clothes that I class as work clothes from hangers and flinging them onto the bed. I stand and stare at the pile and then stuff the lot into a plastic bin bag and go back to bed still smiling my Joker smile.

My biggest fear about leaving this all behind was that I would lose my identity. But I don't feel I have. What I do feel is unfettered. Someone suggested I could do a *Mr Ben* and choose a new identity and job title every day. But I don't want one. Unless, of course, I can be a pirate.

Another thing astonishes me. For the last six months I've been stressed beyond belief with the packing and organising and the wondering what the hell I'll do for four hours a week that will make me as rich as Tim Ferris. Imagine my brain as the mosh pit of the Brixton Academy during a Marilyn Manson performance and you'd be about there. But this morning I wander downstairs. The doors are hanging off their hinges like wobbly teeth, a man is chain-sawing away in the garage, two-dozen boxes lie scattered like an obstacle course in the living room and there is a list as long as a banker's bonus of things to do taped to the fridge door, but I'm so not stressed.

I smile at the mess left in the kitchen. Even the crap that has lodged in the plughole of the sink because John refuses to use the strainer doesn't get a rise out of me.

I am still happy when we leave the house to do some things on the High Street.

'I need coffee,' I say to John.

'Sure you can afford that now?' John asks.

OK, so I knew at some point something was going to take the edge off my euphoria.

TODAY I WAS BRAVE AS A LION

'Where's Daddy going?'

'To work.'

Alula looks long and hard at the train station. 'There?'

'Well, he gets the train from there. Like I do … *did.*' Hah.

'What do you do at work?'

'Er. Well … ' I have to think hard. The memories are already fuzzy. 'Have meetings. Write things.' And that's about it. I can't think of anything else that I do – *did* – at work.

'It sounds boring,' says Alula.

Yeah. It is. I can't tell her this though as I want her to develop a strong Protestant work ethic. Heaven forbid she grows up thinking that it's fine to just drop out of school or quit work and go bum around the world.

'What are we doing today then?' she asks expectantly, now she's got her head around the work issue.

'There's a huge party.' Focus on the party, I tell myself. 'Then we're going to the doctor.' I mumble this last part.

She doesn't focus on the party. 'Why are we going to the doctor?' she asks.

'Er. Well…' I mutter something unintelligible under my breath.

'What, Mummy?'

'Nothing, never mind…'

She doesn't ask any more questions. She is too distracted by the snow and the complexity involved in putting on her fingerless gloves. We get to the doctor's and wait to be called.

'Who's first then?' the nurse asks, raising her eyebrows at me.

For a moment I think of shoving Lula in front of me but some latent mothering instinct kicks in. 'Guess that should be me,' I mumble.

The problem with this is it means I have to utterly not show fear or pain. Not even a whisper of panic. I have to smile as the nurse produces the four needles and I have to act totally nonchalant. This is not an easy thing for me. I fear needles and, mostly, I fear pain.

Lula is speechless, which is rare. It reminds me of how birds fall quiet before an earthquake. I roll up my sleeves.

'OK,' the nurse asks. 'Are you ready?'

'Don't tell me!' I shriek. 'Just do it.'

I close my eyes and thrust my arm in her direction. 'La la la la la la la owwwwwwwww.' I manage not to scream. I hum ABBA instead. I picture poor Katie Holmes staying silent during labour and this gives me strength.

'There, that's two. One more,' the nurse says, filling another syringe.

Jesus. I clutch my throbbing arm.

Now it's Lula's turn. She is wide-eyed in the face of my grimace. 'So you're going travelling then?' the nurse asks.

I wince at her – *shhhh*. I don't want any connection in Lula's mind with needles, pain and travelling. Like those rats that get electric shocks until they learn to take food from a certain bowl – I don't want her brain wiring so that she hears the word travelling and thinks of needles.

Durrr, I want to say to the nurse but she is busy filling a syringe.

I can't look, so focus on pulling down Lula's jeans (her arms being too skinny for needles, they go with the haunch every time). Lula starts to squirm like a lamb in the slaughterhouse. She screams as she is stuck with the needle and I feel the guilt that only a mother can feel.

The nurse gives her a sticker that says: Today at the doctor's I was as brave as a lion.

I stop myself from asking for mine.

FREECYCLING OUR LIVES, BUT NOT MY BUTT

This is what I am currently staring at:

- A Christmas tree, which, if it was a person, would be the drunk at the office party: unconscious, covered in puke, dribbling, while leaning heavily against the wall and flashing obscenely
- A sofa, which is going on Freecycle tomorrow and which I must remember to excavate the TV remotes from
- Speakers, which used to belong to the Royal Albert Hall and which John has eviscerated, and which Lula has since been using as the bases for her ginormous imaginary jam tarts
- A table, still to be disassembled, once I've got the energy to clear

up the ink stamp sets, glitter, glue and carved-up Christmas cards that Lula has done a Tracey Emin on

- One drooping plant, which was supposed to have been picked up 59 minutes ago. I had over 20 offers on that pot plant – you'd think they'd be punctual when it's free, for God's sake. Maybe they thought it was a different kind of pot plant.

We have approximately three and a half days left to deal with the crap surrounding us. Our house is like the magic porridge pot of crap. No matter how much we scoop up and pour into the loft, more keeps appearing.

I wish I could Freecycle John's records. But he'd divorce me if I did. The woman who just picked up some old doors and a wardrobe was angling to get her hands on John's records too. I hesitated before I prized them from her fingers and told them they weren't available.

She then tried to steal off with our canvas – you know, the one featuring my naked butt. It's still in the house because strangely the Tate never got back to me.

'Wow, fabulous,' she said, admiring it.

'Yeah, we made it,' I said, trying to distract her from it before she figured out that the particular splat she was admiring was a part of my anatomy.

'So this is the plinth. Do you want that too?' I asked.

'Plinth?' she said, looking at me weirdly.

'Yes. On the phone, you said you wanted the plinth.'

'No, I think I'll leave that. Is this the print you mentioned?' she asked, turning back to the canvas. 'Can I have it?'

'Plinth! I said *plinth!*'

I glare at her until she backs away from the canvas and out the door. Honestly, the type of people you get on Freecycle! They're the human equivalent of locusts. The kind of people who'd strip the supermarket bare in seconds during a riot or in the midst of the zombie apocalypse (I think I'm maybe obsessed with this zombie apocalypse idea).

Still, in this particular circumstance I'm quite grateful because our house is finally empty.

PART 2: **THE TRAVELLING PART**

INDIA

JANUARY 2010

GETTING TATTOOS IN MUMBAI

It is my first day in India and I have just been to a tattoo parlour in Mumbai. Not just any old tattoo parlour but 'Al's Tattoo and Cappuccino Parlour'. I like that. As you get Tweety Pie tattooed on your ankle you can sip a frothy caffeine beverage. I'm sure that's what most people love to do while having sharp needles jabbed beneath their skin – hold a mug of steaming hot liquid over their laps.

An American girl, Tara, who is also staying with my friend Pooja, decided she wanted a tattoo and I thought I would go along with her to check she knew what hepatitis was (I'm a pro on diseases, after all, having read the *Lonely Planet*'s health risks and annoyances section). Also, I have decided that I am going to say 'yes, Fuck It' to everything. Except to the question: 'so you want a tattoo too?'

On the way there we walked (though I have found that you don't walk in Mumbai – you leap, dodge, jump, hop and skitter) past a church, which had a big sign outside saying: 'Who of you by worrying is going to add a single hour to his life?' I liked that but I'm not sure it's really sage advice. Worrying about getting a tattoo in Mumbai might not add an hour to your life, but getting a tattoo could very well subtract a few.

We checked where Al gets his needles. He told us they come sealed in plastic and are all clean and brand, spanking new. But I've seen the bit in *Slumdog Millionaire* where they fill up the water bottles from the tap and superglue them shut. Just saying.

Then we asked about the measurement for a circle – that's right, a circle – and the tattoo man said: 'So, four inches by three inches'.

Now, I'm no mathematician but that would make an oval, I think. If I were Tara, I'd be concerned.

I'm approaching 13 hours in Mumbai without John and Alula. They are joining me in three weeks' time (there was a small issue of a family birthday party that John didn't feel he could miss* but I weighed up three more weeks in an arctic UK and a family birthday party against a Goan beach and, well… I'm sure my father-in-law won't mind, right?). I'm not yet sick and I've visited a tattoo parlour. So far India is getting lots of ticks in the 'yes' box. My favourite thing so far: tuk-tuks. These are basically like kamikaze bumper cars on an enormous track going head-to-head with buses and pedestrians and cars but they cost about twenty pence a ride – a pretty damn exhilarating one at that.

*OK, fair enough, it was his dad's 70th.

What else? We're in the middle of the city but the sounds of animals are all around – birds, dogs and mosquitoes outdoing each other like a battle of the animal bands. You know that film *I Am Legend*, where New York turns all Serengeti in three years and Will Smith saves the world for the what, fifth time? I reckon if everyone in Mumbai died overnight or just vanished from the face of the earth then this city would take about three days to become a jungle. And, finally, it's *hot*. I love it. I was meant to live somewhere hot.

Last week I was sitting in seven layers (two of them thermal) next to a fire, with a blanket wrapped round me. Now I am sleeping in knickers and a vest under a fan. Let the mosquitos bite me. They can have me. Every inch. I would gladly accept a life of itching over a life of hypothermia. Can we live here? Well, too early to tell and it wouldn't be very fair to make that call when John and Alula haven't even taken their first step on Indian soil. But if I don't become road-kill in the next few days I'll let you know my thoughts.

MY SWIM TO PALOLEM

From nowhere comes a surge of national pride. I cannot let the English side down. And that is the reason that I find myself diving off a boat a mile from shore into open water where I most definitely cannot see to the bottom. Let me just point out here that open water that I cannot see to the bottom of is my biggest phobia. I am utterly terrified of it.

I want to point out too that I've never had a surge of national anything before, least of all pride. However, it isn't the thought of the fathoms below filled with fins and tentacles and Jaws that gets me moving – a sort of sideways scurrying crabstroke towards the beach – or the fact I'm stranded and drifting slowly towards Madagascar, it's the sound of jet skis that makes me think instantly of Kirsty MacColl.

Blood in the water will attract sharks. Even though I've been reassured there are none in these parts of the Indian Ocean, I don't believe it. I have a theory that I'll be safe from sharks so long as I always make sure that there is someone fatter than me close by, so I look over my shoulder at the boat and factor in where the Swiss yoga couple are (though disconcertingly they're rather on the thin side). I swim closer to the Venezuelan film-maker (fatter) and the Italian (fattest), avoiding the Indian swami and his partner (the two of them are just skin and bone – neither would make so much as a canapé). No matter how fast I seem to be swimming, however, the shore doesn't seem to be getting any nearer.

Tara, in the boat, has disappeared into the distance. Hmmmm.

At some point I start thinking I might just have to drown. Then I look up and I see a sign on the beach. It says – I joke you not – *PUB*. I haven't seen a sign for a pub in about three weeks.

I can hear celestial voices singing 'Swing Low, Sweet Chariot.'

You can take the English girl out of the pub but you can't take the pub out of the English girl. I swallow several pints of salt water just laughing. I stagger to the shore feeling victorious. I have conquered my fear of deep, dark water, sharks and jet skis, and in doing so I have found a part of myself I never even knew existed.

A MAN GAVE ME A PEDICURE

I get the Tibetan boy. Tara gets the woman. I sit. And smile politely. And think that at least it's not a bikini wax. It's just feet. Though my feet are so gross right now he might prefer to give me a full

Brazilian. That comes from walking around barefoot in the sun for two weeks. They are as calloused and scaly as a lizard's claws. I'm almost too embarrassed to put them on his lap. *Almost*, I said.

Tara has a moment with the implements. 'Are they sterilised?' she asks anxiously. This from the girl who almost got a tattoo in Mumbai from a man who didn't know that a circle has an equal radius and whose first words to her were, 'I like pink thongs.'

I look at the plastic container holding the nail scrubber, the file and the pumice. They look communal.

'Just ask them not to cut your nails if you're worried,' I say.

The woman just waggles her head and says: 'yes, file, massage, polish.'

'No,' says Tara, 'I'm asking about sterilisation.'

That might confuse the woman, I think in alarm. You might not get a pedicure and I don't want to see what implements they'd bring out for that. Let's just move on. Move on. It's clear the pedicure tools are strangers to the Dettol.

They don't cut our nails. But I found out that oval is the shape-de-mode in India. For toenails. That's just wrong, right? I walk out with red, oval toenails. Courtesy of Diana of London nail polishes. And then we walk across the beach and by the time we get home we wonder why we bothered.

I SEE DEAD PEOPLE
'222-223-598'

'Yeah,' I tell the taxi diver. 'I don't need the phone number, thanks. There's the map on that page – can you just take me there?'

'Surrounded – by – pot – plants – and – set – in – a – beautifully – restored – yellow – Portuguese – townhouse.'

'Yeah, thanks, I've read the description. Do you think you could just drive me there… some time today perhaps?'

I am in the taxi. I have given the driver the book with the map in. But he's more interested in reading me, in halting English, the description of the place I want to get to rather than actually driving me there.

'1500 – rupees. Hot – water.'

Eventually I have to get out, run up to a local woman and ask directions. By the time we get there all the rooms are taken in the beautifully restored, yellow, Portuguese townhouse (the *Lonely Planet* people like their adjectives, don't they?). I am tempted to smack the driver around the head with the book. But this is why I've ended up here instead; in a place which makes me think of cells – of both the Holloway and monastery variety.

Similar to a monastery, the Panjim Park Lane Lodge (don't get misled by the words 'park' and 'lane' in the description) also has a curfew – 10pm – which is OK because I wasn't thinking of sampling the local disco.

Also, just like in a monastery, there is a picture outside my door of a rotting corpse. It's OK to put pictures of rotting corpses in your house if the corpse belongs to a saint, I've discovered. And also I have to be out of here by 8am.

The bathroom, free of beatific corpses, is outside, communal and has a corrugated roof. It does have hot water, which, when I stood under it, scared the shit out of me (again handy, because the shower was over the loo). I'd forgotten what hot-water showers felt like. It really was a surprise.

You want to know why I'm staying here and not at the slightly superior Panjim Inn with balconies, no curfew and no dead people on the wall? Because I forgot my PIN number. Which I am actually laughing about because I think that that is proof of how good the last two weeks on the beach have been. My brain has atrophied to such an extent that I have forgotten a four-digit number. And now my card is barred. And I'm stuck in the middle of Goa on my own (Tara flew back this morning) with just £15 in cash to get me back to Mumbai.

Hmmmmm.

WHY TAKING A TAXI IN INDIA SHOULD ONLY BE DONE IF YOU HAVE A DEATHWISH

I am going to die in leopard-print shoes.

The man on the London-Bristol bus who molested me when I was 21 and then grabbed my palm and told me I was going to die aged 62 in a car crash got his dates confused thanks to all the weed he'd smoked in the piss-pot cubicle that passed for a National Express toilet. He meant 32.

Don't look, I tell myself. Better to just close your eyes. If you meet your oblivion in the form of a herd of emaciated cows or a Coca-Cola lorry, best do it with eyes shut.

But I can't. My eyes flash open... just in time to see the driver swerving out of the way of a chundering, belching bus.

Dear God, Jesus Christ... I invoke every Christian saint, archangel and then the whole trifecta of God one more time, before starting on the Hindu deities. But hang on, is it wise to call on Shiva? Is he not the god of destruction? And what about Kali? If I call on them won't they just want to join the fun and throw in some extra carnage?

Vomit calcifies in my throat. It's like that Universal Studios *Mummy* ride I took Alula on by mistake that left us both mute and whimpering. Foot-to-the-floor, rocket-fuelled acceleration is interspersed with whiplash braking when the driver chickens in his game of chicken with the lorry that says 'Blow Horn OK' on its rear end.

Oh God. I have a chokehold lash mark across my sternum and a five-pointed bruise on my leg from where my fingers have been trying to twist off my own kneecap.

I'm usually laissez faire about death. A *your time's up when your time's up* kind of attitude, but now, as the driver weaves his way over the central reservation and into oncoming traffic, my laissez-faire attitude wavers and dies. I want to live!

And I'm going to die.

I start crying. I actually start crying. I think of Alula's perfect cheeks, her adorable double-jointed limbs. I say a prayer of gratitude for being her mother.

Then the tears dry and I feel an eruption of rage. At myself mainly, to be fair. I am going to die because I'm too damn British and too polite to yell, 'stop the fucking car, you utter lunatic, and let me out!'

As the driver stamps on the gas, then the brakes, and fires his headlight beam into the faces of oncoming cars as though it's a magic ray that will whisk other cars into another dimension before they smash into us, I start making Faustian pacts with whatever gods are still listening. A person walking the steps to the guillotine or falling on their tortured kneecaps in front of Tony Soprano has never bargained so hard. Please keep me alive. I want to see my first book on the shelves of Waterstones... I promise I'll never say fuck again...

Fuck! Please stop driving in the middle of the road! And that's the fucking brake, not the clutch, you moron! And that big metal thing heading straight at us is a fucking *bus*!

Weeping; still weeping, still mute. Though in my head I rage and rage against the dying of the light.

And oh shit. An epiphany of just the wrong sort. I only bought the budget travel insurance, the kind that covers you only if you lose a limb and then only after years of haggling with the insurance people. I'm an idiot. And now I'm imagining a tear-streaked John on his knees explaining to a bewildered Alula what life support is and why it's too expensive to keep it switched on.

And sob. If it's meant to be, it's meant to be. Stop focussing on the road, I yell silently at myself. Take out your notebook. Write it all down instead. This inner monologue will drive you insane if the driver doesn't drive you off the road and into an early grave first.

FEBRUARY 2010

WARM CRABS, DEAD CATS

The Tupperware container of crabs is warm in my hand. I am warm in the taxi. It is nearly midnight and the taxi is… wait for it… lost.

I am getting quite tired of taxi drivers waggling their heads and telling me yes, they know where they are going and then getting lost. If I emptied the warm crab curry over the driver's head I wonder what would happen. But I just wonder about it because I've read *Shantaram* and I don't want to go to prison in India. It doesn't sound like much fun.

I know, you're wondering why I am holding a Tupperware container of warm crabs in the back of a taxi at midnight in Mumbai while we cruise the now-emptying streets asking strangers the way to Pali Naka. Well, so the hell do I.

After arriving back in Mumbai I went out for dinner to the home of a lovely Indian woman I met through my friend Pooja. She gave us an eight-course meal with crabs as the pièce de résistance. This is my doggy bag that I'm clutching on my overstuffed lap because not even I could manage eight courses and there were a lot of crabs left over.

The woman runs a programme that provides support to night schools in Mumbai. These night schools are basically for young people from slums such as Dharavi who work all day and who then come at night to study to get their High School Equivalency (like GCSEs). With this certificate they can increase their chances of getting more highly paid work. Or any work. So we went to one of the night schools in a building so decrepit and falling apart it looked like it belonged in the Gaza Strip.

All the kids were bent over their work, scribbling away (actually they were bent over their work at first and then they were one-and-all staring at the weird white girl who'd wandered into their classroom) and I felt so overwhelmed. There were fluorescent lights and crumbling walls, and I knew that the kids had already worked a 12-hour day and were staring at me wondering what over-privileged planet I came from. And I was wondering the same thing too. (*White girl has eyes opened in India!* – It's like a headline from *The Onion*).

We passed by hundreds of shacks on the way there. From two-storey solid ones, to corrugated iron and plastic ones, down to cardboard and tarpaulins stretched over the pavement and over people lying sleeping on sheets of newspaper, to, finally, people in rags just lying stretched out on the pavement. And then we saw a kitten so newborn it was still covered in mucus. And it tumbled onto the pavement mewling and then fell under a bus.

And now, in a cab, with my warm container of crabs, lost in the back streets of Mumbai, it all feels a bit much.

Guess that's India for you.

ALULA MEETS MUMBAI

'What did the lady want?' Alula asks.

'She wanted money.'

'Why?'

'Because some people don't have any money.'

'Well, why didn't you give her some, Mummy?'

Alula has been in Mumbai less than 20 hours and it's not the heat or the noise or the smells that have blown her away, it's the dresses. She doesn't see the poverty or the outstretched arms begging for alms. She just sees the blues and the pinks and the reds and the greens of the saris, and thinks she's arrived at a Barbie fashion convention.

You think I'm joking but right now she's standing on the coffee table in a sun hat, a pink tutu and with freshly painted red toenails, and is choreographing a dance-off between Barbie, herself and My Little Pony.

Her question gives me pause because it's a valid question. It's valid in her world because she thinks money just comes out of machines (at least, when I remember my PIN number) so why on earth wouldn't these people have money? But it's also a valid question because, like everyone says, there is no place like India for realising the quintessential truth about the unfairness of life and how fortunate you are. So why aren't I reaching into my purse and pulling out the rupees? Is it because I'm already immune to the begging and the deformed limbs and the burnt, scaly skin of babes in arms?

Is it because the aggression with which the beggars prod you makes you switch off? Is it because you realise that you can't help everybody so you decide it's easier to not help anybody? Is it because, as Pooja says, most of the money doesn't go to them, it goes to the mafia bosses who run the whole begging industry? Or is it that I'm just a hard-hearted bitch? What did the Buddha do? That's what I want to know. In the end I tell her, 'Because Mummy and Daddy give money to organisations, not directly to people.'

'What are organisations?'

I look at John but he doesn't throw any lifelines my way. So the conversation continues via 'heducation, what's that?' to 'why don't people have jobs?' to 'why is that man (the rickshaw driver) wearing that hat?' – 'Because he's a Muslim' – 'What's a Muslim?' – 'It's a religion' – 'What's a religion?' – 'It's like a fairy tale' (that was John, that last one).

So that's Alula's first day in Mumbai.

NOBODY PUTS ALULA IN THE PICTURE

Baby, baby. Everywhere we go it's to a chorus of 'baby, baby'. It makes me feel like an extra in *Dirty Dancing*, like I need to be carrying a watermelon with me wherever I go and then maybe someone will tell John not to put me in the corner.

The 'baby, baby's aren't said to me though. They're said to Alula. Alula's response is to narrow her eyes, jut out her chin and stomp off. If you know me, you'll know exactly where she gets that from. But to be fair, we can't blame her. Since she breezed through the arrivals doors at Mumbai airport atop a mountain of bags she has been at the epicentre of an attention earthquake. She has taken to wearing her sunglasses everywhere, like a precocious Anna Wintour.

I now appreciate why celebrities are sometimes rude to paparazzi. Because Alula has been papped at least 300 times since arriving in India just a few days ago. She's had camera phones shoved in her face, she's had zoom lenses trained on her from afar and she's had several leery older men digging their knuckles into her cheeks, which makes me want to karate chop them in the nuts.

'Baby, baby,' they say, marvelling at her blonde curls and blue eyes.

Now she buries her head in our legs every time she sees a camera.

'Can we take her photo?' sometimes people ask, having failed to get the shot through subterfuge.

'Let's ask her, shall we?' I say. 'Alula, sweetie, do you want your photo taken?'

'No,' she mumbles, her head still buried.

'No,' we say. 'Sorry, she's a bit tired of having her photo taken.'

John and I discuss it in bed one night. We think we might have solved our financial issues. The rights to Alula's image could be sold to finance our way around the world. If we charged 20 rupees a shot by now we could have paid for a week-long stay at the Taj – the poshest hotel in Mumbai (at least, for me... John could couchsurf).

We just need to convince the baby baby.

DIET COKE BREAK...

Past the paddy fields, through the palm grove, down onto the beach, through the fishing village, around the sleeping fisherman by the boat, up onto the path, down past the nets, across the beach, up the hill, underneath the eagles, dodging the rabid puppy, avoiding the yogis with their rolled-up-mat sabres, quietly past the lotus-sitting meditator, down the path, over the rubble, up some steps, head-butting the hanging curtain of Walkers crisps. And, after all that, they only have full-fat Coke.

John has brought me to the middle of nowhere. A place so remote, Diet Coke hasn't penetrated it. I am a character in *Heart of Darkness*.

John wanted authenticity and to be close to nature. I ask him if termites in the bed is close enough for him. I like my nature at a distance. Usually a celluloid distance.

I thought we were OK, that I could manage, because I could see the giant towers of what looked like a mega-luxury hotel just 15 minutes' walk down the beach. But then John told me it was actually a mosque. I had been dreaming of a mosaic-bottomed turquoise infinity pool and a mojito waiter service. My fantasy is undone.

Our neighbours are a praying mantis and a meerkat. The chef here at the guesthouse ran away yesterday so there's no food. The termites have hatched their eggs. The water has just gone off while I am naked in the shower, half covered in sand and half in soap. There are two lizards, a mummy and a daddy as Lula points out, scurrying across the ceiling.

Still, John insists it's just what he was imagining and hoping for in the Kerala part of our India trip. I don't say anything.

And yes. That does take a large amount of willpower on my part.

LAKSHMI GETS MEDIEVAL ON MY ASS
The Hindu goddess of wealth gave me a wax today. Well, she was called Lakshmi. But she should have been called Shiva after the god of destruction.

When I was lying there on the bed atop a flowery tablecloth, the line in *Pulp Fiction* about getting medieval on an ass sprang to mind.

I was thinking Lakshmi should use that as the tagline on her leaflets.

If we are to choose a location to live based on the waxing/beauty facilities available, then India is last on the scoreboard. Anyway, after that experience, I hobbled out of the dilapidated hut behind the restaurant, past all the Nepali waiters kicking dogs, smoking beedies and heckling me, back to the beach. (Why do I go to such salubrious beauty parlours, you ask? That was the posh beauty shack. You should have seen the others.)

Then, at the beach, I had a big fight with a giant wave. It was the sunglasses or the child. I lost my grip on both. We all ended up somersaulting underneath the sea and for a split second I was like, 'My glasses!' then, 'My child!'

I let the ocean take the glasses – a sacrifice worth paying. They were only £12 from Boots. Maybe if they'd been Chloé or Versace I would have sacrificed the child. But I didn't, I hauled Alula scream-ing out of the waves. She now refuses to go near the sea with me, only with daddy. While wearing her life jacket. Fair dos.

To top it all off my mother-in-law witnessed the whole debacle from the safety of the beach and I'm sure is now questioning my mothering skills. I went back to the room carrying a dripping, hys-terical Alula, feeling like the day wasn't going too well. Which is when the cockroach appeared. Inside John's T-shirt. He reacted calmly. If it had been me, if it had been *my* T-shirt, I would have run screaming off the balcony. He just turned to me and said, 'What was that?'

It scuttled like an alien over his back and down his leg. I screamed and pushed John towards the door, towards the balcony.

John had more sense. 'Can you get it off me?' he asked.

Oh yes, hadn't thought of that. I grabbed a pair of Alula's drying shorts and swatted it until it flew to the floor, backpedalling its gazillion legs whilst trying to flip over onto its front.

Hah, cockroach! You might be able to survive a nuclear apocalypse but you can't roll over. I imagine a billion cockroaches lying on their backs kicking their legs in the air over a landscape of grey, burnt nothingness, just Viggo Mortensen pushing a shopping trolley over it talking about the fire inside. Evolution has its flaws.

Then, finally, we went to a Hindu festival. There were 17 elephants. Alula now wants to convert to Hinduism. Actually there wouldn't need to be a conversion because she's nothing now except maybe a hedonistic worshiper of the goddess Barbie, but you know what I mean. It was so hot that the sweat was pouring in rivers from places I didn't know sweat could pour from. You could have panned for salt off my body by the end of the night and put Maldon out of business. Then the elephant looked at me resentfully, unfurled its fire-hose-sized willy and peed all over the road – about 50 gallons of wee cascaded towards us in torrents.

So I'm thinking that the gods and the animals and the whole of the earth has it in for me today.

WE START TO MISS THINGS...

'Wellllllllllll… ' She draws out the *wells*. 'What I really miss is *Numberjacks*. Especially the pink three. Yeah,' she sighs, '*Numberjacks* is what I really miss, Mummy, and *Mister Maker*. You know? *Mister Maker*. I miss them.' She sighs again.

I sigh too. Not for *Mister Maker*, though I do quite like *Mister Maker*, but because I've started missing something too. So I can empathise with her, which is something I've been trying to do lately because it's Buddhist and that's what I am trying to be (which is really difficult when you live in a land filled with mosquitoes).

The thing that I am missing is something that I calculate I haven't seen, touched, tasted or smelt in five weeks, three days and six hours. I'm not sure of the minutes or seconds because I'm not quite that much of an alcoholic.

Yes. Lula might miss *Mister Maker* and *Numberjacks* but I doubt she'd give her life savings for an episode, whereas I might be tempted to do just that for a condensation-lit glass of Chablis.

The craving hit me only yesterday, sitting in a windowless kitchen surrounded by chillies, in front of a gas burner, with a child like a hot-water bottle wriggling on my lap on the hottest day Kerala has had in many, many years. Lukewarm beer just wouldn't cut it. I needed wine and I needed it now. Which was a bitch because we're in Kerala – the state so dry it's practically Saharan – in India – a country not renowned for its wines.

You want alcohol? Then you queue with the rest of the alcoholics outside the one liquor shop in town, wait your turn and hand over your 25 rupees for some hooch. Actually I did think about doing that. Then I heard about how in the mornings people tap the palm trees for this honey-type liquid, which they ferment during the day and then by evening it's ready for drinking – with an alcohol content close to meths.

I scanned the back garden for palm trees, wondering whether my Venus razor might be able to tap one. I am that desperate. I freely admit it.

But tonight, at last, we get wine to celebrate my getting a book agent (hurrah!). John and I can't afford to buy wine because, as John keeps reminding me, we are on a budget, one that only allows for us to eat rice and drink water. But the mother-in-law is treating us to dinner on this, her final day in India with us. And let me tell you, that the first sweet gulp was like… I'm not going to sully it by describing it as nectar or ambrosia… I'm just going to say that it was like dying and going to heaven. Except better.

MARCH 2010

SWEAT AND TEA

We're high. Not that sort of high. Mountain high. For the first time in three weeks I'm not walking around with a meniscus of sweat draping my body. This is what it is like to not sweat. I had forgotten what that felt like, but it is lush.

Normally I don't like mountains. I don't like anywhere covered in snow on principle. Or anywhere with an incline of more than five per cent. Or anywhere that people ski. But this is a South Indian mountain. Or maybe it's a hill. Whatever, it's beautiful. There is no snow, no skiers, and best of all I can take a tuk-tuk up the inclines. Or just admire them from my veranda. Which is wonderful until you realise that the picturesque vision of tea plantations covering the hills like a patchwork, intersected with colourful, bobbing tea pickers carrying baskets of tea on their head – quick, take a picture – is rather less picturesque up close.

The tea pickers earn 110 rupees a day and have to pick 20 kilos of tea in eight hours. If they get less, even 19 kilos, they don't get paid a single rupee. One hundred and ten rupees is approximately £1.50. That's about the price of a small box of PG tips.

Think about that next time you make yourself a cuppa. I don't drink tea so I think about being self-righteous and then I realise that, from my planter's chair with a gin and tonic in hand, that's a bit rich.

AN IMAGINARY PARADISE

'I think my daughter goes to nursery with your daughter,' I say to the British woman on the beach in Goa where we've returned for three more weeks.

'Oh right', the woman says looking me over. 'Are you on holiday here?'

'No, we're travelling and working remotely.' (Well, I'm doing the travelling and John's doing the working but why go into detail?) 'We've rented a house in the village,' I tell her.

She doesn't reply but I notice her edge further away from me.

'So are you here for the season?' I try again.

The woman looks at me like I've just asked if she eats children. 'No. We've lived here for six years. We have a house in a *real* Indian village.'

I guess she means as opposed to the imaginary Indian village that we live in.

'Away from all the tourists,' she continues. Subtext: YOU.

'Oh OK,' I say. I turn to John and make a face then I wade over to him standing in the shallows. 'About as friendly as a swarm of piranhas,' I whisper. 'She totally snubbed me.'

We glance over at her, now sitting with a coven of other mothers at a beach bar while their naked kids, all with names like Xavvy and Skye, run around re-enacting *Lord of the Flies*.

'Have you noticed there are no men? That's weird, right?

63

Where are their partners? Are they some sort of species that procreates by itself?'

I tell myself it doesn't matter and reflect on the fact that I did say I didn't want anything to do with these Londoners who have made this little slice of Goa their Notting Hill-by-Sea.

But even though John and I laugh, it makes me realise that every paradise is slightly imaginary.

GOING NATIVE AND GOING TOPLESS

Apparently, leaving your knickers out to dry makes you a slut. In which case, the locals must think I'm running a brothel. Where else are you supposed to put them though? If I left them inside to dry, our house would turn into a sauna from the water vapour evaporating off them. So the knickers stay on the line outside. Which isn't doing my image any good in the neighbourhood. But that could also have been affected by my household attire.

The other day our landlady came around and I answered the door in my bikini. It is about 40°C in our house during the heat of the day. She's lucky it was my bikini I was wearing and not my sweat-draped birthday suit. But that didn't help dispel the brothel myth any.

The social norms of Indian vs Western people are about 5m light years apart. It's not just knicker-laundering etiquette either. Indian people use the beach in the late afternoon only and they swim or, rather, paddle in their saris.

Europeans sit on the beach from sun-up till sun-down. The other day we saw someone sunbathing topless and I felt as offended as if she had slapped her boobs in my face covered in Angel Delight.

It's not that I'm becoming a pretend native like some of the Western hippy contingent (you know – the kind who wear bindis and ankle bracelets with bells on and who change their name to Shiva and start chanting in Hindi), or even a real native like Alula is becoming (she picks her nose in public and, taking a cue from the fishermen at Varkala, even did a poo on the beach yesterday before we could stop her) – it's just I'm starting to see the tension, to feel offended on the local people's behalf by such things. Though not enough to bring my knickers inside, admittedly. Just enough to tut loudly as I walk past the topless woman and mutter something about it not being Benidorm.

CHASING BOYS

'Alula, don't chase after a boy. Ever!' I yell after her disappearing back.

'Why not?' she calls over her shoulder.

'It's not ladylike. Always let them chase you.'

She doesn't listen. She is off tearing after Noah. The thing is, Patnem beach is about three kilometres long. OK, I'm rubbish at distance. Maybe it's more like half a kilometre. It takes me about 25 minutes to walk end-to-end. But then again it takes me about 25 minutes to walk an aisle at Sainsbury's – especially if it's the chocolate one. It seems to only take little Noah about three minutes though. But then, on the fourth lap, with Lula tiring in his wake, they disappear into the twilight.

The beach bleaches out at this time of evening and it's impossible to see anything. I am not wearing the right outfit to appear on the Indian *News at Ten*, tearfully sobbing about my toddler that got washed out to sea by a rogue wave or who decided to play hide-and-seek down a well. So I get up and start running down the beach, calling out for them.

I actually become one of those mothers who grabs passers-by and shakes them, asking if they've seen two small children about yay-high running past. I'm trying to look casual about it but I must look panic-stricken. I can see people looking at me thinking 'what kind of a mother *are* you? You've lost *two* children?'

I'm thinking all sorts – I'm thinking *Jaws*, I'm thinking wild dogs, I'm thinking about what I'm going to tell John when I get home in half an hour, hysterical and childless.

And then they reappear in the twilight, like two ghosts, grinning, stained with lolly drips, oblivious to the panic and to the sheen of sweat I am now wearing.

'No more ice cream for you!' I tell Alula, as I pull her into a hug. 'And don't chase boys.'

SARAH (OR THE BOTTLE OF CIF)

I am lying in my sickbed, dying of consumption. Or that's what it feels like. John Keats had nothing on this. OK, I'm not hacking up blood. Yet. But I do spew up some sputum and then collapse backwards onto the bed, one arm flung out across the thin mattress. I just need a billowing white shirt for the look to be complete.

I have succumbed, like the 70 per cent of people that visit India do, to a chest infection. The *Lonely Planet* did warn me about this but I was too focussed on the RABIES to pay it any heed.

Alula comes in, climbs on the bed, pokes me in the boob and says: 'Mummy, your boobies are getting smaller.' Because what I need when I feel this ill is a small, truth-telling child analysing my anatomy.

In my feverish state I start imagining things. For some reason I start imagining that I have a bedside table. It couldn't be Alexander Skarsgård. It had to be a bedside table. This fever sucks. I want my money back. I start to imagine a bedside lamp. Not this fluorescent one that burns my eyeballs and that cuts out so much that Alula now doesn't even notice but just keeps on talking about my small boobs while we sit in the pitch dark. I long for these things. I long for them more than Keats longed for Fanny Brawne.

It's when you're ill that you miss the luxuries; a bath, a dimmer light, sheets that are crisp and cool and sand-free, a bedside table on which to pile drugs, a TV remote that renders you one push away from the drama of *Coronation Street*, carpet, hot water, running water you can drink from the tap, a pair of knickers that isn't one of the five, a bra that fits.

But mostly I want drawers. And cupboards. I'm not sure why but I find myself agonising over the fact that I have no drawers. I miss my laundry cupboard stocked with clean towels and linen. I miss my wardrobe. I am sick of rooting on the floor and the chairs for clothes – clothes that have sand ingrained into every stitch. I miss my under-the-sink cupboard stocked with Cif and bleach and things I have forgotten the names of. I miss clean.

My decaying lungs are a metaphor for how dirty I am. Beat that, Keats. I am filthy. I mean sand, dirt, grease, sweat, filth. It's everywhere. You sweep it and it comes back meaner, harder...

You breathe it in every breath – dust, sand, fumes, pollution.

You walk in it – dog shit, cow shit, cockroach shit.

It feels like I'll need ten colonics and 50 hours in a Turkish bath with a loofah and an industrial bottle of Cif before I ever get clean again. I could put my drying pants inside the house to achieve the Turkish bath but there is no loofah. There is no Cif.

There is no clean in India, or so it feels. So I'm dying of consumption.

CANOES WITH DOLPHINS

'You are not a *Hardy Boy*, John.'

He is pointing with his oar at a giant scrub-laden hill that he wants me to climb with him. 'Urghhhh,' I groan, letting the oar flop.

'It will be an adventure!' he enthuses.

'I don't want an adventure. I'm tired.' I am still getting over my chest infection.

'You're so no fun,' he complains.

'And you are not in *The Famous Five*.'

Every time I get in a canoe I think of *Last of the Mohicans*. That's what makes me get in the canoe. Then, after approximately three seconds, I decide Daniel Day Lewis made it look much sexier than it actually is. I am not sure I am going to 'stay alive no matter what occurs' in this canoe as John steers us towards a great big bloody boulder in the sea.

'Mind the big rock!' I call out.

'Thanks for that. I can't see anything at all, so it's great that you're navigating.'

I struggle to turn with the oar in my hand. 'You can't see?!' I exclaim, then I realise he is being sarcastic. I stop paddling. Not that John notices. Our speed remains the same.

We head towards some rapids. 'Ahhhh, rapids!' I yelp.

'Why are you worried?' John says, still paddling.

'Because we might overturn. I might smash my head on a rock and drown.'

'They aren't even rapids,' he sighs.

He's right, they are more like the little waves you make when you get in the bath. We ripple through them. And then we see them! Three dolphins start dancing around our boat. I have never been this close to a dolphin. And for some reason the only thing I can find to say is: 'Why don't we eat dolphins?'

'You're watching dolphins play five feet away and you're asking why we don't eat them?' John asks, shaking his head. 'You are unbelievable.'

'I don't mean I *want* to eat them – I've been vegetarian now for eight whole weeks, a feat that I'm rather proud of – I just mean that we eat most things in the sea – urchins and ugly stuff like squid – so why not the dolphins? Why is there no dolphin nicoise on the menu? Have you ever wondered about that?'

John ignores me and keeps paddling after them.

'If I were a Native American I'd be called "Canoes with Dolphins",' I tell him.

John doesn't say anything but, hazarding a guess, I think he's thinking his Native American name would be 'Canoes with Idiot'.

ARE WE BAD PARENTS?

They row canoes across the beach searching for tigers and fairies called Happy. They climb mountains and make princess castles in the sand. In the meantime, we parents sit, drinking cold beers, talking and pay the nearest five-year-old five rupees to make sure the little ones don't drown. Does that make us bad parents? I keep asking this question a lot lately and I'm not sure I like the answer.

When I first paid a visit to the German-run, free-play-rules nursery (there is a suprisingly large number of expats living in Goa) I sat gingerly on the packed-earth floor and thought, hmmm, this is nice, rustic, lovely... my *God*, the children are *filthy*.' Then I picked up Alula after her first day and it gave filthy a new name.

I almost didn't recognise her under the grime. I guess that's what happens when you combine free-running snot with free-play in the dirt.

Every day reminds me of that scene in *Aliens* when Sigourney Weaver finds that girl Newt and tries to clean her up.

'There's a girl underneath there,' I say as Alula streaks naked through the house screaming like the shower is the mother alien come to get her and lay its eggs in her brain.

Does that make us bad parents?

Then we were invited to our tuk-tuk driver's house for lunch – a strange, awkward affair under a corrugated iron roof, Lula playing on their plywood bed while we ate off a plastic table and tried to make small talk about Hindu gods and Hindi music – and his kids were trotted out, pristine, polite, perfect. Hair oiled, parted just so, white shirts pressed, handkerchiefs safety-pinned in triangles to their shirts, huge white smiles.

I looked at Lula, filthy and barefoot, wild and singing to herself about fairies, and thought in horror about what they must be thinking about us as parents. So I asked Cami, a local Indian girl, how come Indian kids are so clean and polite.

And she said it's because their parents beat them.

So now I don't feel so bad.

A SLUM – BUT NOT AS YOU KNOW IT

Dharavi, in Mumbai, is the largest slum in Asia. It is 2km² and home to 1m people. Yes, you heard me, one *million* people.

People are staring at us like we're another life form come to probe their planet. We are on a walking tour of Dharavi. I have issues. Not least with the walking part. But mainly my issues are with the part where we pay money to go stare at poor people. It feels like an update on the Victorian practice of going to stare at the mentally ill people locked up in Bedlam all in the name of entertainment. But I am doing it because Pooja recommended it and because the money from the tours goes straight back into the local community via a community centre and a kindergarten.

And also… because John said I had to.

The guide zigzags us through alleys so narrow only the faeces can run through it freely. The rubbish dump burns day and night. A toxic plastic smoke sears our lungs. Children use the place as their playground, scampering around and darting down the alleyways they call home.

Yet, for all its dirt and crammedness (it's apparently the most densely populated place on earth), Dharavi is a hive of activity and micro-industry and that's what the tour is at pains to point out. This is not a slum as we would imagine one to be.

Dharavi has an economy of around $800m (US dollars) a year. Though the workers in the sweatshops earn about $1.80 for a 12-hour day. And these are literally sweatshops. Now I get why they're called that.

We stop in a workshop where men were feeding ground-up aluminium cans into what looks like hot lava, producing at the end of it ingots of aluminium, which get sold back to the canning factories so our Coca-Cola can be reborn.

Over 250,000 Dharavi inhabitants are employed on recycling initiatives like this one. We wander through the Gujarati part of town next. It reminds me a little of the garden section at Homebase thanks to the thousands of flowerpots stacked in the sun.

We finish up with a visit to the community centre. There are lots of Dharavi residents there learning English. We hand over our rupee notes in payment. It amounts to four days' work for a Dharavi resident. Then we take a taxi back to Pooja's fan-cooled, maid-serviced, security-guarded, fully utilitied-up flat and eat the lunch the cook has prepared, and shower in clean water and lie down on freshly laundered sheets for a nap.

India makes me feel a lot of things: hot, tired, elated, frustrated, delighted, angry, stressed and relaxed. But mostly it makes me feel enormously lucky.

And, in equal measure, guilty.

SINGAPORE

APRIL 2010

THE PLANET SINGAPORE

Somewhere over the Bay of Bengal, while John and I were busy decanting our Cabernet Sauvignon complimentary wine into plastic glasses and grinning manically at each other (it was the first red wine we'd had in two months. The fact that it was 10am was inconsequential, I argued, as somewhere else in the world it was 10pm) Qantas diverted our flight to a planet that Natalie Portman might have lived on in *Star Wars*.

It's immaculate and shiny and perfect here. I half-expected our taxi to the hotel to be a space pod with a robot at the wheel. Everything is pristine and clean like the world has been rinsed in floral-scented bleach and then buffed with a chamois made of unicorn skin. Even the radio playing in the taxi is sanitised: Phil Collins croons to us softly as I sink back into the cool leather seats with a sublime smile.

'Is this still earth?' I ask John.

'No. It's Singapore.'

Just eight hours before this we were in a creaking death trap of a taxi spluttering and honking and careering our way through the streets of Mumbai to the airport, passing slum after slum and beggar after beggar along the way.

There are no slums in Singapore. There are no beggars either. Or, if there are, they're very well hidden. Considering they fine you here for jaywalking I can't imagine what they'd do to you if you stood on a corner and asked for small change.

It takes a while to realise what else is different here. Then I realise it's the noise of a billion tuk-tuk drivers honking in unison. It's missing. Here the cars swish. They stop in a neat line within their lanes. And they are silent. The traffic light beeps for the pedestrians. There is actually a green man. I stare at him like an old boyfriend I haven't seen in a while, unsure of what to say or how to treat him.

The cars rest patiently, indolently, before cruising smoothly off into the night. There is a pavement on which to walk. A smooth, poo-free pavement. How is this real? How does Singapore exist in the same world as a place like Mumbai?

Our bed is made up of crisp white sheets and clouds for pillows. White feels like a brand new colour. Our bed seems to sparkle. It makes my eyes water just to stare at it. And it makes me cry to lie on it. It's a mattress! Not a hard plank of plywood.

There's a duvet, not a sand-encrusted sarong! It's soft and warm – like lying in a cradle of swan feathers.

We pass by Raffles hospital. 'I want to get ill just so I can go in there,' I tell John. It looks like the Ritz through beer goggles.

Later, I enter a coffee shop and three people rush, smiling, towards me as though I'm the Queen come for tea. I sit. The waitress brings me some iced water without me asking and then she compliments me on my necklace. In the USA when customer service people are this nice I want to slap them because it feels like they're just faking it (I say the US because in the UK this would never even happen. It's not even a hypothetical) but here, here I want to take this girl home and make her my best friend.

But you want to know the best bit, the very best bit about Singapore? There's a Topshop. That holiest of places! It gives me chills just to enter it. But that could be the air-con. I'm not used to air-con. I want to fall to the floor and sob in relief and gratitude and happiness at the sight of all these pretty clothes and shoes. Which are definitely not, in any way whatsoever, too young for me.

And then I check out the price tags and realise that even if it wasn't made in Dharavi, and even if they weren't in any way whatsoever too young for me, there is no way I can justify spending £40 on a bikini. Not any more.

I turn my back on the bright, enticing lights of the shop of top and walk away.

Maybe something happened to *me* over the Bay of Bengal as well.

DODGY POOS AND COSMIC KARMA

Even though we've just spent two months in India, John is insisting we visit Little India. While we are in Singapore.

I don't want to visit Little India. I want to visit malls and clean sparkling buildings. I want to get reacquainted with all these lovely things. Not with samosas.

'Dude,' I say, 'you dragged me out of air conditioning to see this? To see what exactly? Some streets with skanky backpacker hostels on them? Because that seems to be about it. Even Disney World could have knocked up a better Little India than this.'

John asks if I'd rather be somewhere like a mall. He is being sarcastic and I narrow my eyes as if to say no, I'm not that vacuous or superficial, thank you very much, but in fact I'm thinking, *yes*! Yes, a mall! I want to be *in a mall*. A mall with air-conditioning!

It is hot. I am bothered. I am bothered that John has made me get off an air conditioned bus and deserted me on a street corner whilst he goes off to rummage for vinyl in an outdoor market, leaving me with a child who won't walk, who is now folding herself double, screaming 'I'm tired!' in the middle of the pavement *and* who has, as she so eloquently puts it, 'dodgy poos'. All in 5,000° and 1,000 per cent humidity.

'I need a poo,' Alula announces. She puts on her thinking face. 'I think I've done a dodgy poo.'

We couldn't have been in an air conditioned mall with marble-floored bathrooms and silk toilet paper. Oh no. We have to be in a replica of a Mumbai street with equivalent bathroom facilities. If we were actually in the real India – the big, grown up India – I would have no qualms about squatting her over the gutter by the side of the road, but this is Singapore and you'd probably get hung, drawn and quartered for that here, so instead I grab her hand and march her across the road (jaywalking – a lesser fine, only $1,000 Singapore dollars, and a three-month jail sentence) and into a back-packer hostel.

The staff waves us towards the back. I nudge open the door to the bathroom and Alula and I flinch in horror from the scene, but there's no other option. I manage to hoist her somehow over the toilet bowl and, holding her there suspended, I crane my neck and look around for toilet paper. There is none. Of course there is none. This is Little India.

Anyway, Alula leaves the place commando-style as there is no salvaging that particular pair of underwear. I have attempted to use the hose provided to clean her up but it's not been that successful because the water was so cold she almost hit the ceiling when I fired it at her.

'I'm tired,' she says as we start walking up the street to find John

clutching some vinyl in his hands. I give him a dark, dark look.
John does his fatherly duty and picks Alula up and deposits her on
his shoulders.

I open my mouth to warn him about the danger that might rep-
resent then I shut my mouth again.

That's called karma.

LAUNDRY AGAIN

John and I are open-mouthed with awe and wonderment. We are
like two Neanderthals staring at a wheel or fire. I appreciate that
Neanderthals don't talk but work with me. Imagine our knuckles
scraping the lino and me grunting.

'Wow.'

'How does it work?'

'Wow.'

'How does it open?'

'Wow. Just wow.'

'Where does the detergent go?'

It has been three months since we've seen a washing machine.
We literally stand and stare at the one in front of us for five minutes.
Then we run. We run for our bags and we pour their entire con-
tents into the machine. I stop just short of climbing in myself.

I have not missed doing laundry. Just in case you missed that fact.
However, our clothes are so dirty they have their own rating. They
are almost sentient they have so many life forms crawling through
the fibres. The desire for clean clothes is momentarily overcoming
my loathing of laundry-doing.

In India we would take a bag of dirty clothes to the nearest
shack and hand over 50 rupees (about 50p) in exchange for the

promise of a machine wash. In Hindi that translates as *bashed against a rock*. So all our clothes are bruised and dulled. It's why I was almost blinded by the colour white when we arrived in Singapore.

And here before us stands a washing machine with beeping, flashing lights, a place for detergent, even a setting for delicates.

We add the detergent and I stand and watch as water – *hot* water – and soapy detergent pours into the drum. I have to suppress a tear.

Sixty-three minutes later the machine sings to me and I sprint into the kitchen and unload our clean mountain of clothes. I spend approximately the same amount of time hanging them up on the balcony in soporific heat. I end up more wringing than the clothes. And that is when I remember exactly why and exactly how much I hate doing laundry.

SINGAPORE DOESN'T MAKE THE LIST

Singapore feels like visiting a Christian university for the weekend. I suspect that even the Amish would find this place too straight and would jump into their wagons and head straight back to Pennsylvania for a good old barn-raising.

No wonder Changi airport is the number-one visitor attraction. It feels as if the powers that be drew up their constitution after reading *1984*. Unless you are Bill Gates you can't even afford to buy a bottle of wine to liven things up, thanks to the 400 per cent tax (I'm not very good at maths so this is approximate).

But both these things are why I can't live here. It is too wholesome. Too sanitised. If Singapore were a pop group it would be the Jonas Brothers. If Singapore were a food it would be uncooked tofu. If Singapore were a drink it would be Perrier (because it looks nice, it's chilled and it's expensive but ultimately it's boring and kind of eighties). If you need further proof, check out what I'm flicking through on TV right now… Justin Bieber is on prime-time news. This is followed by a much-hyped report on the evolution of Singapore's public housing. I flick over to a daytime soap, which I mistake for an infomercial on a wedding-planning service.

Wanting to find some edge, some badness at its core, to find out if I am wrong about Singapore (John argues that there's a badass underground scene here but he's yet to show me where), I visited the Social Innovation Centre and posed the question: 'But what social issues are there to innovate on in Singapore?'

The man thought about it for a whole minute before replying (and, people, it is his *job* to study these issues); 'Well… people treat their domestic help really badly.'

He pointed to the posters adorning the walls advertising a campaign to ensure that Philippino domestic staff are given holidays. Don't get me wrong, it's a really important campaign – but is that it?

'We also have a problem with teenage pregnancy,' he hastened to add.

I raised an eyebrow. 'I come from the UK.'

He smiled embarrassedly and moved on quickly, telling me about Singapore's number-two visitor attraction: the zoo.

On the one hand, it's amazing that Singapore is so on top of its social issues, that crime rates are so low and the quality of life is so high. However, after London and the UK, it just feels a bit scary and I can't help but notice when I Google it that Singapore has a lot of people currently sitting on death row, so clearly not all is clean below the sparkling surface. Singapore feels like a giant mall where consumerism is used as a form of mind-control. I even fell for it myself for a little while, so overwhelmed was I by the colours and the shininess and the air conditioning.

So, Singapore, it is decided by all of us, is definitely not a place we can live.

Let's face it, a city where the airport is the number-one visitor attraction and the lion enclosure the second, was never going to make the list.

BALI

BALI: IS THE SEARCH OVER?

The question 'can we live here?' becomes rhetorical in Bali. It's followed by a silent 'Do bears shit in the woods?'

We have been here a month but within about a day of arriving we knew it was a place we could call home.

Ubud, Bali, is like Brighton crossed with the Hamptons crossed with an ashram. It's like a lusher, less stressful version of India. Alula has started at nursery – a place so perfect John pronounced it the most gorgeous school he'd ever seen (because prettiness is so much more important than academic standards). It sits amidst rice paddies and all the lessons are in Indonesian and English. So everything is perfect. Except for the fact John is making me cycle everywhere.

John's brother Rich has joined us for a few weeks.

'So,' he asks, 'do you think you'll go back to the UK?'

We've only been gone three months but the question makes me want to fall to the floor in a fit of laughter.

'This place rocks,' I tell Rich.

Every morning I feel like Snow White. A squirrel ran across the living room as I ate breakfast today. Two butterflies waltzed over my head. The gecko family (Money and Hula Hoop – named by Alula) sit sleepily on the ceiling, observing us.

Eight years ago John, Rich and I were all cramped in a London flat. There were no geckos on the ceiling, just a patch of damp. Now we are all here in Bali. This is totally an upgrade. So no, I can't see myself living in London permanently again. We do, however, need to find a way to make it work because Bali is not cheap and I am still not sure I have any discernable talents that can be harnessed to create income.

But I will tell people when they ask why we're leaving the UK permanently and moving to Bali that it's because I don't like the weather in England. I won't mention that it's because I don't have to do my own laundry here.

KARMA INSPEKSI

'Do we just text 118 118?'

'Where in the Yellow Pages would you even look for one?'

I tweet to see if anyone can help but Balinese priests don't hang in the Twitterverse apparently, so no joy there.

Richard, John and I are in a van touring the back lanes of Bali. We're talking priests because we need one urgently. Not for the last rites or anything. No one's dying. And anyway, we're not talking the Catholic kind of priest, we're talking the Balinese kind – the kind that come in the dead of night and tell you whether your land is haunted. We need to know whether the land we're vaguely considering buying is inhabited by evil spirits, the type that might make Lula's head spin around 360° or burn our house to the ground for fun. It's called a *Karma Inspeksi*. It's the equivalent of getting a survey done in the UK to check for subsidence.

A priest comes along, just like in *The Exorcist*, and he tells you if there are evil spirits haunting the land that might cause subsidence, thus doing away with the need for an actual survey.

We pull out our laptops and start strategising. Who do we know who might know a priest? We email and call all our Balinese contacts. Eventually I get an email back – it says this: *I know priest. He has very clear sense and can heal people. He can do some predictions as well. He burnt his temples when he was grade 11 and was in jail because of it. He did not want to be a priest. But now he returns to be priest. Crazy young priest, by the way…*

Needless to say, we're parking that guy for the moment, until we need someone who can commit arson. We find another priest eventually. It turns out that when you start asking it's like rent-a-priest around here. We got three in half an hour. So tomorrow it's all set. In the dead of night, John, Rich and I are meeting our chosen spiritual surveyor on the land for our *Karma Inspeksi*.

I'm wondering if there will be chicken bones, slaughtered goats and a Ouija board involved and secretly hoping there will be.

MAY 2010

VOODOO IN THE WOODS

It is the dead of night. The moon is shrouded with cloud. Eerie Balinese gamelan music is drifting through the trees. John, Rich and I are stalking through mud, smacking into branches and tripping over ditches. The high priestess is ahead of us, springing like a mountain goat over the puddles and broken ruts.

She is balancing a basket on her head and I wonder if the Ouija board is in it. I have no basket and am managing to lose my balance as well as my flip-flops, which are being sucked into muddy ditches. I am stumbling like a drunk and cursing loudly. John tells me to stop swearing because the spirits might hear. I look at him to see if he is taking the piss. He appears not to be. Huh. Usually I am the superstitious one.

The priestess is old and toothless. She babbles something at me. I smile and nod. She could be saying anything. In fact, she could be anyone. I have a niggling suspicion that the landowner has just brought his grandmother along, told her to say some gobbledegook, light some incense and chant a bit. There are no chicken bones or Ouija boards involved, not even a slaughtered goat. I have to say I'm kind of disappointed.

After about five minutes of us standing in the silent darkness our translator comes over and tells us: 'The land is good. She says it is good place for build.'

I look over at the priestess. She is laughing with the landowner. I lean over to John. 'She's saying, *these stupid bule, they believe all this voodoo shit? Now, how much are you going to pay me for this non-sense? I could be at home right now in my slippers watching* Corrie.'

John tells me to shhh again.

'I think we should get the arsonist priest over here. You know, for a second opinion,' I say. I'm guessing he'll do some real voodoo shit. Or at least some pyrotechnics. Then at least I'll feel we got our money's worth.

In the end we don't buy the land. Even though the spirits have given their blessing we are not sure our bank manager will and we're not sure we can blag another gold-plated bathroom so soon. And something else holds us back too. While we feel sure that Bali is somewhere we want to make home, we're not so sure that invest-ing money into land here is a wise idea, not to mention an ethical idea. Though foreigners can't buy land, only lease it – a wise pro-vision by the Indonesian government – it does feel as though a lot of foreigners are coming in, leasing land cheap and profiting from it by building monstrous villas, while the locals seem to end up shafted. With little in the way of financial education, most families blow through the pay-out in months using the money for ceremonies, new bikes or just on family and healthcare, leaving them with no sustainable income. Even though this land isn't rice-paddy land or otherwise used for agriculture, it still doesn't feel right.

We've heard horror stories aplenty about foreigners who have 'bought' land and ended up being totally fleeced, with land deeds apparently being invalidated once the money has been paid, death threats being laid at their doors, black magic curses rendering them impotent or paralysed or bald, and even Mafia-style gangsters moving into the spare bedroom.

I don't much fancy any of that. So perhaps it's all for the best.

FIRING THE BABYSITTER AND MYSELF

We are going to have to fire the babysitter. It's either that or one day soon coming home and finding her dressed as Lula's very own gimp.

We've already been through one babysitter. We didn't fire her. The Balinese woman who found her for us fired her. Because she was cross-eyed. According to her, being cross-eyed is a sign of some kind of moral or mental deficiency. We didn't ask her to fire cross-eyed Made (pronounced 'Maday' not as in 'I made this'). We actually liked her a lot, but the agent fired her without telling us, replacing her with a non-cross-eyed version – Ketut – who we're going to have to fire.

I came home earlier today and heard strange noises emanating from the living area – squeals and squeaks and roars. As I walked into the room, heart already sinking, I found Lula playing baby tigers. That's fine. I applaud the imagination involved and her dedication to method acting, but what I didn't expect to see was a fully-grown woman squeaking and roaring too, while on all fours.

I took sweet Ketut aside and said; 'Listen, Alula will push your boundaries. You need to be firm with her. You are free to tell her off if she is naughty. And by the way, you really don't need to crawl around in the dirt with her.'

Ten minutes later I came downstairs and found Ketut shadowing Alula, who was no longer a baby tiger, but now method-acting the role of Scarlett O'Hara and Lindsay Lohan's lovechild, and flouncing around the living room. Ketut followed behind her, picking up her littered toys, lifting her cup for her whenever she wanted a sip, cooing and fawning over her like she was a deity or A-list celebrity. Naturally, Alula was embracing her new-found star status like a winner on *The X Factor*.

'The nanny is Alula's new pet,' I said to John. 'If Ketut was a cat, the RSPCA would need to be called. It must stop. We must do something.'

When Ketut leaves, I have words with Alula. 'Alula Alderson, you are not to treat Ketut like your own personal plaything. And also, she is not there to pick up your things. Who do you think should pick up your things?'

Alula looks at me like I'm stupid or something. 'The cleaner?'

'No! Not the cleaner,' I answer, appalled. '*You* pick up your things.'

I look at the mess she's made and think I must act now. Immediately. Before this behaviour becomes ingrained and she starts giving me her rider every morning detailing the number of cornflakes she wants in her bowl, the exact shade of pink her princess knickers must be and the angle at which her bunches must be tied.

'Pick up all this mess. At once.' I demand.

Alula looks at me and thrusts out her belly, 'I'm not your slave, Mummy,' she says.

Needless to say, the babysitter must go. Maybe I should fire myself too while I am at it. I'm obviously helping raise a monster. Perhaps we need to hire an animal tamer.

Then I have an idea. Let's hire the exorcist priest instead!

UBUD, BALI: LAND OF THE MASSAGE

1. JACK BAUER STYLE

The alarm bells should have started to ring when he straddled me. It wasn't sexual, don't get me wrong. It was more like he was getting ready to carve a particularly large Parma ham. And it hurt. This man knew pain. He was on first name terms with it. There was a point where I actually thought I was going to dig my own finger-nails right through my palms until they came out the other side. There was even a second when I wished he would just get out the meat slicer and finish me off.

Why didn't I say anything? Why didn't I say, 'Excuse me, I don't think finger joints bend *that* way? Maybe you need to go back to your anatomy textbook and turn it the right way up?'

Why didn't I leap off the massage table naked and holler at him when he stuck his elbow joint into the place on my hip where three years of mangled nerves meet and where I'd told him specifically in both signs and simple English to not go near? You want to know why? Because I'm British and I don't know how to complain in any way other than under my breath, in the medium of a blog or behind a back. And never, ever, in a million years, to someone's face.

2. YAKULT STYLE

I can hear John groan and am hoping that I made it absolutely clear that our double massage was to include no 'happy finish' for him. I peek over. It's OK. He's only groaning because the woman has just slapped some yogurt, straight from the fridge, onto his chest and is now slathering it in great lobbing handfuls over his body.

And then I realise he's not groaning at all. He's yelping. My laughter gets cut off when my lady pours half a litre of Rachel's organic yoghurt over my boobs. Seriously. Are you kidding? But guess what, people? I don't say anything. I don't question the wisdom of the friendly-bacteria body mask. I stifle the yelps and just obey when they tell me to get up, inching gingerly off the table and walking like a cowboy to stop it sliding into places it should only go when you have thrush. I follow their directions to the bath. Filled not with the milk of asps but with tepid water. Mmmm, lovely.

Another one chalked-up to experience.

3. HOLLYWOOD STYLE

Massage Ubud Wayan (as she is known in my phone so as not to get her confused with English-speaking taxi Wayan, non-English-speaking taxi Wayan and cleaning Wayan... interesting fact about Bali: Wayan is a name given often to the first-born child whether boy or girl, hence the preponderance of Wayans) is recommended to me by the person who trained her.

She comes to my house (bonus points), she charges half the price of the other masseurs in town (more bonus points), she doesn't use yogurt, she doesn't straddle me and she understands enough English that when I say 'please don't touch my herniated discs' she doesn't touch them. This is progress, I think.

The person who trained her runs a massage company. In Hollywood. For film stars. His masseurs work 24/7 on film sets massaging the talent. I so am in the wrong business. I want to be talent. I want Massage Ubud Wayan to massage me 24/7. My massage takes place in a room overlooking the rice paddies. But I don't notice because I'm drifting between two realms. One is pleasure and the other one is the same place I go to when I watch *True Blood* and pause on the bits with Eric in them.

When she finishes, there is a pool of drool beneath the massage table, I don't smell like a Fruit Corner and I don't have crescent-shaped cavities in my palms.

Result!

DOWNHILL FROM HERE

For the first hour my feet didn't do one single rotation on those pedals. And I spent that hour smiling to myself at the genius of the entrepreneurial Balinese who've set up downhill cycling tours. I mean, what a canny understanding of Western culture. We're fat and lazy (or a lot of us are). Obviously there are some people for whom the idea of cycling uphill or even on the flat appeals. I'm just not one of them. I used to be. John and I once cycled 300 miles across Cuba. It wasn't really across. It was mainly *up* Cuba. It was character-building and also the only time I've ever tantrumed full-on in public since I was three years old.

We've also cycled all over the south of France with tent, sleeping bag, baguette and a bottle of wine strapped to our panniers.

Those were the days. The hazy, crazy days of our pre-child twenties.

There are about 50 downhill cycling tours to choose from in Ubud. They drive you to the top of the volcano and then you cycle down. Clever, huh? So I start off feeling great. I get the best of both worlds. I am cycling but I'm not really cycling. There is no sweat involved, in fact; there's no muscle movement involved other than my thumbs, which are permanently squeezing the brakes. But then, after one hour, it stops being downhill. It stops being flat. It starts to incline.

I start shooting lasers at the guide in front of me. He is wearing a green T-shirt. He is pedalling. His T-shirt says 'Downhill'. I want to holler to him about the Trade Descriptions Act and his company's flagrant breach of it. I want to but I can't because I'm out of breath and I've now fallen about half-a-mile behind everyone else.

I am panting up the hill in the lowest gear, or is it the highest? I don't know. It feels like the wrong gear but I work my way through all the others and they feel even worse so I work my way back down again. But the worst thing is that now I can hear the car behind me. The support car. The one that follows the last person, curb-crawling them, just like in the Tour de France.

I can feel the driver's eyes on me. I know he is wondering whether he should just get out and rescue me and I seriously think about throwing off a flip-flop (I cycle prepared, huh?) and claiming I can no longer ride on shoeless.

Ahead of me, the others are now out of sight. I glance over my shoulder. There it is. The car. Breathing down my neck. Behind it are about six mopeds and two other cars. I hear honking. I want to die of both pain and embarrassment but I don't even have enough breath left to do that. We finally arrive at our destination.

'Did you enjoy?' says our beaming guide.

'Downhill, huh?' I pant in reply.

He hands me a wet towel straight from the fridge.

I really want to chuck it at him but I am so sweaty I don't. I just take it and glare.

MALAYSIA

MAY 2010

RUPEES, DOLLARS, RUPIAH, RINGITTS. CAN'T COPE.

I'm having difficulties with noughts. Four countries, four currencies, four months, four billion noughts between them all. I thought I had it sorted. One thousand rupees is roughly £14. One Singapore dollar is roughly 50p, 10,000 Indonesian rupiah is roughly $1 (for some reason I switch to American dollars in Indonesia). Then we got to Malaysia and it all fell apart.

It's 2am and we've just disembarked in the centre of Kuala Lumpur after a five-hour bus ride from Singapore, having taken a two-and-a-half hour flight from Bali. It's weird continuing on our *Can We Live Here?* quest when we know we've already found the place we want to live, but we're committed to the journey. Plus, our flights are non-refundable. And besides, we need to make doubly-sure that Bali really is the place we want to call home. What if we're wrong? What if it is in fact Kuala Lumpur?

We stop at an ATM en route to our hotel as we are currency-less.

'How much do I get?' John asks as he hops out the cab.

'Er, I think the exchange rate is seventy ringgits to the pound… is it ringgits? I can't remember. So er, get maybe 20,000 or something?'

John slams the door and runs off leaving me with a taxi driver who seems intent on asking me a lot of cash-based questions.

'How much is your hotel? How much was your flight? How much was your –'

I cut him off before he can ask me how much I weigh or how much I earn (precisely no zeros in either answer). I'm wondering if this is how all Malaysians start conversations and I'm feeling weary already.

After about 20 minutes John returns to the taxi. He looks confused. 'I don't think I've got enough for the taxi.'

'Why how much did you get?'

'I only got 500.'

I do a quick calculation. 'That's about eight quid. It's not going to be enough.'

'I tried three times,' he counters. 'The ATM refused to give me any more.'

Huh, I wonder. 'There is maybe, perhaps, possibly a chance that I have the exchange rate wrong.'

The taxi driver has fallen very quiet.

Once we get to the hotel I check the rate. Turns out it's 4.8 ring-itts to the pound. Barclays text us at three am. Apparently someone has tried to commit fraud on John's card. Some fool has tried to withdraw several thousand pounds from an ATM in Kuala Lumpur. Duh.

But at least I now know why the taxi driver was asking me so many questions about how much our hotel cost and why he fell silent. He was clearly weighing up whether he could get away with telling us it was three thousand ringitts for the two-mile journey.

THE BUS, THE WEE AND THE TROPICANA BOTTLE

'Move round. Face the window. OK. Pull your knickers down.'

Lula looks at me aghast: 'But Mummy, people are watching.'

I glance around. 'They're all sleeping. No one will see.'

John shakes his head at me. 'This is all going to go wrong,' he mutters.

'Well the only other option is she wees on me. Given that, I'd rather she tried to wee in the bottle.'

'It's going to go all over the bus,' John warns, handing me a Tropicana bottle that he's beheaded with a penknife. Very MacGyver. Lula crouches in the gap where our feet and bags are. I position the bottle underneath her.

'I can't hold it any more,' she shrieks.

'OK, go!' I say as though it's the start of a steeplechase.

A slick of liquid starts to cascade down the aisle. The bottle isn't filling.

'Mummy, my feet are wet,' Lula says from her crouching position among the bags.

'It's running down the aisle.' John hisses.

'No one will notice,' I hiss back.

Lula pops up to standing. 'MY DRESS IS ALL WET,' she yells.

Five minutes later...

'Mummy. I need another wee.'

My eyes are shut. I'm trying to sleep. 'Hold it,' I murmur menacingly.

'I can't hold it,' she whines pitifully.

I open my eyes. The poor love is wide-eyed and teary. 'Hold it,' I beg.

'I can't!' Lula's voice is panicky.

'Well you have to. There's no loo on this bus and we're not doing the bottle thing again.'

One minute later…

'I'm leaking,' Alula announces.

She is sitting on my lap. I poke John. Now my voice is panicky too. 'John, wake up. She needs another wee.'

He opens one eye. 'She isn't having another wee. She will have to hold it.'

'Can't hold it.' Lula tells him straight.

I look at John. 'We'll have to use the bottle again.'

'No way.'

'Have you got a better idea?'

I think he'd rather she used me as a nappy but I've already shoved her off my lap and grabbed the bottle. 'Right, crouch down again.'

'Hold it in the right place this time, Mummy.'

I am not sure what the right place is. I thought I had it right the first time. 'OK. Wee,' I say.

We hear the sound of tinkling liquid hitting plastic. Result!

'I'm finished,' Lula announces.

I hold up the cap-less bottle. Three millilitres more and we'd have been in trouble.

'What are you going to put it in?' John asks as though I'm on my own on this one. He looks around then hands me another bottle. 'You could decant it into this.'

Why am I suddenly having to do all the danger work? So much for MacGyver. I rest the lip of the wee bottle against the empty bottle. It shakes. I feel like the bomb disposal guy in *The Hurt Locker*.

'Just do it in one swift move,' John urges.

I contemplate how this is going to end. Two hundred and ninety-seven millilitres of warm urine running over my hands and feet.

'I'm not sure this is a good idea. My hand's jolting. It'll go everywhere.'

'Well, what are you going to do?' John asks.

I notice the continued use of the second person singular rather than the first person plural in this situation.

'I guess I will just hold it until we get there.' (Unlike Lula…)

ALULA INVENTS A NEW GAME

We have gone up in the world. We are staying in a dead-posh hotel in Georgetown, Malaysia. We know it is posh because Alula's first words upon tearing through the room and discovering the bathroom were, 'Yay! There's loo paper!'

Mine were: 'Yay! There's a minibar!'

John's were: 'Yay! There's wi-fi!'

That says it all, really, doesn't it?

In the last few days Alula has invented a new game. It goes like this: as soon as we arrive in a place she gathers any and every bag she can get her hands on and places all the things she possesses and then some things she doesn't into these plastic bags. She then deposits the bags around the room in strategic places that we must step over, leap over but never, under any circumstance, move, look in, or God forbid, *empty* out. Not even if our toothbrushes are in one buried under dirty socks and her wet board shorts.

Our morning routine goes something like this:

'Alula, have you seen the hairbrush?'

'Mary had a little lamb…'

'Alula, focus, where is the hairbrush? Have you moved it?'

'Little lamb, little lamb…'

'Alula, darling, where is the hairbrush?'

'Mary had a little lamb...'

I turn my back on my selectively deaf child in frustration and start checking under desks and beds. And there, invariably, I will find her shrine.

Alula's shrines are created by placing her Barbie on the mountain of her tutu and positioning, all around the plastic D-cupped deity, the coins pilfered from my purse, an entire pack of playing cards laid out face-up, her My Little Pony, my hairbrush, whatever shoes happen to be handy, a handful of hair clips and some sweet wrappers. Basically anything that won't fit into the bags. I've not yet found any human or insect sacrifices.

I've started calling Alula 'magpie', since these little shrines are more like nests where she collects her stray belongings (and our not-so-stray belongings) and hides them from our prying eyes. And the bags containing her possessions she calls her shopping bags – so either she is learning some really bad habits from me or she's actually manifesting some anxiety behaviour due to all the changes being foisted on her.

We're starting to worry about the lack of stability in her life and the constant change. Up until now the pros have outweighed the cons, but then up until now we've been slow travelling, spending a month in one place and allowing her time to make friends and go to school. When we're on the road she struggles. We had better settle somewhere before we find her trying to hitch a lift back to London with a plastic bag containing her Barbie, her float suit, a pack of cards and my hairbrush.

I jest, but actually for once I'm not laughing. It really is time to move to Bali.

MALAYSIA – CAN WE LIVE HERE?

We have 24 hours left in Malaysia before we get back to Bali or 'home', as I'm tentatively starting to think of it. We've changed our itinerary and are going back there for six weeks to make sure the honeymoon isn't over. I haven't loved Malaysia. But maybe after Bali that was a tall order. I've been trying to rationalise it, though being rational isn't one of my strong points, as John will attest.

So herewith my *For and Against* list for Malaysia – *Can We Live Here?*

FOR

- Handrolls. It sounds like I'm bigging up something off a brothel's menu when in fact it's just something off a Chinatown menu. Like spring rolls except much nicer.
- Er – let me keep thinking.

AGAINST

- The beaches we've been to are pretty dirty.
- When buying alcohol in a supermarket you are made to feel like you are buying hardcore fetishist pornography involving scatology.

This list lacks lustre. I turn to John. 'I'm writing a list of reasons for and against living in Malaysia. What are your thoughts?'

He pulls a face. 'There's only one reason we can't live here as far as I'm concerned: it's not Bali.'

It's true. Bali ticks all our boxes. Sunshine, great school, amazing culture, beaches, easy visas, beautiful scenery. In a Eurovision-style contest, Malaysia would get *nil points*. Bali would be taking home the trophy.

WHY DO WE KEEP DOING TRAINS?

I'm on a train right now. The light is dying outside – and the clouds are glowing rosy pink over the limestone hills. Enough with the pretty. Inside the train it's prison strip lighting, tacky floors and toilets that make me yearn for a penis (as in, that I had one for peeing with; I don't get turned on by prison strip lighting).

Hell, these toilets – they even make me yearn for India. I never thought I would say I missed Indian trains but here I am saying it. I miss Indian trains – same strip lighting, probably more filth and more cockroaches but there's something so epic about an Indian train ride. I think it's the chai wallahs. And the men who bring you your pile of laundered sheets to spread over your ripped lino plank. And the samosa sellers. Yeah, maybe what I miss most is the never-ending stream of food and tea straight to your bunk.

I've just trekked through ten carriages to the buffet car on our express to Kuala Lumpur and ordered nasi goreng and fried noodles, hold the spice. I trudge back, leaping heroically between the gaps in the cars, and find Lula having a meltdown and John threatening to take her to the naughty step in the prison carriage of the train.

As Lula sits and starts eating, I wonder whether I should tell John that possibly the reason for her dynamic shift in mood is that ten minutes ago she helped herself to the bottle of Sprite into which I had decanted the remains of our duty-free whisky.

But before I even open my mouth, I am thwarted by Alula's scream: 'It's spicy!'

'It can't be,' I say. 'I expressly asked for no spice. Like, three times. I said, NO SPICE.'

John tastes both plastic containers. They are spiced to the eye-balls.

'But I'm *so hungry*!' Lula starts to scream, jump up and down and cry hysterically.

I look at John. 'They have Western food too...'

He gets up and trudges the ten carriages, returning with a burger. This is the man who rolled his eyes at me this morning for ordering Lula a banana pancake because she wasn't getting enough fruit and veg. Banana, hello? Burger, hello? But options are limited and something needs to soak up the 'Sprite'.

She takes a bite into the flaccid chicken patty and I watch in disgust, images of abattoir floors dancing in my head.

'Ahhhhhhh,' Lula screams. 'It's spicy! My mouth is all fizzy.'

I take the burger and dissect it and then lick it tentatively. It is indeed slathered in a chilli sauce.

I wonder, not for the first time, why John and I ever think trains are a good idea. They are only a good idea retrospectively. Even Indian ones. But coaches are worse – let's not forget the weeing episode on the one we took from Kuala Lumpar. There are some benefits to trains I guess, even if that benefit is just a hole in the floor.

I resort to wiping the sauce off the reconstituted burger with a piece of toilet paper.

Lula eats it. I cringe. Then she passes out.

BALI (AGAIN)

JUNE 2010

SPACE INVADERS

Driving in Bali is like playing Space Invaders. Cars, dogs, scooters, chickens, trucks and bikes are all sharing the one-lane road with you and they're coming at you from every direction trying to kill you.

If you get distracted by the seven-year-old driving past you on his scooter with his three-year-old brother perched behind him then more fool you, because you're going to plough into the family of five – all sharing one helmet – that are weaving dangerously in front of you.

So I'm not sure putting me behind the wheel of a huge 4x4 is a good idea. But I'd rather be there than be the chicken on the road. That's a literal chicken I'm talking about – not a wussy kind of driver. The chickens seem to get a bad deal in Bali. Roadkill or just plain kill, grill and served on a plate next to a pile of rice. They don't stand a chance. The poor cockerels might look like they're getting the better deal – often seen being washed and lovingly groomed at the side of the road by their owners, but that's so they look their best when appearing in the ring later – the cockerel-fighting ring, that is. Anyway, driving here, it's kind of invigorating. It's better than driving in south-east London because here no one gets out of their car with a baseball bat and smashes your car if you cut them up (that did actually happen to me and my brother in Brixton once when he was driving me to my Maths GCSE exam).

In Bali they expect to be cut up and just smile about it. Also, here if the police see you do something bad you can pay them off with

101

the 50,000 rupiah (around $5 US) you stash in your glove compartment, whereas if you tried to pay 'cigarette money' to a policeman in the UK you'd be arrested.

I can hear my dad and my brother reading this and going 'She's driving? She's driving in Bali? *Jesus.*'

Well, huh. Yes, I'm driving, and so far no deaths, of the human kind – though I make no claims about the poultry kind. And the thing is, getting in a car, I felt like I was 17 again – the same crazy, stomach-wobbling feeling of liberty and lip-biting excitement at having the means to explore the world and to be able to ditch out of school whenever I felt like it (which was frequently).

Having a car is like being given keys to the kingdom. And, in this case, the kingdom is Bali. It's heaven and I've got a hall pass. I drop Lula off at school in the morning then go for a drive. I just like knowing I can go wherever I want whenever I want. Then, after a day of writing (I am working on my second book in the Lila series), I mooch on back to pick her up after school and we're like Geena Davis and Susan Sarandon – Lula and I. We head out on the open road keeping one eye open for Brad Pitt.

Let's just hope it doesn't come to a nose-dive off a canyon.

FEELING INFERIOR

I was already feeling like an inferior human being. This, mainly thanks to having spent Sunday at Ku De Ta, a place so painfully striving to be cool it can't even spell itself correctly. A place so filled to the brim with beautiful people that it hurts to look for too long in one direction. A place so dripping in its own narcissim that the floors are slippery.

Anyway, a day spent hanging out there next to the sylph-limbed, perfectly-breasted, made me feel like a blubber whale and a slightly inferior human being. Wanting to remedy the fact that I turned up to the most glam venue on the island wearing a hot-pink shorts jumpsuit and fake Ray-Bans (sum total of outfit 40,000 rupiah - around £2) from the local market, I decided to make myself feel better and more sylph-like by reinventing my wardrobe.

I spent Sunday night diligently trawling the internet, bookmarking several Marc Jacobs and Missoni dresses. On Monday morning I hunted the streets of Ubud for fabric. Within about half an hour I had 20m of cotton, silk, batik and ikat in my possession, and was standing in front of a tailor with my laptop open, pointing at the images I'd saved of sylph-like models.

'Can you make me look like that?' I asked as the tailor measured me.

She stared at the image, she stared at me and I could just imagine the thoughts flitting through her mind, the silent laughter she was suppressing. Without saying a word, she unfurled her tape measure and started jotting down measurements.

'Oooooh. *Big* hips,' she announced patting my butt. 'Nice. Very nice.'

So that mission worked then.

FAST BOAT TO THE GILIS

In 1997 I spent a week on Gili Meno – a tiny dot of paradise resting in the Lombok Strait. Geek facts: the Lombok Strait is 3km deep, a breeding ground for tiger sharks and full of treacherous currents.

Lots of divers go drifting out into it and have to rely on the Bali-to-Lombok Ferry to pick them up before they hit the ocean/get eaten by a shark/drown. You like those odds?

Anyway, around 13 years ago I took a Chinese floating tin pot over this strait to get to Gili Meno. I remember that journey because I needed the loo more than I have ever needed anything in my entire life before or since. And I couldn't go for four hours because the loo on the ship was knee-deep in piss and when I stood horror-struck before the unlit cubicle, urine washing around me, a cockroach the size of a kitten ran over my foot.

So I spent four hours on a deck as hot as a frying pan wondering how I could position myself over the railing to pee without falling into the 3km depths below and wishing not for the last time that I had a penis. This is why 13 years later I insisted on taking the fast boat to the Gilis, the one that costs about forty quid for a return, as opposed to five. The one that has a toilet and air-conditioning and comfy seats and even, wait for it… life jackets.

Now, safely deposited on the other side of that fast-boat journey on an island almost unrecognisable from the tropical paradise it once was – layered now with concrete and rammed with huts – I can tell you for a fact that I shall be taking the slow boat back to Bali.

Every vital organ in my body has been repositioned – my stomach now sits where my left lung was; my left lung is somewhere near where my bladder used to be. I am bruised and dazed, and my right hand has cramp. John's has several hairline fractures from me squeezing it in terror as we bounced and jolted over what felt like tsunami-sized waves.

At some point on the fast-boat journey I realised that if Lula needed a wee or to be sick she was just going to have to do it right where she was, wedged tightly between us, because I couldn't twist my head away from the window and the boiling, vertical horizon for even so much as a nanosecond to aim her in John's direction.

Luckily the whole experience seemed to be too much for Lula. She fell silent and then passed out within 60 seconds – no puking or peeing. The boat was smashing into the waves so hard my sunglasses actually broke. *While I was wearing them.* Think about that.

At one point an Irish girl screamed out, 'Fucking bloody fucking hell Jesus man!' at the captain.

About half-way in, I was contemplating a leap over the side and a 3km freedive – anything to get off the boat. But I couldn't stand. I couldn't move. I couldn't even scream at the captain like the Irish girl had. My lips were clamped shut to stop the chocolate peanut butter Oreo cookies they'd given out as an in-cruise snack from reappearing down my front.

So the options are such: we could drift-dive back to Bali, we could take the Chinese kettle boat, or we could just stay here forever. Tempting as that last one is, there's no hot water and Lula has collected every shell on the beach already... so it looks like we're taking the slow boat.

A PILLOW TALK WITH GOD

Only in Bali do you hear the words 'colonic irrigation' and 'ecstatic dancing' in the same sentence. Actually, only in Ubud.

I was feeling down, despite the fact I was at the time eating the most succulent ribs a pig ever parted company with, then someone suggested some ecstatic dancing. I thought, why the hell not? I'm back on the saying 'yes' and 'Fuck It' to everything. When I do that, things tend to get better, or, at the very least, interesting.

I turn up late for my date with ecstasy. I find 30 or so adults on the floor – some lying prone, others waving their limbs in the air like seaweed caught in a current. The music is the kind you usually find in new-age spas or among mating whales.

I realise immediately that I am not dressed for the occasion (from slum tour to new-age dance session, I never seem to get it right). I am wearing my knock-off Missoni, which is definitely more knock-off than Missoni, and which looked way better on Giselle in the picture than it does on me. The people at my feet are all in stretchy yoga clothing, though some of the boys are wearing baggy fisherman's trousers. Bare chests seem *de rigeur* for the men, though in one case I do spy a waistcoat over the bare chest.

I lie on the floor... as near to the exit as I can get without actually crossing the threshold.

The teacher tells us (over a trance version of *Amazing Grace*) that we must 'open our hearts and have a pillow talk with God'.

I roll over onto my stomach and use the wooden floor as a pillow, not to talk to God but to stifle my giggles. Then I open one eye and squint across the room. Everyone else is now on their knees taking their seaweed moves up a notch. Clearly, their pillow talk with God has moved on to third base.

I close my eyes and start waving my arms, arching my back and generally looking like someone with a powerful voltage charge being shot through them. I stagger to standing, sneaking more peeks at the rest of the class – some of whom are now spinning wildly, doing headstands and leg-slapping their way through some electro dance beats.

Mid-dance (I'm now thoroughly getting into it despite myself) I hear the sounds of someone having an orgasm. I sidestep quickly in case I'm in the firing range. The sound of heavy panting, sighs and screams starts to echo around the room. I'm too scared to open my eyes in case I see everyone naked and writhing around me in an orgiastic froth. God *really* delivers, I think to myself.

For the final five minutes we are invited by the teacher/DJ to open our dance to others in the room. Being English, I shuffle over to the corner, keep my head down and eyes averted and dance with myself in my own space, sending out 'fuck off don't come near me' signals. I watch with building hysteria as the waistcoated guy starts trying to dance with a stunning Chinese girl.

He is rolling her onto his back, stretching her legs up in the air, flopping her over like a bedsheet he's having problems folding. They are trying desperately to co-ordinate but it's like watching a comedy skit of two people with lots of self-delusion auditioning for Rambert Dance.

I want to die laughing.

I am so going back next week.

THANK YOU, BALI

The Balinese like their ceremonies. Every day offerings are laid out around the house – little palm-leaf containers holding incense, petals, rice and small bits of food for the spirits. And then there are the big ceremony days, which occur several times a month: on the full moon and new moon, and then on odd days in between and for a plethora of reasons.

Poor cocks, is all I can say.

To claim the Balinese are spiritual is like saying that the Dalai Lama is some kind of peacenik. Bali is the only Hindu island in Indonesia – an archipelago of over 17,000 islands where the predominant religion is Islam. However, the Hinduism of Bali is not like that of India, it mixes in elements of Buddhism and animism too, and the result is the most fascinating religion I've ever come across; a religion that permeates every facet of life.

Houses are built in such a way as to confuse evil spirits (who can't turn corners), with fishponds to absorb any evil spirits that happen to cunningly make it around the corner. Offerings are made every morning outside every house, laid out by sarong-clad women, to keep the spirits happy.

These offerings are made at dawn following the belief that no one in the house can eat until the spirits have. There are three tenets at the heart of the Balinese belief system: respect and love for God, respect and love for humankind, and respect and love for the earth. If any of these are out of harmony then chaos reigns.

Made, our neighbour, explains that all Balinese try to live with these three tenets guiding them.

'If only the rest of the world did,' John remarks.

I feel humbled. Most of the time I barely hit one out of three. Actually, most of the time I don't even get one.

Made takes us to the temple in his house's compound. It is a big ceremony day – well, averagely big – there are maybe 60 people present, not all the 160 families who live in our village who would show up if it was a wedding or cremation.

The offerings are only stacked three-high. I am feeling lucky that I bought so many sarongs (to give as gifts of course, there was no intention of making them into dresses, you understand) because I am now wearing one the way it was intended to be worn: as a ceremonial sarong and not as a cute little Marc Jacobs-style dress, and having to shuffle along like a geisha because it's too tight.

John is next to me dressed like David Beckham circa 1999.

An old lady (it turns out she's actually the priest) flicks some water over me and slaps some rice on our foreheads. Lula starts eating it (not off my head, off the offering) but that is apparently what you're meant to do. Made explains that the ceremony is about giving thanks for all that we have. We are kneeling on the wet ground and I can't help but feel suddenly overpowered by how apt it is that we are here, among our new neighbours, invited into their home, into the heart of their community, to offer thanks.

There is so much to be thankful for: the bank manager's gullibility; the fact we are here at all; that we have made new friends in such a wonderful, peaceful and beautiful place; that Lula is happy and healthy; that I have discovered ecstatic dance.

When we get home, Alula starts wandering around the house gathering up petals and leaves. She disappears for five minutes, then comes back and takes John by the hand and points out all the little offerings she has made – several dozen in every corner.

'They are offerings to say thank you,' she says, 'for ice cream and chocolate.' She gives him a very stern look. 'You mustn't ever move them.'

EXCESSIVE USE OF THE WORD 'DUDE'

For those of you who don't know me so well, I use the word 'dude' quite a lot. I use it occasionally as a term of endearment as in 'hey, dude' meaning 'hello, my friend', but more often I use it in lieu of the words 'for fuck's sake'. I figure that by using the camaraderie of the D-word no one will be able to haul me up on the subtext and punch me.

Examples: 'Dude, you just cut me up!', 'Dude where are the keys?', 'Dude where have you been? I've been waiting in a hot car with a screaming child for hours.'

The funny thing is that until now I never figured what the

subtext was. It took an episode with our friend Jay to realise. He and Natasha, parents of Lula's crush Egg and her nemesis Noah have just moved into a stunning house perched over the Campuan river.

We decided (stupid rookie mistake) to swim in the river. In my head I'm already picturing myself in a Natural Essences commercial and so I run off to don my bikini and grab my shampoo bottle. I flip-flop my way down the riverbank with Jay.

The first *dude* occurs within 60 seconds.

'Dude, where are we going?' I ask.

'Just down here' Jay replies.

I frown at the tangled undergrowth and follow after him, biting my tongue. A flip-flop gets sucked into the abyss. My foot is covered in slime and coated in mosquitos.

'Dude, where's the path?' I yell, surveying the sodden, dank ground – a haven for cobras and pythons. My heart rate is upping frantically. A friend's nine-year-old daughter got bitten four times by a python not two weeks ago, very near to here. She's been left with a very impressive scar in the shape of fang marks and is hoping she can now speak parseltongue.

'I'll go ahead and see if we can get down,' Jay shouts over to me and off he goes, leaving me with just my panic and the mosquitos for company.

A minute later he calls to me that he has found a way down. I take a breath. He is not my husband so I cannot go hysterical on him. I cannot swear or yell or turn back. No, I have to act all Bear Grylls about it.

I follow until I reach him, and when I do, I look around at the waist-high undergrowth and the 6m drop to the brown, churning river below, and then I look back at Jay and say, yeah you guessed it,

'Dude, where is the path?'

Jay hacks a way down and I slip and slide after him until I come to rest on a rock overhanging the muddy rapids.

A collection of rubbish has dammed the river in front of us.

'So, you coming for a swim then?' Jay asks, already wading through the trash.

I look at him carefully. 'Dude, you have got to be kidding.'

HOW MUCH MONEY DOES IT TAKE TO TRAVEL AROUND THE WORLD?

So it turns out there is a point when the ATM decides to say 'NO'. Or, in my case, 'NO. NOW BACK THE HELL AWAY FROM THE TERMINAL, TURN AROUND AND GET OUT.'

It could be that withdrawing thousands of dollars worth of rupiah (which runs into the billions, so high that I can't even count it without getting vertigo) over the course of five days is not a wise thing to do before checking your bank balance. The little minus sign next to the big number? That apparently means something.

Then John goes and hops off to Singapore to investigate work opportunities, taking his plastic with him and leaving me with a stinking Jeep, which now ain't getting a clean, a small child who is going to be dining on fruit Mentos tonight, two episodes of *Mad Men* till the end (hmmm, what would Joanie do?), and not enough cash, it turns out, to pay for the taxi to the airport tomorrow, the exit visas for Alula and I, the small issue of our rent and the cost of our return visas (and if I don't pay that one I don't get our passports back).*

There you go. That's how long it takes to travel the world before going broke: six months and nine days. One time in Greece, when

---

* As per the terms of our visas, we need to leave Indonesia every 60 days.

I was about 20, I ran out of money on the last day of the holiday. I called my dad, reverse charges, and begged him to wire me some so that I didn't have to sleep on the streets of Athens and prostitute my way back home. He told me he was busy in a meeting and hung up on me.

So the path to daddy is closed. I'm going to have to man-up and figure this one out all by myself.

AUSTRALIA

JULY 2010

WANTING

We've had to say goodbye to Bali for the time being, and continue on our round-the-world trip. I say 'had to' but it isn't like anyone was forcing us. We do have these round-the-world tickets, though, that must be used and we do need to verify that Bali is indeed the place we want to move to. So now we are in Australia, comparing and contrasting.

The thing about being back in the West is that it's quite stressful. The capitalist gene kicks in and everywhere I look I see things I want to buy or consume: pork belly, ludicrously priced organic skincare, a house with gables and a veranda. It makes me stressed. So stressed that I can't breathe properly. It makes me think about money. And the fact I am unemployed with only my book advance to sustain me until John manages to woo Singapore's design companies into employing his genius.

Wanting things is stressful. In Bali and India there was little to want and what I did want I could generally afford – partly because back then my bank balance was still sort of flush with bathroom slush funds and I was sort of completely deluded and tricked by all the noughts. In Indonesia I was a millionaire with just $100 in my pocket.

There's a lesson here in wanting. It's certainly true that I was happier in Bali. But was that because I wanted less or because I got what I wanted (barring wine)?

The Buddhists are right whichever way you look at it: wanting things is the root cause of unhappiness.

I gotta figure out a solution to that one. One that doesn't involve meditating.

BEING SARAH ALDERSON

I kept telling people that the one thing I wanted to have in Bali was my collection of recipe books, that I really, really missed cooking, that I was going to excess baggage my way back to Indonesia with a suitcase filled with garlic presses, Le Creuset pans, working can-openers, my juicer and even a few cake tins.

Except we get to Australia – to a house stocked with non-stick pans and sparkling counter tops, with Philippe Starck lemon squeezers and silver cheese slicers, with an oven and a coffee grinder, and six types of olive oil and a larder of delicacies and Jamie Oliver recipe books – and, you know what? I cannot be arsed to cook. Can't even manage to melt chocolate in the microwave in a feeble attempt at dessert. I put it on for 20 seconds and forgot about it. Came back half an hour later and put it on for a minute. Came back when I smelled it burning. Gave up. Ate the strawberries as God intended. (And have had to hide the bowl with the burnt chocolate on it until I can figure a way of drilling it off.)

I would argue that, after dealing with ant-infested kitchens for six months (we are talking so ant-infested that you'd come down-stairs in the morning and find a line of them walking off with the S-bend), I've lost interest in kitchens and cooking. But I think it goes deeper than that. I think that's just an excuse I made up to cover up the fact that really I've lost any kind of interest in the domestic.

Tonight I watched our lovely host wash up. She looked at me

standing there and said, 'The tea towel's over there on the side.'

I stared at her confused for full on ten seconds wondering why she was telling me this. My hands weren't wet. I didn't need to dry them.

'I think you've gotten too used to having help,' she laughed when I finally twigged that it was being suggested I dry the dishes.

It is true. I have not washed or dried dishes in a very, very long time.

I then went into the bedroom. It was rather messy. My excuse for this one is that we've been living out of a bag for six months and moving a lot, even in Bali where we seemed to move from guesthouse to rental to new rental every week or so, so what is the point of unpacking? And if I do, Alula just comes and takes everything and rearranges it anyway into little shrines around the house. Best off just keeping it in the bag. Or at least piled on top of or around the bag.

'You're so messy,' John said to me.

'Oh my God,' I replied. 'What are you saying? Are you saying [pause for indignation] I've become a slob?'

John didn't answer – kept his back to me, in fact.

'Oh my God!' I tried to sound appalled and outraged. But, oh my God! He's right. And there is no excuse. Except maybe to say: 'But my hand hurts. I can't pick anything up.' (I have a very bad case of tendonitis as I've just written a book in very short order).

But we all know that's an excuse because I can still manage to pick up my glass of wine and lift that tub of ice cream out of the freezer.

So there we have it. I am a slob. This is making me wonder what use I am to the world. I am too scared to voice this out loud, though, in case John doesn't answer and keeps his back to me.

PERTH – CAN WE LIVE HERE?

Yes. I could live in Perth… If the apocalypse was looming and/or I had just been told I had six months to live. Or if the people we are staying with wanted to maybe, say, give us their house to live in because it is rather stupendously lovely.

Perth is absolutely beautiful. Blue skies, stunning beaches, awesome bike trails (for all the cycling I just love to do), a gorgeous waterfront. But it can't help reminding me of that scene in *Beaches* where the dark-haired woman who isn't Bette Midler is dying. I keep expecting to hear John singing that I'm his hero and everything he wishes he could be (I'll keep waiting on that). It is beautiful and peaceful and sedate. It's the kind of place where you could sit on a veranda in the sunshine and listen to the kookaburras all day and not do anything. And be perfectly, serenely happy. If I had to wait for death to claim me I would do it here for sure.

Here are my other fascinating observations on Perth:

1. You could play 'What's the Time, Mr. Wolf' on the freeway blindfolded and not get hit by a car.
2. You get called a lot of things, like: champ, darling, sweetheart, love, beauty, you beauty, darling and mate. It's quite nice.
3. It is exceedingly expensive. I'm sure it wasn't this expensive when I was 18 because I managed to enjoy myself quite a lot back then, but now it is the equivalent of £8 for the cheapest bottle of wine and £5 for a bottle of Garnier Fructis. And I am not resorting to drinking shampoo as a cheaper alternative. That's what meths are for.
4. Fashion seems to have entered a strange vortex here. Ripped jeans, mullets, sequinned tops, singlet vests over tight T-shirts

116

and knee-high stiletto boots with silver buckles are everywhere I look.

5. There are drive-through liquor stores here, called bottle shops. I mean why have we not thought of that in Europe?

6. It seems that in order to be able to afford to live here (and buy shampoo), you need to get a job in the oil industry, which rules Perth out as an option.

So, goodbye Perth, see you again, I hope. Or not, as the case may be.

THE USA

AUGUST 2010

OUR THIRD WEDDING ANNIVERSARY GOES WELL

'It is not my fault. It is the map's fault.'

'A-ha,' John murmurs from the driver's seat.

'No. Seriously. This map is totally fecking shite. Joshua Tree could be five feet away, it could be five miles away, or it could be 5,000 light-years away. Want to know why it could be any of those? Because this map that you bought from Target is so shit.'

'Right, so it's my fault that you can't read the map?' John asks.

'I can read the map. I can read a map better than you can, Mr. "Turn it upside down to check whether to go left or right".'

'You get us lost more than I do.'

'I'm sorry? Did you or did you not take us on a 150-mile detour yesterday through the Mojave Desert?'

'That's because the scale was off in the *Lonely Planet*. Anyway, it was fun. We got to see the desert.'

'It was fun for you because you got to work on your computer. I was the one driving through the desert. It wasn't fun for Alula either, who had nothing to do but stare out a window and look at desert. Look. This map is shit. I am buying a new one.'

'It's a waste of money. We already have a map.'

'We have a shit map. That is getting us lost a lot. If we spent $20 on a new map, we would save that in petrol money for all the detours.'

'Well you didn't even buy a map. You couldn't even find the maps in the store.'

'Yeah, well actually it wasn't that I couldn't find them. I forgot to look.'

[Silence]

[For 50 more lost miles]

DISNEYLAND: THE FATTEST PLACE ON EARTH

Disneyland – the happiest place on earth. Also, possibly, the fattest. I didn't know fat like this existed. It's astonishing fat. It's six-belly-folds fat. It's humungous fat and it's queuing in front of you at the ice-cream place ordering a triple chocolate sundae. It's possibly more pronounced to us because we've spent so long in Asia where, for the most part, people are thin.

I can say this with something like authority because I just Googled it and 34 per cent of Americans are officially obese (compared to the UK where it's about 17 per cent).

The queues in Disneyland are so long because lots of the rides were designed in the eighties when America was thinner – now they can only squeeze one person in per row, when before three people could fit. Hence queues three times as long.

Walking down Main Street, trying to avoid being squashed, John looks at me: 'This is your idea of hell, isn't it?' he asks. He is smirking. He and Alula are both dancing down Main Street like they're auditioning for *Fame* while I am covering my eyes and wishing there was a dark room nearby that I could lie in.

I am too busy scowling to answer John, but he is right. I hate crowds, I hate noise and, most of all, I hate smiley people.

I do kind of hate smiley people though. I think that's quite British of me. There are many smiley people in Disneyland – the staff/visitor ratio is about 1:1 and all the staff manically grin. That's all they do. They just grin. It's like they know Disneyland Big Brother is watching them and if they stop grinning they'll get shot. Right there on Main Street.

I wonder whether when they wake up in the morning they have to swallow a bucket of Prozac just to get up. Every night I imagine them going home and injecting muscle relaxant into their cheeks. It makes me depressed. It makes me want to cry.

Alula is in heaven, though, and this is the point, John reminds me. Alula is silently, worshipfully in awe of the princesses. I try to look at Disneyland through her eyes. Instead I'm thinking things like: 'Oh you poor dear, you probably graduated from LAMDA and they have you dressed in that absurd Princess Jasmine get up' and 'Tinkerbell looks just like Kelly Osbourne' and 'Peter Pan has terribly bad hair'. I hope for his sake it's a wig and if that animatronic of Johnny Depp is lifesize he's really, really small. Like an elf.

Disneyland should have made me nicer. It should have filled me with the spirit of celebration – it should have made me want to unite with all humankind. 'It's a Small World' still rings in my head like a Guantanamo torture tune. But instead of making me nice it just made me (more) misanthropic and evil.

And, now I think about it, the only bit I liked and that made me smile was the evil Maleficent strutting her way through the crowds scaring the children.

NO GAS

There is only the road: long, dusty, hilly, desert-y and deserted. Then there is the fuel gauge: red, flashing, beeping and two miles till empty.

'Crap, crap, crap!' I hiss.

'Don't stress. It won't help,' says John.

'But what if we break down out here?'

'I'm so not walking' is the subtext. I'll be like those people who break down in their cars in the snow and get found six months later desiccated inside them. It's not snowing but that's what I think of. I start thinking, too, of John hitching to find fuel and a lonesome truck driver pulling up and a whole horror-movie scene plays out in my mind. I really wish I hadn't watched *Wolf Creek* or *Halloween*.

'Coast. Don't press the gas,' I tell John.

'We're going uphill.'

'Well, put it in neutral when you get to the top.'

'Where's neutral? It's an automatic. Do automatics have neutral?'

It would appear not, because we coast downhill in drive and the gauge rides to empty.

'Pull over. No, don't pull over! No, not here! No, don't stop in the middle lane, what if we conk out right here at the lights? Look! Look! A petrol station!'

We slide into the forecourt. I hop out, jubilant, and run inside. (I hate this whole having to get out the car to pump gas* – look at me, sounding all American – I mean, put petrol in the car – but this time I don't care because they also sell ice cream inside and we need to celebrate our victory over the fuel gauge.)

'Forty dollars of gas, please,' I tell the man behind the counter.

I insert my card into the machine.

'Sorry, we don't take credit cards,' the man tells me.

'Err, that's all I have,' I answer. 'Hang on. I'll just get my husband...'

*We've been spoiled in Bali with gas-pump attendants (who would often cheat you by filling you up with air and pocket the extra cash, but, still, I did get to sit down while they did it).

John tries swiping too. The same thing happens.

'Is that a European bank card?' the man finally asks us after numerous failed attempts.

'Yes.'

'Yeah, we don't take those.'

'We have no gas.' We have no cash either. Only about $2-worth of quarters, with which I plan to buy my ice cream and which I'm keeping my fist tightly curled around in case John hears the coins jangling.

'Sorry,' the man says, turning to the next customer.

Turns out there is an ATM though just behind me, right beside the jerky stand, and I thank God for overdrafts, and Ben & Jerry's for the invention of Cherry Garcia ice cream.

A LITTLE INTERLUDE WITH A BEAR

'I'm going out there. I have to move that potato.'

'OK,' I whisper, thinking, 'you are on your own, buddy'.

John disappears through the canvas flap. He is gone a long time. I hear rustling. Then I hear gallumping, paw-pounding sounds right near my head. Then I hear John breathlessly re-entering the tent.

'Did you get the potato?' I ask.

'There's a great big fucking bear,' he replies. 'I need you to come outside with me.'

I sit up in bed. 'Are you fucking kidding me?' I hiss. 'You just said there's a great big fucking bear outside.' Not even the fear of a $5,000 fine can persuade me outta that bed and through those canvas flaps.

'But it's our fault,' John says. 'The bear is going to keep coming back until it gets the potato.'

I open and shut my mouth.

'Fuck, fuck, fuck,' John repeats like a prayer.

'What? What is it?' a frightened little voice pipes up from the darkness on the other side of the tent.

'Nothing, darling, go back to sleep,' we whisper.

'But what is it?' Lula asks shrilly and loud enough to wake the entire campsite. 'Is it a bear?'

'No, no, it's just daddy, he needs a wee. Go back to sleep.'

She flops down on the bed and consents.

'Look, come with me,' John says again.

I have to go. I cannot stay in the tent clutching my knees, my ears pricked for the sounds of growls and shrieks and leg-bones snapping like twigs. It's like the Blair Witch is outside and John wants me to leave the tent with him. I am caught between a rock and a bear. I am not dressed for facing down bears. I'm in a T-shirt, knickers and flip-flops. 'When am I ever dressed right for the occasion?', I think in some recess of my mind that isn't processing BEAR.

'Turn on the outside light,' I say to John.

We tip-toe outside the tent. I stand guard, convinced that every boulder is, in fact, a bear.

John rescues the glowing potatoes from the embers of the fire. Well, he rescues one. The other three have mysteriously vanished.

John puts the lone potato into the metal container. The one that says on it in big, bold letters: PLEASE PUT ALL YOUR FOOD INSIDE. FAILURE TO COMPLY WILL RESULT IN A $5,000 FINE. DON'T BE RESPONSIBLE FOR KILLING A BEAR.

We skitter back inside the tent and grip each other tight beneath the sheets.

'Well, you're not getting your Junior Ranger Badge,' I tell John. 'You're supposed to yell "NO BEAR, GO BEAR!"'

'Says the girl who left the potatoes in the fire to cook overnight.'

A LETTER TO ALULA

Dear Alula,

Today you are four and you just told me the following things: that you love me as many houses as we have lived in ('that's such a lot isn't it, Mummy?') and as big as the waves and as dark as the night when you are sleeping and how big the moon is and how hot the sun is.

I wonder whether you will be a poet or a songwriter. Although you resolutely refuse to learn your letters. 'BORING', you say.

'But if you can't write', we say, 'then how will you be able to read signs that tell you where buried treasure lies? Princesses read. It's part of the job description.'

'No. Not interested,' you insist. 'But "banana" begins with B.'

We don't really care. We know you'll do just fine. I kiss you and tell you how much we love you and how glad I am that you're my baby – that you chose me to be your mummy. You look confused at that.

I ask you if you'll always be my baby, even when you are 40 or 80 or a 100. You tell me you'll love me even when you are a billion and a hundred. And ask if you will have stopped growing by then.

'Yes,' I say, 'you'll stop growing when you are about 18. And you will be taller than me and undoubtedly beautiful. And, you know,' I tell you, 'four years ago I was lying in bed with you and cuddling you and the doctor's first words were, "look at those eyelashes".'

'Why?' you ask.

'Because they are long,' I say.

'I just can't sleep, Mummy. I want back strokes.'

'OK,' I say, because we do this every night. 'Lula bean, Lula bean,' I start to sing.

'You're my mummy forever,' you finish (this to the tune of 'Edelweiss'.) 'Please, Mummy, I just need to not sleep and look at all my birthday presents.'

You stroke back my hair and it feels like you're not four but much older. And you say, 'I'm sorry I was naughty today, Mummy. Thank you for all my birthday presents.'

And I say: 'That's OK, my darling, you're good 99 per cent of the time. Everyone's a little bit naughty.'

And you kiss me and ask, 'What's a per cent?' and I breathe in deeply and say, 'Go to sleep now.'

And now you are four and a big girl and we will hold you to your promise that now you will brush your own teeth and walk every-where. No more carries. But secretly I'm hoping you break that last one a few times more.

Happy Birthday, pop pop.

I AM A SAGITTARIUS, YOU KNOW – THAT SORT OF EXPLAINS IT

I'm not ready to hang up my travelling boots. I have started discuss-ing with John a plan we are hatching for some time in the mid-2020s when Alula no longer needs stationary parents (or nearby parents, for that matter) when we will buy an old Airstream and drive across and around the Americas for, say, maybe ten years.

We will own a husky dog which I think we will call Lobo and a gazebo we can put up outside for evening dining, possibly draped with fairy lights, and by then everything will be technologically advanced and I won't need to yell at John for navigating us to

Canada instead of Mexico because Google will be driving the car. I think maybe I'm planning too far into the future, which is something I'm prone to do. I keep forgetting to enjoy the present.

But am I ready to return to London? What do you think? Does it sound like it? Would I ever be though? The answer to that is no. I have tasted sunshine and ecstatic dancing and canoed with dolphins and eaten grapes off the vines in the Napa Valley and faced-down a bear and written two books and started a third and found that there is a whole world of amazing opportunity and potential and incredible adventures out there so, no, there's frankly no going back that I can see.

Plus if we did I'd have to get a job because being a writer only pays well enough if you live somewhere like Indonesia or if you're Stephanie Meyer (working on that plan). And then there's the little issue of laundry too.

So I have an idea: why don't you come join us out here instead? You could be the cool people in the airstream next door. Oh come on, you know you want to. Or maybe you don't. Maybe it's just me. I'm Sagittarius, the renowned traveller of the zodiac, and I don't like doing laundry.

TOP EIGHT THINGS ON OUR ROUND-THE-WORLD TRIP

We have seven days before we head back to London. I can't believe we've been away for seven months. It's been easily the best seven months of my life, so I'm kind of reeling with premature holiday blues while also enjoying the best time of the trip so far. Not that it's over. On the one hand it feels like London will be a brief hiatus before our return to Bali in October when the next chapter of the adventure begins. The chapter called 'No, Really, Can We Actually

Live Here?' is the chapter the bank manager is no longer funding.

Anyway, on one of our endless and endlessly beautiful car journeys through California, I debated the highlights of the trip. So herewith, a list, for any of you out there following in our footsteps, of things not be missed on a round-the-world journey.

1. CALIFORNIAN HOT SPRINGS
Only I'm not telling you where these are because they are too, too special and I want to keep them all to myself, just like I do Green & Black's chocolate.

2. THRIFTING
The unsung joy of our American trip has been the thrifting. Like shopping at Ikea, it allows you to think you're not spending anything… until your card gets declined. At a thrift store. That's embarrassing. Best thrifting? Mission Beach in San Diego, Monterey and Santa Barbara (rich pickings).

3. CALIFORNIA WINE COUNTRY
Take a picnic. Don't take a child.

4. CHAI AND SAMOSAS IN PATNEM BEACH, GOA
Life was great in Goa. My day consisted of tripping out of our pink house, piggy-backing Alula to school past the cows and the rubbish dump, stopping by for 4p-samosas and then heading to the beach to sip chai as the sun warmed my face. This would be followed by some writing, some swimming and some eating. There were so few distractions: no television, no shops, no choices. Everything was simple and basic, but joyful.

5. CYCLING

John says cycling up the volcano in Bali. If you recall, I once cycled down the volcano. Except it wasn't all down. So that doesn't feature on my highlight list. But cycling around the riverfront in Perth does. Because it was flat.

6. SWIMMING TO PALOLEM

Purely because I did it and didn't get eaten by a shark.

7. INDIAN TRAIN JOURNEYS

A trip to India is not complete without spending 12 hours in a non-air-conditioned second-class carriage. Seriously, it was one of the best days of the trip. Not that I'm keen to repeat it in this lifetime.

8. PILLOW TALKING WITH GOD

Ecstatic dancing was probably the funniest and most fun thing I've ever done in my whole life. I got a chance to pillow talk with God, which isn't something you get to say very often, and I also got to see things that normally you only get to see in the outtakes from *The X Factor.*

BACK IN THE UK

SEPTEMBER 2010

Welcome Home! says the helium balloon that welcomes us. Except it's not really home. Or it doesn't feel it. But then after a day it does. Having had an emotional breakdown at the baggage carousel in Heathrow where I almost climbed onto said carousel, rotated through to the runway strip and tried to stow away on the next flight to anywhere, England is slowly working itself back into my affections. Not enough to make me stay for long, let me add, but enough to soften the blow of returning. Partly, I think it's down to once again being within range of Percy Pigs.

But then, just as I start to get comfortable in my new M&S knickers, exploring the new ranges of fizzy pig tails and other gelatinous farmyard creatures Marks & Spencer, in their infinite wisdom, have seen fit to create, I have an encounter in south-east London that removes my Pig goggles.

I am walking down my old high street. A boy of about 14 is coming towards me pushing a pram (I don't think the progeny therein is his own – possibly it belongs to the woman behind him – his mother?) and he's weaving the pram straight at me like a drunk driver. He thinks it's funny. I don't. I dodge out his way and give him a look. A look I had forgotten I could do but that has nonetheless lost none of its power.

Alas my 'look' does not have the power to turn people to stone, or smite them to ash.

He swears at me. I, of course, call him something unprintable.

His mother says nothing. I cannot believe two things: one, that kids these days are such little shits in this part of the world, and two, that within minutes of re-entry into my native land I'm as aggressive and mean as everyone else who lives here.

It's a Darwinian response, I tell myself. Kill or be killed.

I go into Boots the chemist with my mum and we get elbowed out of the way by two twelve-year-olds in school uniform who proceed to plaster themselves with green eye shadow and pink lip gloss and then steal the testers – completely ignoring the fact there are several adults with actual money to spend trying to choose products for which they will pay.

I get in the car and start driving and immediately realise that I shouldn't be behind the wheel. Especially not having gone back to a stick-shift, especially not with jet lag, especially not in south-east London. With the moves I'm making – reminiscent of Bali driving – I might cause serious injury or get involved in a road-rage incident.

Halfway through overtaking a bus on a residential road I have a moment of clarity and brake hard, pulling-in behind it with cheeks burning. I'm driving like a South Londoner again but one that's been hybridised with a Balinese driver. It's lethal. I could audition for *Fast & Furious 18*.

I have a sudden longing for Bali. I want to live in a country where no one loses their temper or shouts, which is a hugely uncool and largely unthinkable thing for a Balinese person to do (though some will happily smile to your face and then go away and put a black-magic curse on you behind your back, so I hear). I'm hoping if I live there long enough that kind of laid-back, happy attitude will brush off on me.

I long for the me who smiles and waves at strangers and gives way at stop signs and never swears (well, not quite as much) and rarely eyeball-rolls or death-stares. Honestly, she does exist, just not in this country. London Sarah is not half as nice as Bali Sarah.

'God,' I say to my mum, 'why on earth would we move back here?'

And the thing is, even though we've taken her only granddaughter half-way across the world to live, she agrees with us wholeheartedly.

ANCESTORS AND ROOTS

It's not so easy to get nostalgic about your roots when your grand-father grew up on the Old Kent Road. And generally speaking I don't hold with anywhere north (of the equator, let alone the M25, that is). But visiting Cumbria with John, land of his forbears, I find myself getting all family-minded and feeling misty-eyed about the UK. Don't get me wrong, I'm not about to suggest we ditch Bali for Cumbria.

It's September and the rain is giving the windows a good whipping, the stonework is about six foot deep and even that's not enough to stop me from sitting on top of the Rayburn oven drinking in the heat, and once more I find my driving skills unsuited to one-lane winding country roads. ('Maybe slow down a bit?' John suggests, with one hand wavering over the handbrake.) But, amidst the weather and the dodgy driving, I do pause to think that there's something rather lovely about a churchyard full of Aldersons, which there is here in Cumbria.

There's even a John and Sarah Alderson, our ancestors (well, John's – there I am again, claiming them as my own, but Sarah Alderson from 1732 wasn't born one either and there she is in the graveyard laying claim to six feet of Cumbrian soil). And the old Alderson farmhouse, standing bluntly over the stunning Eden Valley, is now no longer a rambling stone shell but the site of the world's most incredible shower (a shower so good I contemplated actually sleeping under it, rather than in my bed).

It feels good to connect Alula with her roots; she's been so rootless for so long. And even though she's oblivious to the sense of history (she still thinks she's going to live to be a billion and a hundred) I'd like to think it will give her some grounding in the future. Then I'll take her to the Old Kent Road and let my dad take her to Millwall football ground ('The Den') so she can connect with her other roots and learn some proper hooligan behaviour. She is, after all, half-South Londoner.

A big part of me is happy to vagabond my whole life, with no desire for one home and no calling to set down roots in one particular place. Yet here I am, confronted with centuries of one family (my husband's family, at that) living in one place. It's kind of mind-blowing.

I think I need to think about it for a few days before I figure out what family and place means to the sense of self we create. How does the place we live in, the place we come from, the place our family comes from, affect our own identity? I am a South Londoner born and bred, and it's definitely affected who I am. I think there's a certain hardness – a shell – you build around yourself to survive in any city, but in London it's Kevlar-impenetrable. There's a fast-paced-ness too, an impatience (get out of my way you daft tourist, standing on the left of the escalator), a cynicism that gets seeded early on. Or maybe that's just me, and the particular circumstances of my life.

I can see those elements of me have, however, started to erode while living in Bali, but not completely. I think they're too entwined with my DNA to ever fully vanish.

The thing is, I might start a trip back to the UK by strolling through the streets of London feeling like an alien, smiling at everyone I pass, but within half an hour I'm back to huffing loudly as I push past slow-walking tourists and avoiding eye-contact with everyone on the tube.

It's hard to hang on to the new identity – the vision of myself I want to be – when you're back in the place that formed and moulded you to begin with.

Home, or, rather, the place we inhabit, really does define and shape you, and in ways I never realised before.

WORK WARDROBES

'Honey,' I say, 'do you like my new bikini?'

John pauses to look up from his computer, which oftentimes I think he should have married instead of me. It certainly gets more attention and is probably worth more than I am. Not that that would be hard. Anything worth more than approximately £10.34* would be worth more than me.

'Where's that from?' he asks.

'The Shop of Top,' I say. OK, OK, I know I said I was way too old and that it was immoral to spend £40 on a bikini after seeing poverty in India… but, but, but in my head I'm still 17, and as I mentioned before, as soon as I got back to England it was like the consumer devil inside me switched back on at the same time that

---

*Possibly the amount of money in my bank account right now. Though, possibly, I missed the little minus sign in front of it.

the cynical bitch did. I hate myself and I despair that all the things I thought I'd shed: vanity, materialism, an obsession with trivial, unimportant matters – weren't shed at all, but merely shoved to one side momentarily. Being back in the West has thrown open the Pandora's box and everything's come rushing out again. It's a darkness that will overtake the world and destroy it.

But at least I will be wearing a cute bikini when that happens.

'How much did it cost?' John asks.

'I can't remember,' I mumble.

'Do you really need a new bikini?' he asks.

I scrunch up my nose. 'It's work clothes,' I tell him, giving him what I hope is a winning smile. 'I needed a new outfit for the office.' This time my grin is genuine, because it is pretty awesome to know that I will never have to buy proper work clothes ever again (hopefully...) and that my office is a house in Bali.

But then I glance at the price tag and sigh. John's right. Do I really need another bikini, and one probably made by someone in Dharavi? Reluctantly I take it off and put it back in the bag. I glance over at John. He seems to be doing much better than me at holding onto a more Eastern mindset of non-attachment.

Though I wonder what he'd do if I hid his laptop?

LONDON JUST EXHAUSTS ME

Last night I found myself drenched, numb, bone-tired and hating on the whole London transport system. And all I could think about – to the point that I almost burst into tears as I stood at South Ken tube staring at macaroons in the window of Paul that cost £3.30 each – was the golden Californian sunshine, or sitting on a Goan beach with warm sand trailing through my fingers, ordering an entire succulent spicy pig for less money than a sugary French treat and the fact I never ever, ever feel an ounce of cold in Bali unless I'm standing beneath an air-conditioning unit naked having just showered in cold water.

My friend Nichola found me drizzled upon and unhappy, wrapped me up in her scarf and stuffed a Berocca vitamin in my mouth. It wasn't a macaroon but, hey, it's probably better at halting death.

I think if you live in London for a time you adapt, because I used to do it daily and, yeah, I was tired, but now I can't even manage to travel around London for half a day without feeling like I need to put myself into a coma for a month to recover. Which leads me to equate London with a disease to which you build up immunity. And if you're away from it for too long your immunity decreases and you come back and you're decimated in seconds. It's like the Black Death.

How did we ever do this, day in and day out? It feels unreal, and totally insane. No wonder everyone looks so tired and harried. No wonder everyone seems so grumpy.

Get me out of here.

GET ME TO THE PLANE ON TIME

Before – once upon a time, when I used to be a professional – I knew what punctuality was. It seems that in the last nine months punctuality and I have become estranged. Possibly permanently.

It's quite amazing how quickly it happened. John and I have never worn watches and for a time while travelling I didn't have a phone either. As a result we lost all sense of timekeeping. And really – what did we ever have to be on time for? OK, there were flights and the occasional train, but usually we had a taxi booked, which meant we had an alarm-call, so to speak.

John was always challenged in the time department. I used to get annoyed by it. Now I just sit or lie and read a book until he says, 'Right, are you ready?' And then I still don't move. I don't move now until John is out of the house, in the car, engine running and has done his two return trips to the house for forgotten items.

I have learned the hard way. We've almost divorced at every airport we've travelled through because John will amble along to the gate, and then decide to go to the bathroom when they are screaming, 'Final call!' over the PA system and pulling the tape across the gate.

In our first week back in the UK we had to get to a wedding. We were already running late (or we thought we were; we didn't know for sure because we don't wear watches and the clock in the car was saying something like 43.18) and when we turned into the multi-storey car park close to the church John decided that now would be a good time and place to get into his suit, change his belt, and his shoes, and his shirt, and choose a tie... I don't know, probably shave too.

I got back in the car and read five more chapters of my book. When we finally made it to the church the bride was just about to enter to the wedding march. John tried to get around her and the bridesmaids. I had to grab his sleeve and hold him back. Anyway, all this is to illustrate that we rarely make anything on-time these days.

Same goes for our flight back to Bali. We made it to check-in with about 30 seconds to spare. The man at the check-in stared at our two trolleys and raised a perfectly over-plucked eyebrow.

'We have paid for excess,' I panted (we'd run).

Our three check-in bags weighed-in at almost 100 kilos. Six kilos over the excess. So there we were, on the concourse, unpacking the beasts and scattering items all around, trying to work out what to purge. It was like the final of *The Crystal Maze* – the clock ticking and some pen-tapping, disapproving staff member tut-tutting all the while as we stacked things onto the scales to make up six kilos.

Needless to say, I lost all my books (one of which was a recipe book, so no loss there) while John purged what, exactly? I'm still not entirely sure – some laptop screen cleaner I believe.

We boarded with about 45 kilos of hand baggage, claiming 'laptop bag, laptop bag' at whoever barred our way and questioned our three bags a piece.

We ran through security and then guess what? *Final call.* John goes to the loo.

We were the last to board.

Ironically, I now recall, the one item John did empty out of his bag and purge was the alarm clock.

PART 3: THE LIVING PART

October 2010

SHIT, WE'RE ACTUALLY EMIGRATING? WHY DID NO ONE TELL ME?

I don't think I've ever been so scared. And that's nothing to do with reading the Air Asia in-flight magazine in which they discuss what happens when planes crash into the sea and try to comfort you with all the rescue paraphernalia that would ditch into the watery abyss with you. (It's OK, you'll plummet 37,000 feet but you'll have a whistle. And seasickness tablets. So what's the big fuss?)

I'm scared because I think we might be mad. And it's only suddenly occurred to me, 37,000ft in the air and over water, that we're emigrating. I swallow hard. And then clutch John and demand to know what we were thinking. Our previous wanderings seem suddenly like a two-week Thompson holiday in Spain compared to this.

This is monumental. And a part of me longs for the crazy, lazy days of mooching around the planet with just a rucksack, a bank account a-slosh with money for a fake bathroom and a round-the-world ticket in my hand. I miss the lightness of that, the vagueness, the freedom, the possibilities. Now I will be a stayer-putter.

Am I ready to have a home again? A routine? Won't that feel like prison? For the whole 14-hour Air Asia flight, when not trying to stave off hypothermia by clutching tightly to Alula (Air Asia: that'll be £50* for a comfort blanket, please), I kept thinking, what have we done? What have we done?

And then we land. We're picked up. We're driven to the house we've rented in Bali. And within seconds it *is* home. The restaurant next door rustles up a pancake for Alula and delivers it to us. The neighbours all pop by to say hello. I do a supermarket sweep and bump into three people I know. Oooh, I think, I can do this. This is actually rather wonderful.

And then I unpack the mugs, the fridge magnets and the Marmite. Oh, and the 5kg of Percy Pigs I had hidden from John during the suitcase purge at the airport. I sit back on the balcony admiring the view, eating a gelatinous pig while listening to the sounds of a real one being slaughtered.

And I really do feel at home.

NOVEMBER 2010

LEARNING INDONESIAN

'Shower', I say (in Indonesian).

Wayan nods.

*This might be exaggerated but it was certainly more money than we could comfortably part with.

I flick hurriedly through the pages of the dictionary while I stand in the bath demonstrating. 'Long' I say, pointing as I say it to the shower lead. I search frantically for 'shower-head holder'. It is nowhere to be found in the concise Indonesian-English dictionary.

I settle for 'to hold'. So we have: 'shower long to hold'. I add the Indonesian for 'to buy'. Should be enough, right? You get the gist, don't you?

Wayan says something. I recognise the word 'Nyoman' – his sister-in-law who lives behind us – who speaks an iota more English. I run around to her house and explain that I'd like Wayan, if possible, to buy a longer shower lead (because at the moment the shower lead is so short that the head reaches my belly button) and then drill in a shower-head holder over the bath. I would do this myself (well, maybe not the drilling, as I'd probably drill through my own hand) but I have no clue where to locate the parts or a drill. And we're paying Wayan a monthly wage and so far all he's done is drain the pond every day and fill it back up again.

I stopped him from burning the rubbish – his only other job – and installed some recycling bins, which get collected weekly, so he doesn't even have this job to do any more. (The only waste we now have is compost and this gets fed to Wayan's pig, which I've been told we will later get a chance to eat.)

Anyway, Nyoman says something like, 'OK, OK, sorted.'

I go home. Five minutes later an out-of-breath Nyoman arrives. Not Nyoman who lives behind us who I've just spoken to, but Nyoman a man – the husband of our landlady. It's confusing, I know.

'Is there problem with shower?' he asks.

'God, no,' I say. '*Tidak* problem. Just, um, we need longer lead for shower.' (You get in the habit of dropping pronouns after a while as there are none in Indonesian.) 'So if people want shower they can have one.'

'Aahhhhh, OK,' he says, and disappears off.

Ten minutes later Made arrives (not the old nanny, the landlady) and says: 'What's the matter with the shower? Is it broken?'

I bury my head in my hands. There are three options but two I'm not prepared to consider: learn better mime skills or learn DIY.

The time has come to learn Indonesian. Or at least a little bit more than 'shower', 'hold', 'long' and 'to buy'.

2011

UBUD: TOWN OF ECCENTRICS AND SOAPNUTS

A list of the people I have met in the last five days:

- Iridolgist
- Raw-food cook
- Colonic irrigator
- Sexuality-through-yoga teacher
- Tarot reader
- Theta balancer
- Ecstatic-dance teacher
- Feng-shui balancer
- Soapnut evangelist

Where are all the accountants and lawyers? They are not here, because there is no place for them in Ubud. No one is interested in money here because they are too busy meditating in a rice paddy and balancing their karma to balance their books. And the law – well, the law seems to have no place in Indonesia, full stop. I am thinking of working on a novel based here. I wouldn't have to make anything up because you really couldn't make any of this stuff up. No one would believe it wasn't fiction anyway. It would be like a Jilly Cooper romp, only exchanging the polo field and double-barrelled surnames for The Yoga Barn and chosen names*.

The only problem is that I shall have to write it when we're ready to leave because it's a small town and I don't want to find myself sent to Coventry. The thing that stops me from picking up a pen today and starting on it, however, is what I'd have to do in the name of research.

THE LAST TIME I DISCUSS CREMATION AND DEATH WITH A FOUR-YEAR-OLD

Alula and I drive past a fifty-foot-high horse made of papier maché and Alula asks: 'What's the horse for?'

'The King of Ubud died,' I tell her.

'A real king?' she asks in wonder.

'Yes,' I tell her. 'He died and they're having a cremation.'

'What's a cremation?'

'It's something they do when people die.'

'So, will they take him to the not-dead doctor and make him better? Will they make him alive again?'

'Err, kind of.'

'What do they do to the horse?'

'They burn the horse.'

---

*A lot, and when I say a lot, I mean practically 90 per cent of the expat community in Ubud have ditched the name on their birth certificate given to them by their parents and chosen a new name. Most chosen names seem to follow the pattern of Indian God + a reference to the moon or an animal. For example: Shiva Moonbeam, Kali Jaguar, etc.

'And the King is in the horse?'

'Yes.'

'But if they burn the horse, won't he die?'

'He's kind of already dead. He died two months ago.' (I don't mention the digging-up of his body by his relatives after two months, which is how long it's taken to prepare for this event next Tuesday.)

'But what happens to him?'

'The horse takes him to heaven.'

'But you just said they burn the horse.'

'Err. That's after.'

'And will he come back after that?'

'Yes. Hindus believe in reincarnation.'

'What's re-instarvation?'

'It's when you die and come back as somebody else. Your soul transfers into a new body. Kind of.'

'What does "soul transfer into a new body" mean?'

'Err... It's kind of like... Well... Err... Oooh look, a cloud. Shall we sing a song? Ten green bottles...'

STICK IT UP YOUR BUNGHOLE

Our lovely housemate who is staying with us for a few weeks comes into the kitchen one morning and asks: 'What time does Bintang open?' Bintang is the local supermarket. It's on a par with Lidl if Lidl existed in Siberia during the Cold War.

'Eight, I think,' John says. 'But if you need anything for breakfast just help yourself.'

'I need butt lube,' she answers.

'Right,' says John, beating a hasty retreat.

'They sell butt lube in Bintang?' I ask.

144

Sunset in southern India, 2010.

Alula contemplates life and keeps an eye out for bears in Yosemite National Park, 2010.

It's a hard life in the tropics, 2013.

The view from our balcony across Ubud's rice paddies, 2012.

Beginnings and Endings. The magical spot in Goa where I wrote *Losing Lila* in 2010 and where I returned in 2014 at the end of our *Can We Live Here?* journey.

Exploring S.E. Asia together during the school holidays, 2013.

Alula and I modelling for the 'Keep Bali Plastic Free' campaign. (Picture courtesy of Tina Stoneking.)

Enjoying our last few days together in Bali, 2014. (Picture courtesy of Aubrey Cody.)

'Well, vegetable margarine,' she says.

'You use vegetable margarine? Urgh.'

'It's better for you than petroleum-based gels,' she responds sagely.

I nod silently because there's one thing that our housemate knows and that is butts and putting things inside them. No, it's not *that*. She is a world-renowned colonic irrigator. And she's trying to get me to cleanse and irrigate. And by 'cleanse' she means raw juice three times a day, and by 'irrigate' she means stick a hose up my bum.

Ubud is the kind of place where people accost her on the street and start begging her for appointments and I just stand there wondering how embarrassing that must be, having a stranger who's on intimate terms with your anus stand and chat to you while the traffic honks.

But it would seem that it's only me who has such issues and who's squeamish about having vegetable margarine slathered on my butt and a tube pushed up there. It seems that most of the rest of Ubud wash out their butts as often as I wash my hands.

Everyone tells me it's really good. That you drop 3.5kg in half an hour. That you feel like a light being once it's over. And really I must, must, must try it.

Yeah. Isn't that the same feeling you get after drinking ten shots of tequila? I muse. Apart from maybe the 3.5kg.

And then, how would I be able to spread Flora on my toast and sit down to breakfast with my housemate ever again knowing that she was on such intimate terms with my colon and what was inside it?

DEALING AND HEALING

It's amazing. You think you can travel 13,000 km and never have to deal with the shit that drove you crazy ever again.

But guess what, folks? Turns out you do. Turns out you could move to a whole new galaxy a million light years away and that shit would still find you. You'd still be dealing.

Luckily, I'm living in Ubud, land of the crazy, land of the tarot reader and the theta healer and the ecstatic dancer, where you're only a phone call or a green juice order away from someone who can *heal* you.

This is a list of the things I have been told to do by well-meaning people in order to deal:

1. A week-long juice fast and cleanse (involving shoving a hose up my butt)
2. Attend laughing yoga*
3. Be authentic
4. Surrender
5. Chant: 'I am sorry. Forgive me. Thank you. I love you.' Until the person who was mean has a change of heart
6. Read Eckhart Tolle's chapter in *A New Earth* on the pain body and ego. Oh, and live in the now
7. Meditate.

So, in the spirit of trying things, I decide to start a cleanse. I even buy myself a juicer and promise myself that I am only going to drink fresh juice and water for a whole, entire week.

*A yoga class where you just sit on a mat and laugh for an hour. I'm not making this up.

I last three hours before I eat a delicious mozzarella and tomato sandwich.

I was going to attend laughing yoga but I ended up sleeping instead.

I contemplate authenticity but conclude that I hate the word and that people who use it tend to be smug, self-righteous, inauthentic fools.

As for surrendering… I'm not a natural surrenderer. This I have learned. If I was a soldier in a past life I would not have been the one waving a white flag. I would have been the one either a) hiding, or b) running into a hail of bullets. Anything to avoid giving someone power over me.

I try chanting and manage five minutes, but the whole time I am wondering who exactly I am supposed to be telling I love and who I am supposed to be apologising to. I am going to keep on this though because I read a story online (must therefore be true) about a whole ward of criminally insane people who were miraculously cured when one dude started chanting this in the room next door to them. So I figure it's worth a shot, as a control experiment if nothing else, because – not to cast doubt on the story's 'authenticity' – I'm not sure I totally believe it works.

I read Eckhart Tolle and I'm trying to live in the now. This involves not thinking too hard or much about anything, which is OK because, having dropped caffeine from my diet, I'm pretty much a walking zombie anyway, so thinking with any kind of clarity is off the menu.

Meditatation… I've already charted my success with meditating. At the moment my meditations go something like this:

One breath… two breath… urgh… how much longer? Three…

I'm hungry but there's no food in the house. I really want to buy a puppy. No. Puppy bad. Hmmmmm ooooh, woops four… OK, start again… One breath… No, if I start again it'll take me forever to get to 20. Let's start at five. Is that cheating? I'm going to go into town and check the DVD store today because I really want to see if Mad Men 4 has made it yet. I so miss Don Draper… mmmm, yummy. Focus, Sarah, for goodness sake… focus! Try to focus on light and energy travelling through your body…

Nope. Not happening.

Try to imagine laser death rays travelling 13,000 kilometres. No. Remember Eckhart. I forgive. Thank you. I'm sorry. I'm sorry. I love you. Who – who am I talking to? Who do I love? Who do I forgive? I am going insane. I am becoming one of those bug-eyed yogis who inhabits Ubud wearing stretchy leggings and drinking only reverse osmosis water. Next stop, laughing yoga… 18 breath… 19 breath… Bored… 25. Ooooh yay, I've finished.

It's funny because I thought that when I left the UK I'd immediately morph from a caterpillar into a butterfly; a rich, successful, beautiful, thin and spiritually enlightened butterfly.

I couldn't even manage the thin. And that was in India.

Let me be a warning to you.

You can't run away from what's inside you. Remember that before you book a flight. But also, if you do want to face up to it and try to at least find spiritual enlightenment, then Bali's the place to do it.

I NEED TO HAVE A SON (APPARENTLY)

I'm a failure, according to Nyoman and Made, the two women who own the shop over the road. I am a failure because I only have a daughter.

'You have more children soon, yes?' they ask, nodding their heads vigorously.

'Err, no. Not planning on it,' I tell them.

They stare at me with a mixture of pity and horror. 'But you must have son,' they insist.

'Why? I have a daughter,' I tell them. 'And she's just as good as any son. Actually, better.'

But they can't get their heads around this at all and just keep staring at me dumbfounded. I head home scowling, frustrated that this idea that girls aren't good enough persists around the world. And it's not just here or in developing countries either. I get it at home too: from my father-in-law who would dearly love a grandson to carry on the Alderson name. Fair-dos. But he best start looking to the other daughters-in-law because this particular Alderson mare is done breeding.

When will it ever stop though, I wonder? When will the women of the world wake up and smell the roses? If even women think men are better, and believe that they are not equal to men, then we are truly fucked. What hope is there?

But the really bewildering thing to me is that here in Bali it's the women who do the back-breaking field work, who labour on the roads carrying rocks that weigh more than me on their heads, who are up at the crack of dawn every morning preparing offerings for ceremonies, who look after the children and the in-laws. Once married, a Balinese woman must move in with her husband's family… Imagine if that was the case in the UK! I think most women would be serving life sentences in prison.

It's the women here who do all this *and* hold down a full-time job on top, while by comparison a lot of the men seem to just sit around all day stroking their cocks (cockerel fighting is a big thing here) and yelling out 'transport, transport' to any foreigner who walks past.

Yet women's economic value is still relatively tiny compared to a man's. A two-minute taxi ride (only the men seem to drive taxis here) costs the same as a whole day's wage for a woman home-help. How is that fair?

Our landlady, Made, is an amazing powerhouse of a woman. Born into abject poverty in East Bali, she left school and started working as a cleaner at the age of 12, taught herself English, fought her way up the job ladder and now owns three properties, which she rents out to earn an income. She is the sole provider for her entire extended family, as well as her husband's family. She also has to look after her elderly, infirm mother-in-law (there are no nursing homes, so she is effectively a 24-hour nurse on top of everything else). She tells me that her greatest ambition is to see her children graduate from university and that's why she works so hard: to make sure they have the opportunities that she didn't.

'I tell her, marry foreign man,' Made tells me, with regards to her daughter. 'Is only way. If marry Balinese man –' she wrinkles her nose in disgust – 'then life over.'

A month or so later she comes to my house in tears and informs me that her daughter, aged 23, with a promising career ahead of her as a teacher, is pregnant and getting married in a week's time to a Balinese boy with no job and no prospects. She sobs. 'Her life over.'

Her life clearly isn't over but I see my landlady's point. 'My daughter is no longer my daughter,' she informs me. She isn't allowed to visit her family without the permission of her new parents-in-law. She must also hand over a sizeable amount of her salary to her mother-in-law. Divorce is exceedingly rare in Balinese communities and if she were to leave her husband ever then custody of the children would in almost all circumstances be awarded to her husband.

I understand now why Made and Nyoman think it's far better to bring a boy into this world than a girl.

BAD, BAD, BAD VIBRATIONS

'I want you to introduce yourselves and give me one word that describes how you're feeling at this moment in time.'

Bored, I think to myself. Can I say bored? No, that's rude. What about highly sceptical? No, also rude. Resistant? Well, if she can read my aura she surely knows this already. I'll go with tired. Tired is inoffensive. Oooh crap, it's my turn.

'Hi, I'm Sarah,' I tell the group, 'and I'm from London and I'm…' An alcoholic. Say that. Then pretend you've wandered into the wrong meeting by accident. No, you're here now…

I opt for: 'Tired.'

'Now,' says the lady in the kaftan and silk scarves who is leading this 'workshop', 'begin by swaying your arms in front of your base chakra point and imagining a rainbow of light.'

Huh?

'Red light is filling up the room.'

You what? I glance around the room at everyone else. I don't see any red light. But no one else seems to be thinking this is weird; they're all waving their arms in the air like they're swaying to a Rod Stewart ballad. They just need Zippo lighters. I figure I better join in before I start to look like the odd one out.

After about two minutes my arms are aching. How much longer do we have to do this for?

'Now move your arms up to your third eye,' the teacher tells us, 'and start swaying as you visualise the colour purple.'

Oh my God, seriously? My third eye? Where the hell is that supposed to be? My arms are really fricking hurting now. How much longer do I have to sway for? Oh, everyone has their eyes shut. Maybe I can just drop my arms... no one will notice... Hahahaha... Whoops, busted. That teacher has an eagle eye... Sway those arms. Sway those arms. Stop smiling. You look like you're taking the piss.

I *am* taking the piss

'We are balancing our chakras,' the woman intones. 'Feel the energy swirling around you.'

I try. I really do, but I don't feel anything except for intense frustration. Why did I think a crystal chakra healing workshop would be a good idea? I'm hot and I'm starting to sweat and I don't like sweating.

Oh for God's sake, when can we stop swaying? Why does everyone else look like they're in some kind of trance? Why is no one else laughing?

'Everyone take a crystal love necklace,' the teacher finally says.

I drop my arms with relief and move to the pile of crystal love necklaces she's placed on a satin cushion on the floor.

'When we surround ourselves with things that have a higher vibration, like these crystals,' she tells us, 'our cells start to vibrate at a higher frequency and we can heal ourselves from any disease.'

Are you fricking serious? My eyebrows shoot up. I snicker. If my eyes roll any further back in my head they'll sever my optic nerve.

'Now I want you to send out a colour to your partner,' she tells us.

I look around. *You what?* A sweet-faced girl stands beside me looking hopeful.

'Start making the noise of that colour,' the teacher says. 'Send out the intention of that colour.'

Does that mean I can yell? My colour wants to scream. Can I scream?

'Err,' I ask. 'What do you mean, exactly, by noise?'

The teacher sighs and comes over to me, clearly the remedial student in the class.

'Like this,' she says and demonstrates: 'Mmmmmmmmmmhm-mmmm.'

The mmmmm stretches out for about as long as an ad break during *Corrie*. She must have the lung capacity of a blue whale.

OK, I think to myself, cutting a glance at my neighbours who are *ohmmmmming* at each other so loud they sound like two trucks in reverse. I don't want to *ohm*. I want to yell. Good job I didn't do that. That would have been embarrassing.

I realise I can't just stand here in silence while my partner waits expectantly for me to send her a colour intention or whatever it is I'm meant to be doing. I need to make some kind of noise at least. Fake it. *OK, here goes.* 'Mmmmmmmmmmmmmmmmmmm.'

Now I sound like a lobotomy patient. Why am I here? Why am I doing this? I want my money back.

'Now,' the teacher says to me, 'what colour were you sending out to your partner?'

'Red.'

'What colour did your partner see?'

'Green,' my partner answers.

Funny, that. I feel, however, like I've failed some fundamental test. Like I've been told I'm a Muggle and everyone else has a ticket to Hogwarts.

'Well, when we can't express the colour correctly,' the teacher explains with something of a sneer, 'it's because we're too much in our masculine side.'

'What?'

'Our masculine side is limited,' she explains with something of a patronising smile, 'and can only do one thing at a time. You're too much in your masculine.'

Hey, we finally agree on something! I frown. But isn't that a bit rude to say it out loud? I know we're all women here but, err, I think you just likened me to a man – and in an insulting way.

'You need to be more in the feminine, which is boundless and infinite,' she tells me.

'I do?'

'Try thinking of your mother.'

What the serious what? My mother is many things, but 'infinite' is not one of them.

'I see auras,' the teacher informs me.

And I see dead people, I almost shoot back. I narrow my eyes at her. If she's a healer, I'm the Buddha. Shit, I think, alarmed, 'What if she can see my aura right now? Is that why she's looking at me funny? Maybe she can sense that I'm thinking, CRAZY FRICKING CRYSTAL LADY.'

'I hold regular healing sessions using the power of sound and crystals,' she tells the assembled group now that we've all stopped *ohmmming* and she's stopped lecturing me on being too masculine. I glance around again, confused. Am I the only one here who thinks the lady hasn't been taking her Thorazine?

'I also do *Eat, Pray, Love* soulmate love readings too, where you can discover love in your aura and your soulmate.'

I giggle. Translation: I rip-off middle-aged women coming to Bali looking for their Javier Bardem.

'Now, at the end of the session, how do you feel?' she asks, smiling beatifically at us all. Well, apart from at me. She shoots red daggers at me.

I narrow my eyes at her.

How do I feel? Mainly murderous rage at having been fleeced of $15 to be told I'm a man who can't multitask.

Wait? Is this how John feels when I tell him the same thing every other time I open my mouth?

CELEBRATING MY FIRST ANNIVERSARY OF UNEMPLOYMENT

As I was lying on the massage table I started musing on a conversation I had today when I mentioned that I used to be on a senior management team.

I had to pause at the time and try to remember the words in the right order. Then I had to shake my head and blink to check whether I wasn't remembering something from a past life or from a film I watched a few years ago. Then I had a sudden flashback to senior management team meetings. The memory involved lots of biscuits and eyeball rolling, some mild snickering and plenty of grinding of teeth – but not much on the actual detail of the job. It's all so fuzzy. A bit like memories of childbirth become after time. Except, about a year after giving birth you start forgetting the fact you almost split open and died while half the world looked up your jacksie, and instead you start to think what a marvellous idea it would be go through it all again.

But let me tell you now, with employment the memories don't fade; you don't start getting sentimental over Excel spreadsheets, funding applications and performance reviews, and start thinking what a great idea it would be to have just one more job, just the one, because it isn't very fair on your first job if it doesn't get to have someone to play with and because your first job was a girl and you'd really like the second one to be a boy because one of each would be lovely. No, none of that.

I've now calculated that it was almost a year ago to the day that I left my job. I feel like this deserves celebrating. I'm sure everyone I used to manage thinks it deserves celebrating as well. OK, so I'm not really unemployed. I do write everyday. But that doesn't feel like a job. It's never a chore. I can do it when I want. I can, if I choose, decide that for a week all I'm going to do is watch *Buffy*, surf the net for pictures of male models to inspire my next character, and bury my nose in young adult books. And call it research. And, most importantly, I can't get fired for it.

My office is a bed. I can play on Facebook as much as I want without having to do a quick 'Control+N' every time someone walks by. I can work in my bikini or my birthday suit if the mood takes me (it hasn't yet). I can play music until the house shakes and I can dance around to Taylor Swift every time I get bored.

So if you're out there and wondering whether working in an office for the rest of your life is it, or you have an inkling that you could move to somewhere hot and figure out a way of making money that doesn't require sitting in a management team meeting trying to look like you care about 'spending reviews', then remember the power of saying 'Fuck It'. That's all we did. And somehow we ended up here. So go say it to your boss. And see where you end up.

(But if where you end up happens to be unemployed, penniless, with no reference from your ex-boss then, err... don't blame me.)

OH THE DRAMA IN OUR LIVES

I have been busy this week, occupied with pulling dead lice out of my daughter's hair. At times, the three of us have resembled a small troupe of gorillas picking fleas out of each other's fur. Well, not John. He's the shaved-headed gorilla. And Alula might soon be a baby bald gorilla because if they come back then I'm taking John's razor to her head.

I wasn't sure I even had them, but mention the word nit and – weird thing, this – is your head itching? It is, isn't it? Go on, scratch. Scratch that itch. See. As soon as the school told me Alula and half her class had head lice I ran screaming into the bathroom and emptied the lice shampoo on myself without even checking if I had them first. Once lathered up, I turned my attention to Alula. She hates having her hair shampooed even on the best of days – the days where we distract her with a Chupa Chup – so you can imagine how fun this was.

We lathered, shampooed and combed through the screams, the cries and the hollers. And we did this for three days in a row, spending two hours nit-picking, literally, while she screamed and yelled, and I pleaded and bribed and cajoled. And every day, they would be back. Alive. More resilient in the face of death than John McClane from *Die Hard*.

They weren't even bashful about it. It was like they were laughing at me as they careened down her centre parting. Eventually, on the third day, I collapsed in tears when I found yet another live one in her hair.

'I can't do this any more,' I said to John, clutching him by the tops of his arms.

'You do realise,' John said, 'that the lice shampoo you're using says it has no pesticide in it, don't you?'

'What? What?!' I yelled, tearing into the bathroom and ransacking the cupboard. 'But, but,' I spluttered, grabbing the bottle. 'I bought this shampoo in Boots. I asked the lady behind the counter for the most effective one and she said this one.'

I check the ingredients on the back: tea tree oil and neem oil. Basically the shampoo equivalent of asking a nit to 'please go away, we'd be ever so grateful' when what is called for in these terms is a punch to the face and a 'now fuck the fuck off'.

I threw the bottle to the floor and sent John out with instructions to locate the most toxic, FDA-banned, nuclear lice-busting shampoo available on the Balinese black market. 'Preferably one with a skull and crossbones on the bottle.'

He came back with something pink. The ingredients list was non-existent. I hovered with my fingers over my laptop thinking I should Google the brand name but I stopped myself in case it said that it caused irreparable brain damage or had been banned in 243 countries after tests revealed it made your head fall off.

Instead we poured the entire contents on Alula's head and then wrapped her in cling film overnight (her head, anyway).

And guess what? Chemicals work, people! Tea tree oil-based lice shampoo is about as effective as treating a brain tumour with a sherbet Dip-Dab.

SO I WAS GETTING A MASSAGE AND...

I keep starting a lot of my posts with 'So I was getting a massage and…' but, um, I was getting a massage this morning in the downstairs bedroom and Alula wandered in.

'Hello, Mummy,' she said.

'Mgrhrmrmrm,' I answered.

'Is it OK if I sit on the bed?' she asked, clambering onto the bed.

'Yes, OK,' I answered, 'but you have to be silent and shut the door because I don't want the gardener seeing me naked.'

Thirty seconds later I'm aware that instead of a two-handed massage, I'm getting a four-handed one. After a few minutes of Alula patting my shoulders while Nyoman attends to my legs, Alula bends down so her lips are brushing my ear and she whispers; 'Mummy, who's massage is better? Hers or mine?'

I'm giggling too hard to answer. And thanking goodness she didn't come in ten minutes earlier while I was getting waxed.

Then I feel Alula's nose against my back. She takes two giant sniffs. 'Mmmmm, minty superhero perfume,' she says. 'You smell good, Mummy.'

She disappears for a few minutes and I start to think she might have lost interest and gone off to play with her Littlest Pet Shops, but then the voice in my ear returns: 'Mummy, is it OK if I make magic fairy juice?'

'Go and ask Daddy,' I mumble.

She runs back into the kitchen. 'Daddy! Daddy! Daddy! Daddy!' I hear her hollering.

Alula is turning into me in the laziness stakes. She hates climbing the stairs, hence the standing at the bottom in the kitchen, hollering up them. This goes on for ten minutes until I'm so tense that

Nyoman's fingers are practically rebounding off my muscles as if they're made from rubber.

Eventually Alula stops hollering and I hear cupboards banging and the outdoor tap running. I try to focus on drifting into another realm, but all the while I'm imagining the chaos I'm going to walk into in the kitchen when my hour is up. Eventually I manage to forget it for a few minutes and start dreaming up new characters for the book I'm working on (strangely, they all seem to be variations on Ryan Gosling). Then I am startled out of my daydreams when I hear several male voices in the garden.

I know that the handyman is coming by to quote us on a few odd-jobs and I had pre-warned John to listen out for him. I hear a man ask: 'Is your daddy at home?' and another two men chatting. I don't hear Alula answer.

There is only a carved wooden door between my oiled naked body and three strange men. I wonder if I can stay silent enough that they won't know I'm here. But Alula is still not answering (we've warned her about talking to strangers and she's obviously taking this advice very seriously) and now the men have started pacing and I worry that the sound of Nyoman's hands slapping my thighs will make them think John and I are up to something kinky, having first banished our daughter to the garden.

'Alula,' I finally yell through the door, giving myself away. 'Go find Daddy.'

'NO!' she answers and starts hammering her fists on the bed-room door.

'Please,' I beg. *What on earth must they think I'm doing in here?*
'NO!'

'I'll give you three Chupa Chups,' I plead.

'URGH. OK.' She stalks off and I hear her start to yell, 'DAAAAAADDDDDDDYYYYYY!'

After five minutes of yelling I can't take it any more. I am starting to think that maybe John is lying dead upstairs. Or probably, and more likely, he has his headphones in and our daughter is too lazy to climb the ten steps necessary to actually find him. So I jump up from my massage, quickly pull on my clothes, and unlock the door.

The three men stare at me and my wild, crazy hair-do and half undone dress and I can see them peeking into the room where Nyoman is crouched on the bed on all fours, her hands oiled and poised.

I rush past them and tear up the stairs (Alula sitting half way up, still yelling, 'DADDDDDDYYYYYY!'). And what do you know? There's John asleep with three pillows stuffed over his head. I whack him awake then run back downstairs to finish my massage, sprinting past the waiting men who I can't even look at, I'm that embarrassed.

And once again I'm lying on the bed and I'm having my head massaged – *mmmm, lovely* – and I'm sinking back into heavy plot action (maybe the new character should be a cross between Nathan from *Misfits* and Han Solo… and Ryan Gosling) when suddenly all I can hear is John outside, trying to sleepily puzzle out my odd-job requests with the non-English-speaking handyman.

I'm groaning to myself, thinking, 'heck if this isn't the most ridiculously pointless massage in the world'.

'We need a concrete cover built for the washing machine,' I eventually yell through the door as Nyoman moves on to my shoulders.

'Why?' John answers back.

I roll my eyes. Seriously, I am not about to enter into a debate about corrosion of electrical items left outside in the tropics while someone is rubbing down my body with warm, minty, superhero-scented oil. But I do. 'Because the electrics might fry during the rainy season!'

'What?'

I look at Nyoman and I tell her we may as well just forget it; this massage is as pointless as Lindsay Lohan going to rehab.

I pull on my clothes again and exit the bedroom and find John drawing up plans for the washing machine cover, Alula still sitting on the stairs and the three men staring at me quizzically.

THE THINGS I DO FOR YOU GUYS

'I know what you need,' Suki says when I tell her I feel really crappy.

Steak. I am thinking I need steak. When I woke up this morning that was the first thing that popped into my head. *I want steak.* In the same way that most people wake up and go 'oooh I fancy a coffee and some cornflakes.' But Suki begs to differ. She thinks what I need is a hosepipe slathered in lard stuck up my butt and 200 litres of water hosed up my colon.

OK. We clearly have different understandings of my body's needs. I'm hearing 'steak'. She's hearing 'lard'. And we clearly have different ideas of what constitutes a pleasurable experience. Starting with which orifice should be involved. But somehow – and please, don't ask me how, because I'm still thinking that maybe this happened in an alternate universe – I actually agreed.

Partly I think it was curiosity (admit it – you're curious as to what it might feel like), partly it was because I was thinking of what a funny story it would make, and then mainly, I have to admit, it was down to the fact that I heard someone mention you can lose over

162

4 kilos just in fetid faecal matter and I thought that I could do with using a few kilos without actually having to give up chocolate or wine or like, having to diet… or exercise.

I'm not going to go into detail. I'll spare both you and myself the remembrance. Let's just say that the colonic wasn't pleasant. It's kind of strange to lie on a table whilst your good friend inserts a tube and pumps water up your butt, and inspects the poo that comes chugging out as you lie there and try to act nonchalant and chat about boys and shopping.

Halfway through, Alula walked in and wanted to know what on earth was going on and where was the hose going exactly, Mummy, and why?

Why? It's a good question. I think I screeched something about tummy massages but actually I do now have an answer. I feel better. I feel lighter – roughly four kilos lighter, in fact. I feel less tired, less groggy. My stomach is practically concave, my complexion bright and sparkly, my thighs most definitely thinner.

Obviously one colonic is all it took and I am now a supermodel. Move over, Miranda Kerr.

Curiosity is also fully sated. As in, fully. I will never be doing that again. Even if Victoria's Secret offered me a $1m contract. It wouldn't be worth it.

And, for the record, I am still craving steak.

DRESS RESPECTFULLY
This is government office. Dress respectfully.

Oh dear. I look down at my dress: A Topshop maxi-dress with a slit up the thigh on both sides and a slit at the sides to the waist. At least

I am wearing a bra though. And knickers. You can see both. They're black. I think this, however, constitutes a fail in the 'respectfully dressed' stakes.

Shit, I think. I'm going to be deported. And it will be Topshop's fault. At least Alula looks respectfully dressed. She's in a sundress. Mind you, it's too big and you can see both her boobies, as she cheerfully informs me (she calls nipples 'boobies' for some reason we haven't yet fathomed).

Perhaps it is a little much for a trip to Immigration. But I had to literally run out of the house to get here. I didn't even have time to pee. When *Imigrasi* tell you to jump, you ask how high. Although the word 'high' spoken anywhere near an Indonesian in uniform freaks me out.

Anyway, I dashed out of the house and I didn't stop to consider clothing or respect because I was too busy worrying about deportation if I didn't arrive on time but now I'm cringing and wishing I had at least brought a scarf to cover my shoulders. I turn around in my seat and try to gauge what 'respectfully dressed' might mean. The woman behind me is wearing a hijab. Hmmmm.

Finally, Alula and I get called in. I feel like a common criminal. I'm told to sit down and am ordered to give my fingerprints. Sitting is a problem in this dress. It requires both hands to hold down the slits to avoid flashing my thighs. If I cross my legs one side of my dress tends to flap open revealingly. But as Alula is clutching both my arms and refuses to let me go, revealing myself is the only option. *Nil points* so far.

The two men mutter something in Indonesian and then motion for me to stand Alula in front of the camera. Of course, she's having none of it. She tries to claw her way up my body like she's a monkey in the sacred forest and I'm a banyan tree. I have to force her off me but she only grabs onto me harder and refuses to look at the camera. I crouch down, aware that my thighs are now on display and flashing like the bill-boards in Times Square. The men don't seem impressed with my wanton display of flesh or with Alula's general cuteness. They look irritated.

I don't want Alula to think I'm scared but I kind of am. 'They're going to put Mummy in prison unless you look at the camera and say cheese,' I plead.

'No', she squeals.

'I will buy you ten Chupa Chups if you let go of me and look at the camera.'

'No.'

'Please, Lula? Please. I'm begging you.'

'OK. A lolly. If you buy me an ice lolly.'

'OK, done, deal. You got it. Just look at the camera.'

She obliges. I follow suit.

'Done? Are we done?' I ask the man as I stand and try to rearrange myself.

'Yes, we're done,' he says to me rather ominously.

For the moment I have not been deported. But I do wonder what notes might have been written on my file and sent to Jakarta.

ECSTATIC DANCE IN UBUD. AGAIN.

There's a part halfway through where I'm pouring sweat, literally pouring, as if my body has sprung several leaks, and I realise that I can't move my shoulder or neck any more. I decide to take a break. I pant my way to the water cooler. It's ecstatic dance. Everyone by the water cooler is full of ecstasy.

165

'It's amazing, isn't it?' I get asked by some euphoria-fuelled girl.

'Yes', I say, nodding in agreement, and for once I'm not having to stick my tongue so far into my cheek it looks like I'm chewing a billiard ball. Because it actually is. It's the best dance night I've ever been to. It's way better than one I went to the other week where I mistakenly thought I'd signed up for two hours of 'lose yourself in the music and dance like no one is watching (in a corner by myself)' fun but instead it turned out to be two hours of holding hands with 30 other adults, skipping around the room, stroking strangers' faces and sending them the love of the universe. So not my thing. But apparently a lot of other people's thing because no one else was muttering 'what the fuck' under their breath or looking horrified or wiping their hands down their shorts or casting around desperately for the exits or mentally preparing their blog lines. They were all sending the love. And stroking the faces.

But tonight I am high without being high, and I'm loving it. There's no holding hands or swaying or sending love to the universe. Although there are two people sitting on the floor in a lotus pose smiling ecstatically like Buddhas who've smoked one too many. (I later find out that they were 'making miracles happen').

I clutch my neck and realise it really, really hurts. Earlier, I pulled a muscle in my neck while taking a shower. But I ignored it and decided that I needed to dance. So I washed down two Nurofen with two margaritas… and now I'm paralysed.

But this is ecstatic dance. And it's ecstatic dance in Ubud, no less. I only have to wait oooh, 30 seconds, before someone comes and starts healing me with a hands on Reiki session right there by the water cooler. All better – well, not all better but I find that once I start dancing again I am cured. Miraculously.

Then I go home, pass out, wake up and start crying. Because pain has replaced the ecstasy. I go to the local chemist that is decidedly not Boots. I order something over the counter for muscle pain. I take it. Half an hour later I tell John I don't feel so well and go and lie down.

I am unconscious but conscious. I am being hit on the head by Alula repeatedly but I am not able to do anything but drool in protest. After a few hours I prize my dead eyes open with toothpicks and tap the name of the drug one-fingered into my computer.

Google tells me that I have just taken the strongest opiate on the market other than heroin. Also, the most addictive.

Indonesia, where you can be shot for smoking weed, happily administers opiate-based drugs (with no warnings about not driving and no suggestions to not take if pregnant or on other medication) to people with a little bit of neck pain.

But my neck is better now. Which is good because this Friday I intend to dance again.

JESUS COMES TO TEA AND I FIND MY PURPOSE

Jesus came to tea the other day. (I always wanted to write that line.)

John told me that he runs a business in town. I look at him, sitting in our garden: long brown hair, sorrowful face, beard (no stigmata that I can see) and I ask John if at board meetings he sits on the right-hand side of the table. Also, I want to know, what kind of business? Is he a carpenter? Please let him be a carpenter.

Also at tea were two people on day seven of a ten-day fast. This was a good thing because I got to eat both their shares of the strawberry cheesecake. As I forked that cheesey goodness into my mouth, I couldn't help but wonder why anyone would forego eating for even an hour, let alone 240 hours. I mean, *hello?* When there's cheesecake that good in the world? When frozen margaritas can be delivered to your door in less than twenty minutes?

I was told that there are people in this world who apparently have not eaten for seven whole years. All they do is get up, meditate and smell flowers. And this, apparently, is enough to sustain them.

Financially, they are sustained by doing speaker gigs at festivals and telling the world all about how they live on water and air. I smell something fishy. I reckon they sneak to McDonald's at night and stuff themselves on quarterpounders, but hey, that's just the cynic in me talking. It's speaking a lot lately, getting louder. It's almost like I've got a split personality and the cynical me is trying to squash the emerging bliss-ninny me out of existence.

That same evening we went to a party. We met someone there who can plot your human destiny. Or was it Human DNA? I forget. Maybe I'm getting him confused with a character in one of my books. Anyway, he definitely said something along the lines of interpreting our human purpose by looking at quantum physics, our horoscopes and the I Ching. I know he said this because not even I could make that shit up.

When I quizzed him further about what the hell he was talking about he told me he could let me know if my life's purpose was, for example, to be selfish or angry.

'And then what?' I asked. 'Is that so you can work on it and improve your, um, DNA?' I asked, 'you know, become a light being?'

And he said to me: 'No. It's so you can stop pretending to be something you're not and start living your authentic self.'

A muscle by my eye went into spasm. He said the word 'authentic'.

We all know how I feel about that word. 'Authentic' is the most ironic word in the universe. It's only used by frauds.

'You can be selfish,' he explained. 'That's fine. Because that's exactly who you are.'

I looked at him through narrowed eyes. What? What utter nonsense! But then I thought to myself, huh, maybe that explains it then. Maybe my purpose is to be a cynical bitch and there's nothing I can do about that except embrace it, own it… live it. Phew, what a relief, maybe there's more to this human DNA-I Ching-quantum malarkey than I first thought.

THE PSYCHICS AND ME

The psychics are angry. Every time I pass one on the street in Bali – which I have to tell you is quite frequently, say every tenth person or so – I am being given death stares.

From this I've deduced that either:

a) I'm evil

b) I'm going to die very soon

c) They can read my mind (which would make them telepaths as well as psychics).

At ecstatic dance, where several self-labelled psychic-type people congregate, I'm being avoided like the plague. This could be my dancing. Or it could be any of the three options above. I take my problem to my friend and ask her whether she thinks that the psychics in town have it in for me, that they can see something in my aura, or my future, or my irises, or if they're just reading my mind?

My friend takes a deep breath and tells me that I'm just being paranoid, that if anything they're just picking up my very grounded vibes. She tries to tell me that people who are spiritual (and at this point I'm thinking, but not saying, hey I'm spiritual, kind of, I mean I know I eat cows and stuff and I struggle to meditate but um, I'm totally spiritual…) can feel intimidated by people like me who are so grounded in reality.

I bite my tongue from saying, 'Basically you're calling me a cynical, eyeball-rolling bitch with no connection to anything remotely spiritual or deep.'

And then I think about it some more and I realise that maybe all these psychics aren't seeing me dying. And they're not reading my mind.

No. They're reading my blog.

UPGRADING CAR AND DOWNGRADING COOL

We've just upgraded our car. This sounds impressive but really, from the jeep, it was impossible to downgrade, except to maybe roller-skates made out of shopping trolley wheels and some frayed rope.

It's laughable that an upgrade from our tin pot on wheels – with doors that didn't shut properly, brakes that didn't understand their purpose and an engine that made a noise so loud and reverberating as to have its own ranking on the Richter scale – is to a car that if I saw it in the UK I'd cuss out as the kind of car that only grannies with mobility issues would ever drive. It's the kind of car that I would once have scoffed at if I whipped past it on the motorway. A car on a par with a Reliant Robin. But needs must.

It actually costs more than our Jeep. But for an extra $70 a month we get seatbelts, brakes and four doors, so no more of Alula clambering with filthy feet over the seats, or stalling on slopes.

'You can't drive that car,' my friend Leila tells me straight-up. She says it in such a way as to suggest that our friendship may be on the line if I drive it. I know for certain that if I drive this car and bump into her on the street she will look the other way.

'I liked you in the Jeep. The Jeep was cool.'

She's right. I did feel cool zipping around town in the Jeep. I'm kind of sad to lose the Jeep persona. However, given the status of my back, which I put out a few days ago, and the fact I can no longer bend or twist, it's quite useful to have a car I can manoeuver into without having to fold myself double.

Yesterday at the crack of dawn I packed up the car and sped off to the coast by myself. I wanted to get out of town before anyone could recognise me driving something so uncool. But *woah*. A granny mobile it may be, a mobility car it most definitely is, but this car *zips*. My dad will be horrified to hear it but this car can overtake three lorries in a row going uphill on winding roads.

But don't worry, Dad, at least it has seatbelts.

GIVING UP EATING

I'm writing this about friends of ours – friends whose company I enjoy a lot. But I'm never going to have dinner with either of them again. That's because they've given up eating. As in, solids. As in, chewing. As in, *food*.

And you thought *I* was lazy. They're not doing this indefinitely. No, they're doing this 'infinitely'. As in, until the end of time, when God comes a-knocking.

I get the whole eating-healthy thing. I do. Honest. Well, kind of. But juice for the *rest of your life*? I love juice as much as the next person but *for the rest of my life*??

I think about the repetitive strain from passing all those carrots and broccoli stalks through the juicer all day. I ask my friend if she'll just sit in Clear Café and work her way through their delectable drinks menu every day, because if I was her I could do that. That would be OK, for a day or two anyway – especially if I could just drink one of their chocolate smoothie drinks on the hour every hour.

'Will you still poo?' I ask my friend, cutting right to the important stuff.

She assures me that she will. But I'm wondering how that's possible if all that's going in is liquid. Surely you'd just poo water; in other words, squit?

'Won't you die?' I ask next.

She tells me no, that juice contains all their dietary requirements.

Hmmmmmm. I wonder if she's had one too many colonics and they sucked out her brain cells along with the old poo clogging up her intestines.

This evening I read a blog post about their first day doing this juice for the rest of their life thing. I'm kind of in blinking awe. And stunned disbelief. I want to go around to their house and start barbecuing steak and letting the smell waft in through their open windows, or at the very least smother some papaya in coconut cream and cacao (I know they like this) and start eating it in front of them, but I guess they'd probably just liquidise it and drink it as juice (the papaya – not the steak).

And then I read on their blog that the ultimate goal is to stop taking any kind of food or liquids at all, and to live on light.

Imagine how much washing up that would save, I think to

172

myself, and how much money! And then I feel relieved because maybe we can have them round to dinner after all. Because I won't have to try to juice them anything with my broken juicer or cook. I can just give them a plate with a sunbeam on instead.

Update: two years later and both parties are now fully committed members of the carnivore world. No more raw food nonsense for either of them and no more attempts to live on light. In fact, one of them tells me he hasn't eaten a salad or anything green in over a year and he feels utterly amazing. So yeah... 'nuff said.

NYEPI, OR BALINESE NEW YEAR

Roosters, birds, crickets, geckos, ducks, a man shaking the tin cans on the line in the rice paddies trying to scare away the birds. But other than that, silence. Which isn't very silent. Cockerels are loud. We've learnt to block them out but now, on this day of silence, we notice them more.

I'm trying to remember what other noises I normally hear at this time in the morning. The man shaking the cans usually yells too. But today he's silent. Even the dogs are silent. There's no distant noise of traffic or conversation drifting over the walls from the neighbour's house. There's no *kelapa* delivery man dumping coconuts on our porch and calling out '*Pagi!*' This is because everyone (except for a handful of police) is locked inside their houses, hiding with the lights off.

We're hiding from the evil spirits who have returned to earth. We hide so that the spirits are tricked into thinking nobody's home and leave once more until next time *Nyepi* comes around, when they decide to try again. We have to stay inside for 24 hours –

traditionally a time for silence, meditation and fasting (though silence and meditation with a four-year-old in the house? And fasting with John in the house?)

Anyone going out on the street can be fined up to 1million rupiah (around $100 US), including tourists, who are banned from leaving their hotels and can't leave the island because the airport is shut.

Last night we walked up the hill to the football field in the centre of town, following a procession of *Ogoh-ogohs*. These are a bit like bonfire Guys: huge papier-maché and polystyrene monsters made by every village and usually sporting enormous penises and engorged breasts and other interesting anatomical elements that Alula loves to gawp at. The *Ogoh-ogohs* are paraded through town, amassed on the football field and then taken away and burned. Or, in some cases, sold to five-star hotels who like to display them to their guests because when you've paid $1,000 for a room for the night, nothing spells luxury like a giant papier-maché monster penis in your face.

Alula's school made an *Ogoh-ogoh* that looked like a zombie, which explains why for the last three days she's been obsessed with playing zombie games at home. I had been puzzling over that one, wondering if her babysitter had shown her *Dawn of the Dead* while we were out. Glad we've cleared that up.

We took our new dog, Lily, with us on this adventure to see the *Ogoh-oghohs*. It became an impromptu party with other parents and kids. Then we walked home. Alula and Lily and I took a tumble in the crowd as a surging *Ogoh-ogoh*, carried by dozens of teenage boys, came careering towards us. Health and safety? Meh.

Kids of 12 were hoisting up the power lines to let the *Ogoh-ogohs*

174

pass beneath. Crowd control consisted of one policeman blowing a piddly whistle. Still, when you compare it to the Western world, where adherence to health and safety seems to be out of control, this was a lot more fun.

MEMORIES OF AN ALULA

Alula and I are talking over soft-boiled eggs and soldiers.

'Alula, do you remember travelling?'

'Er, no.'

'You don't remember anything – anything at all?'

'No.'

' What about living in India – remember the beach? Remember going to school with Dumpy?'

'Um, no… I remember Egg though.' (Her first big crush.)

'What about getting the train in India when we were squidged up in a bunk together?'

'What's a bunk?'

'OK, what about washing the elephant?'

'Oh yes, I remember that… I think.'

'Right, what about the tuk-tuks? Driving through the streets of Mumbai – remember that?'

'Oh yeah! Tuk-tuks. They're alive!'

'Well, they're like cars. They're not *alive* alive.'

'YES. THEY ARE.'

'OK, whatever. Do you remember going to the zoo in Singapore?'

'No.'

'So that whole day I spent dragging you around in 100 per cent humidity until I wanted to cry, you don't remember it?'

'No. Were there animals?'

'Yes, there were animals. What about America? Do you remember Kerrie and Jamieson?'

'Oh yes, Kerrie, with the long, long hair like Rapunzel?'

'Yes! Do you remember staying with them?'

'No.'

'Well, do you remember Disneyland? It was only a year ago.'

'Oh yeah, we saw Aurora's castle. Why wasn't she at home, Mummy? Where did she go?'

'I think she went off to get married to the Prince.'

'But why didn't they get married in the castle?'

'Because they had to get married in his castle. What about Australia? Do you remember going there? We rode bicycles around the bay. You were on the back of Daddy's.'

'Were you too?'

'No, I was not on the back of Daddy's bike.'

'What about Yosemite?'

'Yo-what?'

'Nonno and Nonna meeting us in Malaysia?'

'No.'

'All those trains, planes and automobiles?'

'No.'

'I'm starting to think we should have just left you at home.'

'Ini tidak kuning,' Lula says. (Translation: that's not yellow.)

I look at her: she's starting to spout random bits of Indonesian and right after finishing her egg and soldiers she speeds out the front door, strips naked and starts running laps around the house in only a pair of pink Crocs, shrieking happily under a monsooning sky.

'*Ini tidak kuning!*' she yells.

She might have forgotten the detail of travelling, but who she is, in every moment, is a sum of those forgotten months.

THE CONTINUING TAO OF ALULA

'*I love you in the morning and in the afternoon. I love you in the evening and underneath the moon. Oh skiddly dinky, dinky rink, diddly rinky do... I LOVE YOU!*' Alula pauses in her singing. 'Mummy, I love you,' she tells me.

'I love you more,' I say.

'I love you most,' she answers.

'I love you to the moon.'

'I love you to the moon and back.'

'I love you to the Pleiadian mothership and back.'

'What's that?' she asks.

'Never mind. I love you to the end of the universe and back.'

'Well, I love you that plus one.'

'You can't. It's not possible.'

'Why?'

'Because when you're a mummy you'll realise just how big love really is. I will always love you more than anything in this whole universe.'

'I will always love you most,' Alula argues.

'One day you'll have a baby. And you'll love that most.'

'Will I have a girl?'

'Maybe. But you might have a boy.'

'No. I don't want a boy.'

'Well, you'll love it either way.'

'I'll love that baby more than anything in the whole world ever, won't I? More than I love my puppy and more than I love you.'

'Yes, you will. And I will love you more than anything else in the world.'

'You know, Mummy, you can't throw rubbish in the sea because the fishes eat the rubbish thinking it's food and then they die.'

'OK, good to know.'

'And at school we all put our hands together and think of our favourite colour and then we say 'whooooooooosh' and send our colour to all the fishes and the animals that are feeling sick. They did it to me the other day when Dil hit me in the head by accident.'

TOO COOL FOR ALL THAT FASHION MALARKEY

The lady over the road who regularly berates me for not bearing a boy-child sells clothes. We're not talking Topshop here. Hell, we're not even talking a market stall in Outer Mongolia. And when we first moved I kind of had a glance at the random assortment of T-shirts advertising beer (in kids' sizes too) and fisherman's trousers hanging up, sighed deeply and silently to myself about the fashion vortex that is Bali, and then went and unpacked my suitcases, figuring it was a price well worth paying in exchange for coconuts and massages.

And it is. Since then (it's been six months living here in the vortex) I've actually come to care a lot less about fashion and what I look like. I mean, we're at the stage now where Alula cares more about looking cool these days… 'But, Mummy,' she says once she's accessorised her morning ensemble, 'does it look cool? Because no one at school says I'm cool.'

'Yes, well, darling, 'cool' is subjective.'

'What's subjective?'

'Being cool is about *not* caring what people think of you, because you're too cool for all that shizz.' At this point I pause to muse that I must be uber cool, because I care not an iota what people think of me. (Fashion-wise at least. In Bali, at least.) I'm wearing flip-flops two sizes too small for me because someone took mine by accident where I left them outside a cafe and I think the ones they took were ones I took from someone else the week before at Yoga Barn anyway. I estimate that I should get my original pair back in a few days.

I wear the same manky old vests and ripped denim shorts almost every day. Most days I forego the bra because, as Alula tells me, I've got no boobs left anyway. And I've given up caring. I like that about here. You can't wear heels – not unless you want to break your neck falling into one of the cracks in the pavement.

The most common look in Ubud is the yogi camel-toed stretchy-leggings look, accessorised of course with feather earrings and a mandala, and tattoos on ankle, lower-back and hipbone of Sanskrit prayers, the yin-yang sign and a tree of life.

Last night I went online and thought I'd have a look at what goodies Topshop is offering these days for women who refuse to act their age. I am going to Singapore next week so this was my recon/ intel mission. I looked at the flip-flops and blanched. Twenty dollars! They're only $2 in town (or free if you happen to find a pair in your size outside of Yoga Barn). Then there is a dress for $50! I gave up and went over the road to the woman who sells fisherman trousers and bought myself a tie-dyed T-shirt with a big heart on the front and a white embroidered top (just like something Star from *The Lost Boys* might wear) and I thought 'hah!' as I handed over my 80,000 rupiah (roughly £4), beat that Topshop!

Partly I bought the stuff because Made, the lady who owns the shop, always tells me I'm *cantik* (beautiful) in between telling me that I need to have a boy-child, and that everyone thinks I'm *cantik*. *Cantik* this, *cantik* that, *cantik* hips, *cantik* face, *cantik* boobs. It's her sales pitch. I'm sure she'd say the same if I looked like the hunchback of Notre Dame.

I'm like: 'OK, OK, you got a sale, lady; enough with the *cantik*, get your hands off my boobs.'

This is what I've come to. Buying clothes from a woman who sells T-shirts with beer logos on to kids and who wouldn't know a copy of *Vogue* if it landed on her lap.

Fashion and I are no longer on speaking terms.

HAPPINESS IS...

Today has been magical. I tried to think what particular thing was making me feel so happy and in the end I realised it was the sum of its parts, starting with a morning cuddle with Alula, where we argued about who loved each other more, and eating a Cornetto for breakfast. (It was a mini one and we were out of cereal. No, we weren't. I just felt like eating ice cream.)

Then spying four volcanoes on the drive back from school. Even Mount Agung – the most shy of all the volcanoes on Bali, normally so cloud-shrouded that when it does occasionally appear it's like it's a spell or an illusion cast for the day and I feel I can wish on it.

Getting to watch an episode of *Prison Break* at 9am because I've finished writing the novel I was slaving over, so I feel I'm allowed do what I like at nine in the morning for the next day or so.

Going swimming and just listening to my iPod by the pool rather than pounding lengths trying to work out who said what and who did what in the chapter I'm writing.

Having my front veranda filled with Balinese friends popping by – one of whom then very kindly knocked down the wasps' nests being built in the rafters over John's desk while I cowered behind the door. He then gave the wasp grubs to Alula to feed to the fish.

Getting new fish for the pond (I killed the last three).

Managing to say 'food for the pig' in Indonesian to the gardener Wayan and have him grin at me *and* understand me, most importantly.

And also learning how to say, 'the fish eat the wasps'. (*Ikan makan tawon.*)

Coming home and having Alula yell, '*satu lagi bu!*' at me.' ('One more, Mummy!' – talking about sweets.)

Phoning the Taco Casa and having them answer it thus: 'Good evening, Sarah. How are you?'

Having a friend make me coffee with coconut cream, cacao and spices.

Eating fresh papaya and drinking a whole coconut.

Bumping into lots of people I know just on the way to buy quinoa.

Finally getting around to buying a bookshelf! A home for my stack of dust-covered books. 'Excited' doesn't cover it.

Lying in bed with my laptop and 16 more episodes of *Prison Break* ahead of me.

BALI SPIRIT

I love that Alula is growing up somewhere so full of magic and wonder. Somewhere she runs around school barefoot, singing songs about love and thanking the Mother Earth and Father Sun for her lunch, and at night counting geckos not sheep.

In the mornings she wakes up and squawks, 'Cockadoodle-doooo!' at the top of her lungs. Normality for Alula is putting offerings out for the fairies and stopping to pat the Ganesha and Buddha statues by our door on the way to school. I know, I know: hippy, much?

There are few of the issues here that plague children back in the UK. That might change when they become teenagers: here experimenting with drugs will earn them a date with a firing squad, as opposed to the slap on the wrist they'd get in the UK.

There's little in the way of one-upmanship (so far), when the only toys to be had are wooden drums from the market or cheap plastic tat from the only supermarket.

There's no fashion, so to speak, so no comparing expensive brands. Hardly any of the kids watch TV so there are no trends to follow – no Bratz dolls, *High School Musical* (excuse me if I'm out of date, I actually have no idea what the latest trend is). Most of the parents living here are eco-conscious, ecstatic-dancing, broad-minded joy-seekers and the children in their tie-dyed clothes, waist-length hair and tri-lingual happiness reflect that. In many ways living here is as perfect a childhood (in our book) as you could give a child. Alula has us with her almost all the time, has made friends with people from all around the world, is learning another language, is being immersed in a culture that respects the earth and honours community and family, is surrounded by nature in her bamboo school and in her house amidst the rice paddies.

But, at the same time, it's a bubble world. It's a tiny part of the globe, which is rapidly changing and shifting as Starbucks and the dollar take hold, but nonetheless a world which remains a happy bubble for the time being.

Today at the Bali Spirit Festival, surrounded by many friends and people wearing an astonishing amount of Lycra, Alula ran barefoot and free, squelching in mud, dancing to West-African rhythms, stroking snakes, eating ice cream, chanting to kirtan.

And then she was with us one moment and gone the next – yelling something about going off to do some magic. We found her 20 minutes later sitting in the children's tent glueing and sticking. When I talked to her at bedtime about not running off ever again she asked why and I struggled with how to explain just enough that would make her understand but not enough to frighten her.

'Because we worry about you,' I said.

'But why?' she said, and I saw it from her perspective. Why would we worry about her when she's among friends in a place she's never felt afraid, where all the children are running happily amok?

'Because while Bali is relatively safe, you can't just run off in places like London.'

'What's "safe"?' she asked, perplexed.

How do you shatter a four-year-old's innocence? 'Just that there are bad people out there and we don't want something to happen to you,' I answered.

'A bad person like the person who took your flip-flops?' Alula asked.

'Yes, like that,' I said. 'And we love you and don't want anything bad to ever happen to you.'

'Like what happened to the flip-flops?'

Growing up in a bubble is wonderful – magical, even – and I feel sure that it's the best thing we could do for her. We just have to hope that she isn't being set up for a massive shock when it bursts as, eventually, one day it must.

ANOTHER CRAZY TALE OF UBUD

I have 12 minutes to make it through Bintang supermarket, buying whatever it was I wrote on the list, which I left in the kitchen, and get back across town to pick up Alula at the library.

I slide the car into a sweet spot in the shade, jump out and am heading, keys in hand, across the car park when I hear: 'SARAH!'

I almost jump out my skin. There, sitting on the steps of the supermarket, is the woman I've been avoiding since, well, since our return to Bali. This woman gives me the heebie-jeebies. She sends my psycho compass spinning. She makes me want to reach for a bottle of holy water. If this was Sunnydale, you'd know she'd stepped right out of the hellmouth. If I were Buffy I'd slay her without asking any questions.

'Hi,' I say. It comes out kind of strangled.

'You need visa?' she asks.

'Er,' I say, fumbling for an answer.

This lady is just trying to part me from my cash. That's her job. She organises visas for expats. But I'm sure she also curses them with black magic when they say no. This is the same woman who fired cross-eyed Made for being cross-eyed.

'No, I'm good right now,' I say nervously.

'I get you visa,' she says.

'No, I'm good, thanks,' I repeat. 'Visa sorted.' *Please don't curse me.*

I'm about to move off, aware that time is ticking, when this American guy next to her with a straggly beard and a cap, stands up. He looks like he just spent the last week camped out in a shack in the hinterlands of Minnesota cooking up some meth. And when he opens his mouth I think I must have the gift of clairvoyancy.

Because the man is clearly high on something meth-like.

'You must come on Sunday,' he says to me.

I stare at him. I stare at the heebie-jeebies woman wondering how these two know each other.

'Um, I must come where?' I ask, thinking he's maybe about to ask me to a cookathon.

'This woman,' he slurs. 'She's amazing. She saved my life. You know Anna, she knows Kali who came here six years ago, she saved so many people and she's having a Tantra workshop and you must come and...'

I know my mouth has fallen open and I'm kind of gaping, whilst also looking over the top of my sunglasses at him wondering how he managed to make the mental and verbal leap from 'visa' to 'Tantra'. Talk about non sequitur.

He rambles on some more about Tantra. In my head this is what I'm thinking: 'What the hell is this guy saying? Think of some excuse. What are you doing on Sunday? Tell him you're going to Singapore. No, don't do that because scary lady might ask questions about your visa. Tantra? With this dude? I feel sick. And how does evil lady know this crazy lunatic? And, God, what are the odds of running into two totally mentally unsound people outside Bintang? And just when I'm in a hurry? Actually, don't answer that. Pretty high in this town. Shit, he's staring at me again. Pull your sunglasses up. Make an excuse. Is it rude to interrupt him? If you don't interrupt him he's going to talk until your ears bleed. Don't make eye contact, back away slowly; slowly now. Smile brightly. Now say it!'

'Thanks,' I blurt, 'but I have to run. I have to pick up Alula.'

And I run. While he's still talking about Sunday and Tantra

to my departing back. When, two minutes later, I rush out of the supermarket clutching my loo roll and milk, he's still there. He's still talking. I dash across the car park, avoiding eye contact.

I might have to start avoiding the supermarket. It's getting too stressful dodging the lunatics in this town.

THIS MANNY'S GOING NOWHERE

'Kadek's good at making pancakes,' Alula says, 'but she can't do puzzles.'

It's true. She can't. And for this reason Alula refuses to accept Kadek as a babysitter. This is a problem as it's the Easter holiday and I have a book to write. And then, as if the universe is listening to my woes, a friend of ours who is visiting Bali brilliantly breaks his leg.

And now I have a manny! A manny I don't even have to pay. And, even better, he can't complain or try to leave because his leg is broken in two places (his foot practically severed from his shin) and he can't even hobble one metre without crutches… (Crutches that I've cunningly hidden behind the door.)

I did think about suggesting a life-swap with him, where John and I'd take his stunning house on the Sayan ridge (which he now can't access as it's down a long staircase), and hang out in his plunge pool while he hangs out on my veranda with his foot up watching cartoons with Alula for the next two weeks, but I thought it might be a little unfair. They only gave him so much pain medication, after all.

Alula, of course, is loving the disabled manny, who has the 70 hours of *The Last Airbender* on his computer. She thinks he is the funniest person in the world *ever* and has taken to drawing him love letters and making me write him notes because after the first 50 her hand cramped.

Earlier she made me write 'I love you and you love me and I will love you forever even when you're dead and I forget you' and then she decorated it with hearts and swirls. So for two weeks I'm able to escape upstairs, leaving Alula curled up by the manny, who doesn't know I'm secretly calling him this.

I catch him trying to book a flight out of here back to Europe and in my alarm I tell him that he really should think about letting the swelling go down first, that, in fact, he really should stay the whole two months it will take to recuperate in case his foot explodes on the plane.

But I think the manny is getting quite anxious now to leave. He says it's because he wants to make sure the metal plate the surgeon in Bali inserted into his foot is actually in the right place. Hmmmmm. Thoughts of Kathy Bates spring into my mind. Today I'm going to the hardware store to buy myself a sledgehammer.

This manny's not going anywhere.

THE SLOW BUT INEVITABLE DEATH OF CYNICISM

A good friend popped around in the week and astrally projected from my balcony. She went to another dimension where she met a three-metre-tall, blue alien. I wanted to know if he looked like Sam Worthington from *Avatar*, but she couldn't say. I should emphasise: no drugs were involved.

But really, only in Ubud, right? I was sort of jealous that I lacked the switch in my brain to turn off my cynicism and join in. I mean, astrally projecting sounds fun, don't you think? I even have a character in one of my books who can do it. Though he never meets a three-metre-tall alien or visits other planes of existence. Clearly I need to work on my imagination.

The funny thing is that, a year ago, if you'd have told me I'd be taking part in a ceremony on my balcony whereby someone astrally projected, I'd have snorted with laughter. Same too for going to Kirtan and ecstatic dance. But somehow, living in Ubud does open you up to the esoteric. Even if I can't quite quit the eyeball-rolling, I find I'm snorting less and less and thinking more and more, 'well, why not?' The cynic in me might be dying hard, but it is dying. And maybe that's got a lot to do with not living in London any more where cynicism seemed hardwired into my DNA.

It is no surprise, really, that moving to Bali would involve some kind of re-evaluation of beliefs, given that Bali is called the island of the Gods, and has always been regarded as a magical, spiritual place. There is a deep mystical connection between the people and nature. The Balinese believe that the spirits are there, but invisible to the human eye. They live alongside us.

The deep-rooted spiritualism and magic of Bali is why so many expats choose to live here. It is not why John and I did. I wanted to live somewhere hot, somewhere I could lie by the pool all day and write, and with sunshine. Yet, here I am, patting my Buddha statue and lying flowers on Ganesha every morning, choosing a card from a psychic tarot deck, putting on my Saraswati necklace (goddess of creativity) and thanking the universe for my Russian book deal before asking if it would please see fit to send more foreign book deals my way. (The cynic in me suggests I am covering all bases.)

When we meet up with people who are just visiting here from London or LA and tell them all the alternative viewpoints and beliefs you're likely to find in Ubud – from raw food (which once seemed to be wack-job crazy to me and now just seems normal – though not something I'm about to take up) to Pleiadian technology, chakra meditation and breatharianism, their jaws drop open. John and I just shrug. We've become used to alternative ways of living, I guess.

Don't worry though, people, there is no need to stage an intervention just yet. I'm not about to sit naked on my balcony and entreat the Pleiadian mothership to beam me up. Nor am I going to ever attempt to live on air alone. I struggle to meditate or do yoga, after all. I think enlightenment and three-metre-tall, blue aliens will continue to elude me.

THEY FUCK YOU UP

When we were travelling, moving around every few days or weeks, Alula started displaying worrying behaviour traits. Every time we arrived in a new hotel or guesthouse she'd gather up a random assortment of belongings – her toys, hairbrushes, shells, books, her tutu – and place them all in a carrier bags, which she would then stash in random places – behind the loo or under the bed for example. It was weird. It was disturbing. And it freaked us out. I mean, when a three-year-old does this it kind of reveals latent displacement issues. What issues were we seeding in her psyche that might manifest at a later date as psychosis? How much did we need to start saving for therapy? At 13, would she throw this back in our faces – 'I hate you, you're not my Mummy ' – she already has this line down pat – 'you ruined my life making me travel around the world, wearing only a tutu!'

In rebellion against her hippy parents, I wondered, would she become an accountant? Would she refuse to board another plane for the rest of her life, move to the suburbs of some faceless city and choose to vote Conservative?

I hated it that she had no feeling of stability. It was the one thing we struggled with while we were on the move, forcing us to slow our pace (a good thing) and cancel some parts of our travelling to provide her with a sense of semi-permanence, at least.

So when we arrived back in Bali we were relieved to finally have a home, to be able to create a space for Alula where she felt safe and secure.

'But how long are we staying?' she kept asking.

'For ages and ages,' we answered. 'This is our home. Look, here's a bookshelf and your own princess bed.' We even bought her a puppy to help cement the idea of permanence.

And then I mentioned to her the other day that we were going back to London for the summer, and not 30 seconds later I find her burrowing through her treasure drawer, frantically emptying the contents into a plastic bag.

'What are you doing?' I asked her.

'I'm packing up all my treasures,' she answered, continuing to stuff things into the bag.

'But, darling, we're not going for ages, and we're coming back here. This is our home.'

But Alula didn't seem to hear. She just kept packing up her stuff.

Philip Larkin was right: they fuck you up, your mum and dad.

2012

AN UNUSUAL, UNDERWEAR-LESS DETOUR

Here is the abridged version of the last four days:

SINGAPORE AIRPORT

'I'd like to check in for my flight to Bali, please.'

'Sorry, your daughter's passport is three days under the six-months validity required to enter Indonesia.'

'You're kidding, right? Kidding, yes? Right?'

'No, sorry ma'am. Please step away from the counter.'

ON PHONE TO FOREIGN OFFICE

'The British High Commission doesn't issue passports any more, I'm afraid. You need to go to Hong Kong.'

'I can't go to Hong Kong. I need six months on my daughter's passport to clear immigration.'

'Oh.'

'I suppose I could tie her up in the butterfly enclosure at Changi and pick her up in four days.'

'You could try to get an emergency travel document. But the High Commission isn't open until Monday, maybe Tuesday. And it costs £100 and I'm not sure if Indonesia accepts them.'

ON PHONE TO JOHN

'ANSWER YOUR BLOODY PHONE.'

CONVERSATION WITH ALULA

'Is this our house now?'

'No, this is where we have to stay for three nights until the Consulate opens.'

'There are no windows.'

'I know. And you can sit on the toilet to shower.'

'I miss Daddy.'

CONVERSATION WITH ALULA, LATER

'Mummy only has her handbag. We have no underwear, no hairbrush, no toothbrush, no anything. We need to go shopping.'

'To Toys R Us?'

'Well, if you're a good girl and let me do all the shopping for everything we need then, yes, we can go to Toys R Us.'

ON PHONE TO JOHN

'I need money.'

ANOTHER CONVERSATION WITH ALULA

'We just saw *'Pung Fu Kanda Two.*'

'*Kung Fu Panda.*'

'*Pung Fu Kanda Two*… But you didn't buy me popcorn.'

'I bought you Littlest Pet Shop, so be happy.'

'What happened to the panda's mummy and daddy?'

'They died.'

'When I die, Mummy, I want to be buried because then Mother Earth will keep me safe.'

YET ANOTHER CONVERSATION WITH ALULA

'Sit up straight. No, don't slouch. Don't smile, either. Tilt your head this way a bit. OK, stay still, don't move… Listen, if you can't sit still and they can't get a good photo they might not issue a passport and then you'll be stuck here in Singapore for the rest of your life.'

'Cool. Will you buy me more toys?'

AT BRITISH HIGH COMMISSION, MONDAY MORNING

'I need an emergency travel document for my daughter.'

'I can't issue an ETD without proof of flights out of Singapore.'

'I can't book flights out of Singapore until you tell me how long it's going to take to issue this.'

'We can issue it by tomorrow.'

'Please, please, please, can you do it earlier?'

'If you can bring me your travel booking confirmation by 11am I can issue it by 4pm today.'

'Please can you put seven months on it, just to be sure?'

AT BALI IMMIGRATION

'Come this way, please, ma'am.'

'It's an emergency passport!'

'What is it?'

'An emergency passport.'

'A what?'

'It's a special passport. For emergencies.'

'Why you need? You have passport.'

'It's not valid.'

'Why not valid?'

'Um, it's complicated. Please can you let me into Bali though? It has been a very long weekend and I think I might cry if you don't.'

'You wait.'

'Hello?'

'Hello?'

'Um, hello? Still waiting.'

'What's happening, Mummy?'

'Err, don't worry. Everything's fine.'

CONVERSATION WITH JOHN, FOUR HOURS LATER

'Next time, *you're* doing the visa run.'

BACK IN THE UK FOR THE SUMMER

Bird song. Cool air. South-East accents (lots of 'fucking this, fucking that' – I'm quite at home). Pints of beer. Kettle chips. Roast lamb. Strawberries and raspberries. Croquet. Beer bellies. It's still light at 7pm! Aggression. Wine, wine, wine. Goat's cheese. An English country garden, complete with roses and, um, I don't know the name of any flowers, but is there anything more beautiful than an English country garden? A stack of shiny new books. A duvet. Carpet. The Sunday papers. Charity shopping. Pavements you can scooter down (and not have to call sidewalks). Smooth roads. Washing up (sucks). Fish and chips (yum). The proliferation of floral playsuits and soft, white flesh.

I do like being back in the UK.

For a short time, at least.

And in the summer.

STRESS AND WORRY AND ANOREXIC CELEBS

I worry about stuff more here in the UK. I stress more about silly, inconsequential things. I have to think more: what time train? What shoes? Umbrella or no umbrella? Where's my Oyster card? Can I really afford this second Frappuccino? Who *are* all these people in *Heat* magazine? Why are they still renovating the same Victoria line escalator that they were last time I was here? Surely it can't take 18 months? (Answer: yes it can.)

It's mentally exhausting. I feel like a character from a Brontë novel – and no, not the plucky heroine, more like her annoying great aunt who's always needing the smelling salts and having an attack of the vapours.

While I'm enjoying the walks along the Southbank, wine, catching up with friends and family, going to the cinema (sugar popcorn!), M&S undies, I am craving a return to my simpler life in Bali. There's less choice, less media to get absorbed into, no TV and no glossy mags, no fashion and no fashion choices to be dictated by the weather; I'm calmer there, and happier. I find gratitude all the time and with that comes a kind of peace I think it's practically impossible to achieve, living and working in a city.

It's hard to feel anything but tired and stressed when you're faced with four-hour train journeys, drunken people swaying into you on the pavement and constant exposure to the following two headlines: 'ANOREXIC CELEBRITIES' and 'AMAZING: Kate wore a Jenny Packham dress on the eighth day of her Canada trip.'

THANK GOD IT'S ONLY ONCE A YEAR

Two four-year-olds have cornered me.

'Is there birthday cake?' one demands.

'Yes,' I answer.

'Is the cake raw?' the other asks.

'No,' I say, pulling a face. Honestly. A raw birthday cake? That's as pointless as decaf coffee.

'Is the cake vegan?' the other asks. 'Because I'm vegan.'

'No,' I sigh, wishing we'd stayed in the UK for Alula's birthday and not come back to Bali, because at least there no five-year-old would ever utter the word 'raw' in relation to the word 'cake'.

'Well, what will I eat?' she demands, hands on hips.

'Um…' I don't honestly know or really care, but one thing I do

195

know is there'll be a lot more cake for me. I edge past the angry four-year-olds.

'Sugar's bad!' they chant in unison to my back.

Shaking my head, I find Alula, the birthday girl, and gather up the fifty-odd other kids who are running wild, and usher them off on a trek around the rice paddies.

'Enjoy the scenery… walk in the *subak*…' the man had explained to me prior to booking. It sounded great. So off we toddle now.

Ten metres in, the first casualty hits. A scream. A child falls into the rice paddy head-first.

Oh shit. Once the kid is rescued I plaster on a smile and usher the other kids along like I'm Mary Poppins on ecstasy… 'Oh look, isn't this fun, everyone?' I beam and clap my hands together like a performing seal. 'It's only a bit of mud!' I tell the child who fell in and who is still trying to scrape slime off his face.

'What are we doing here, Mummy?' Alula asks with a po-face.

'We're on a nature walk, it's fun! And it won't be for long.'

She frowns at me. 'The grass is itchy. I want a carry. I hate this.'

'OK, I'll carry you,' I tell her. It is, after all, her birthday and I am, after all, feeling rather like a failure at this point. Someone else's mother organised a trip to the spa for the entire class. Fifteen girls all had manicures and pedicures while sitting in massaging chairs, each of them with an iPad to entertain them. My effort – this rice-paddy trek – is not really reaching the impossibly high bar that's been set. It's falling quite a little short.

The second casualty happens a moment later. Another child survives a fall into the mud, though barely. The third casualty follows quickly on the second. One of the mothers on the walk with us topples sideways. She is fine but her shoes disappear and are sucked into the muddy abyss. She's lucky she didn't get sucked in after them.

'I'm so, so sorry,' I say, cringing at her mud-splattered trousers and now bare feet.

She laughs, but not before I see the rage behind her eyes.

'This is not a success, Mummy,' Alula announces as I try to tip-toe delicately along the six centimetre width of the rice paddy verge while holding onto Alula and the camera, and simultaneously trying to apologise to women and children who are crying and limping along ahead of us.

'No, no, it's fine, darling,' I whisper, so as not to be overheard, when secretly I'm thinking: Whose bloody idea was this? Oh yes, good one, John. And there goes my shoe. My new leather shoe. Eaten whole by the mud.

Finally we make it back and I do a headcount before moving swiftly on to the cake-cutting part. And I'm thinking, gin, give me gin. Where is the gin? – even as I cut the cake.

'I get the biggest piece,' an older kid announces, shoveling his way to the front and sticking his nose into the icing. He reminds me of *Charlie and the Chocolate Factory*'s Augustus Gloop. If Augustus Gloop had eaten the entire contents of the chocolate factory *and* Willy Wonka.

'Err, actually, I think *I* get the biggest piece,' I say, thinking to myself, who's got the knife, kid? You might want to rethink your strategy.

'Well, I get the first piece,' he counters.

Who invited you in the first place, I want to ask. I don't even know who he is. Is he gate-crashing?

'No, actually, the birthday girl gets the first piece,' I tell him lightly. 'And no one gets any cake unless they say please and thank you!'

He scowls at me. I smile at him. There's a whole field of mud just over there which I'm perfectly willing to throw him in. I'd like to see him get sucked into the muddy abyss head-first.

'Wow,' the kid says, staring around at the balloons and the food. 'Do you know who's paying for all this? This is like, going to cost millions... and millions.'

I'm still holding the knife. OK, it's only plastic. But I could use it to smear icing over his head. Then push him backwards into the paddy.

'Where's my goodie bag?' he demands once I've served him a tiny sliver of cake (last) and I've watched him shove the entire slice into his mouth in one go.

I put the knife down. 'We're all out of goodie bags,' I say, smiling a rictus grin.

When we get home I pour myself a bottle of gin with a splash of tonic. And then I stuff myself with the two extra portions of cake that were leftover and that I hid from the annoying kid.

BLACK MAGIC (AND NOT THE CHOCOLATE KIND)

The day after the astral projecting on my balcony, another friend came over and told me how she had just been to see a healer to have a black-magic curse removed.

I *am* living in Sunnydale. Next I will be hearing of a girl called Wayan, the chosen one, a girl-child born in every Balinese generation, whose mission is to slay the creatures that come through the hellmouth, aka Seminyak and Kuta.

Here in Bali, it might be Hindu but the ceremonies are very

animalist in nature: offerings are laid out every morning outside our house, on our car windshield and at the gates, to protect against bad spirits. Or maybe just against my bad driving. So far they seem to be working, even though the dog eats half the offerings and Alula prefers to lay out her own version of cornflakes and half-chewed prunes to ward off the enemy.

My friend had been hexed by someone she'd had an altercation with. They had, according to the healer, stolen hair from her hairbrush and taken it to a bad priest who had placed a black-magic curse on her. It was a terrifying, very real experience for my friend and hearing her tell it gave me goose bumps. She managed to find a healer who banished the demon. My friend explained that it was like having an invisible snake pulled out of her throat.

So far, so *Exorcist*, right? Except without the spinning head and vomiting child talking in a freaky voice. It's a funny old place, Bali. Fascinatingly magical and creepy at the same time. I just intend to be extra specially careful from now on not to piss anyone off.

LET'S THINK ABOUT THIS FOR A MOMENT

Bali is not entirely without its horrors. Our neighbour Made broke his leg a year ago in a moped accident. It happened just before we arrived. He's still on crutches and can't walk. He's also in a lot of pain. He just came over to show me his leg and I did well to keep my breakfast down. I'm not good with bodily secretions. Least of all yellow, oozing ones.

The thing is, Made and his wife, Nyoman, are poor. They are so poor that they have just enough to feed themselves. They certainly don't have enough money to pay doctors' bills. We provide their only income – paying Nyoman to lay offerings around our house and to babysit Alula on the occasional evenings when we go out. But in a country where I'm told many of the doctors buy their way into medical school (hence the richest and not necessarily the brightest become doctors) and where it's not unusual to bribe your way through the exams, getting good treatment is hard enough even if you do have money. If you're poor, the odds are not in your favour.

Our friend Komang's aunt fell and broke her arm – the bone snapping in two and poking through the skin. Unable to afford the local doctor's fees they took her on a bumpy car ride to the priests at Besakih, the mother temple on Mount Agung, who are renowned for their bone-fixing abilities. Once there, the priests set her arm. Without any painkillers.

Not long ago, Komang's wife, Kadek, was sick for days and days. She went to two doctors in her local village. They told her she needed more sleep. Worried about her, I took her to Doctor Ating at Green School. He took one look at her and told me she had hookworm. He prescribed iron pills and a simple de-worming tablet. All in, the two cost under a dollar over the counter at the local pharmacy. Within twelve hours Kadek was back on her feet, feeling fine.

De-worming is a pre-requisite in the tropics. I realised this only after Alula and I both had dodgy tummies and an Australian friend who is married to an Indonesian and who has lived here 15 years told me that we most likely had a parasite and should get some over-the-counter worming tablets. Up until then I had thought that was just something you gave dogs.

I also heard the other day that allegedly the doctors here are bribed with cars and televisions by pharmaceutical companies.

The payback? To keep babies away from their mothers for the first 36 hours of their lives, so the mother's milk dries up and they are forced to buy formula. This in a country where formula milk costs more than most people earn in a day.

My UK friend has recently returned to Bali with her six-week-old son.

'He's so fat!' the Balinese gasp.

He's not. He's a normal, healthy weight for a breast-fed child of that age. But it seems that the Balinese are so used to watered-down formula or poor diet that some don't even know what is normal and healthy in a child.

This same week I have finally sorted our health insurance – making sure that it includes evacuation – because the one thing I've learned is that if we get into an accident I don't want to be treated here if we have choice in the matter. As I tapped in my Visa number, I felt sick with guilt and also overwhelmed with gratitude at our privileged situation allowing us to just buy our way out of difficulty. Here we are with the means to get the best medical care available while my neighbour cannot afford so much as an indigestion tablet.

I took Made, our neighbour with the bad leg, to the local clinic, Bumi Sehat. It's famous for its birth centre and its philosophy of gentle birth. The founder, Ibu Robin, just won the CNN 'Hero of the Year' award for her work in Indonesia to support maternal and newborn health. She also runs a clinic. In between her hectic round of appointments she took the time to look Made over.

'He needs antibiotics,' she informed us. 'Or he'll lose that leg. It's infected.'

'OK,' I said. 'Where do I get antibiotics from? How?'

She shook her head. 'The ones he needs aren't available in Indonesia.'

'What?' I asked in despair. 'How can that be?' But then I remembered my own brush with giardia (another parasite infection) a few months back. I dropped about eight kilos (beat that, colonic irrigation) and was as sick as a very sick dog for three whole months, waking every morning at 3am to crawl to the toilet and wretch up whatever was in my stomach, followed by what felt like my stomach lining. Constantly nauseous and tired, I can tell you it wasn't much fun. And not a single test or doctor I saw in Indonesia (three in total) could tell me what was wrong.

In the end, and luckily for me, we happened to be flying to join family in Perth at Christmas and my dad, on seeing me at the airport, drove me straight to a doctor, who ordered every test in the book and then, while we waited, wrote me a prescription for the strongest antibiotic on the market, suspecting that I had giardia.

The antibiotics worked. I was cured. If I was Balinese I would most likely still be crawling to the toilet to hurl each night.

Bali has taught me the value of good deeds and gratitude for my circumstances. Then last night I was reading an article in *The Guardian* about the dismantling of the NHS in the UK. It painted a dark future of a private healthcare system discriminating against the poor, providing only the best services (and most expensive treatments, like chemotherapy) for those who can afford them.

The UK could potentially wind up with a US-style system run on market principles, where only the rich can afford treatment and the poor must suffer. Can you imagine, in the UK, having your neighbour show you his puss-y leg and ask you if you can afford to pay his medication bills? How would you answer?

In the end, Ibu Robin managed to locate the antibiotics Made needed at a US-funded health care centre down in Denpasar, the capital. For the moment at least, he's had a lucky escape.

WHY BEING A MOTHER SOMETIMES SUCKS BALLS

I am sitting amidst a pile of cellophane wrappers and discarded shoes – plastic Tweety Pie-emblazoned fake Crocs, Disney Princess bow-clad horrors with heels and sparkly, beaded flip-flops – and I am in tears.

'If you don't choose a pair of shoes by the time I count to ten I am going to send you on the next plane back to England,' I hiss at Alula.

I know I'm not the world's best mother but, by God, I try to be. It's just that sometimes being a mother *sucks balls* and any mother who says otherwise is a big fat liar and I challenge her to a duel. Or to hand over whatever it is she's taking because I want some of it.

Yesterday, being a mother *sucked more balls* than I can tell you about. Alula has four pairs of shoes, including a pair of £30 Start-rites bought in the UK, which she chose herself and which she loved, up until she got bored with the Velcro strap and the three extra seconds it takes to put them on, which stops her from getting to the sand pit first.

Right now, those £30 Start-rites are floating eerily sole-up in our fishpond where I threw them yesterday in a fit of pique. Alula didn't care a jot about their watery demise; her only thought was for the fish I might have brained in the process.

'There are children living next door who have *no shoes*,' I told her, 'and you have a gorgeous pair of shoes but don't want them.'

Did she repent of her ingratitude and haul them out of the pond

203

and put them on, sobbing in anguished shame? Did she heck. She just shrugged at me.

She also has a pair of Crocs, which she used to love but which, for reasons I cannot fathom, have been moved from the endangered to the extinct list. And finally, she has the faux-animal-fur flip-flops she chose just yesterday in the supermarket when, through utter exhaustion, I told her she could just have whatever she wanted; I no longer cared, even if they had six-inch heels and a handy place to stick a flick-knife.

Those shoes lasted a day. They weren't comfortable, she complained. So here we find ourselves surrounded by cheap, tatty shoes, with me in tears and Alula unmoved and still shaking her head at every pair that the shop owner and I thrust her way.

'Fine then,' I say. 'You'll just have to go barefoot to school. I've given your Start-rites to the neighbour's child.'

'NO,' she announces. 'If I don't have shoes I'm not going to school.'

So just let her stay home, you might think, or, just buy a pair of damn shoes and make her wear them, or refuse to buy her new ones and make her wear the Crocs. If that's what you're thinking then yeah, I hear you. And believe me, I wish it was that easy.

I spend half my life online trying to figure out the best parenting approach for Alula and discussing it with John (supernanny, exorcism, the naughty step – tried 'em all). And I laugh at your naïveté. You haven't had the pleasure of meeting our daughter. She makes mules rethink their approach to stubbornness. The words of my mother, said to me when I was about eight, come back to haunt me: *one day you're going to have a child just like you and then you'll understand.*

OK, I want to add something else to my list of things that suck balls. Karma. And you know what else? That no one ever tells you how hard being a mother is. You think women might want to share that little secret a bit more openly. It would help. That too goes on my sucking-balls list.

We have been, by this point, to two supermarkets, the Crocs shop *and* two local shoe shops. We have tried on every pair of size-29 shoes in Indonesia. Flip-flops, Crocs and any shoes with straps have been ruled out. What does that leave? It leaves barefoot. But knowing the hellishness that would result the next morning when this becomes clear to Alula is more than I can handle.

Eventually, she tries on a pair of flip-flops that had attached to them what looked like those little bath oil balls The Body Shop sold in the late eighties… remember them? Kind of squishy like boils?

'Yes,' she says, trying them on. 'I can wear these.'

I hand over the $2.50 and we walk back to the car, me still in tears.

WHO YOU GONNA CALL?

Alula has been doing her best impression of Damien from *The Omen* these last few weeks. And when I say 'impression' I mean that she follows the method-acting school of thought.

Being Ubud, most people's first response when I appear weeping before them, despairing of her behaviour, is: 'Have you taken her to a Balian?'

Not: 'Have you taken her to see a therapist?', 'Have you taken her for ice cream?', 'Have you spoken to her teachers?', 'Have you tried Supernanny?' but: 'Have you taken her to a witchdoctor?'

And that's not coming from the Balinese, that's coming from

the expats – most of whom I count as friends and who aren't the typical bliss-ninny you find here but people I consider practical, sensible and intelligent.

Hell, I'll try anything at this point, I think. And what harm could a little opinion be? And I am a believer in some aspects of spiritual healing (though I have never tried a witchdoctor before, it must be said).

So I email a Balian recommended to me and ask what he thinks. The Balian tells me that two demons are squatting on Alula's astral plane. Yes, you read that right. Two demons. Squatting. Astral plane.

I mean, where do you go with that? Other than to the dictionary to make sure you've understood properly? And then to the bathroom to lie down on the cold, wet tiles, clutching a bottle of vodka? Suddenly I'm Mia Farrow in *Rosemary's Baby*.

So the Balian says he'll do a clearing. I think that's the polite terminology for 'exorcism'... Oh the irony. Our child actually *is* possessed!

'OK,' I say to the guy. I mean, why not? We're also trying Omega 3 fish oils, lavender sprinkled on her clothes, a no-sugar diet, approaches from *The Explosive Child*, daily massages and lots of love and hugs. Having someone chant some words on top of all that sounds fine to me. I'm open to most things these days – except, perhaps, staring into strangers' eyes and sending them the love of the universe. And it beats electroshock therapy, right? And thirdly, in this lurid list of self-justifications, what if, just what if, it might *actually* be true? You'd be breaking out the holy water too, believe me...

And guess what? Alula woke up this morning for the first time in about six weeks and told me in a sweet, angelic voice: 'I love you, Mummy.'

There were no screaming battles, no devil faces, no rages. She was placid as a lamb. Maybe it's the lavender. Maybe she just woke up in a better mood. Maybe she'll flip out again later.

Or maybe Rosemary should have taken her baby to a Balian.

GREEN SCHOOL BALI

Alula has started at a new school. Some of you may have heard of it. It's called Green School and it's sort of famous because it's a) completely built from bamboo, b) Al Gore has visited, as well as Ban Ki-moon, Richard Branson and, my personal favourites, Daryl Hannah and Ben & Jerry, and c) it's the world's greenest school.

Once you see it, you kind of come away wowed and wishing that you could be five years old again with really cool parents who moved you to Bali and were hippy enough to not really care much about whether you were learning your ABC but who thought that skipping around a giant crystal in the jungle, learning songs about Mother Earth and how to make ice cream was the way forward.

It's like Swiss Family Robinson crossed with Mallory Towers, crossed with *I'm a Celebrity... Get Me Out of Here* crossed with an ashram. See, you're nodding, right? Cool, huh? You want to be five again, with me and John as your parents, I can tell.

The place is off-grid, grows most of its own food (each class has its own vegetable garden and rice paddy to tend), has its own farm and conservation project, and uses banana leaves as lunch plates. The toilets are made from bamboo. There is one for weeing and one for pooing. This means you can sit next to a friend and chat while vacating your bowels, so long as the other person is only weeing. If you poo in the wee toilet I think you'd have to reach in and pick it out. It is quite a challenging set-up for a five-year-old who hasn't yet mastered pelvic floor control (hell, it's challenging for me) but despite all this, or perhaps because of it, Alula still thinks that it's the best school in the world.

THE UNBECOMING OF A DOMESTIC GODDESS

On my list of things to do in both 2011 and 2012 I have the following written:

1. Give up cooking

So I'm not sure why I've just spent $100 on an oven that looks like a giant toaster but with a spit-thing in the middle, just in case I fancy spit-roasting a piglet (a whole pig wouldn't fit) for Sunday brunch.

I'm not sure why I've bought an oven at all. I think if I stopped to analyse it, which I'm frightened to, I'd discover the reason is because the ghost of Nigella haunts me. Buried deep in my subconscious is the need to be a domestic goddess with an enormous bosom, even though the chances are nil-to-subnil of this actually ever happening (being a domestic goddess or growing boobs bigger than an A cup).

Perhaps, too, is the idea that if I can cook I will redeem myself in John and Alula's eyes as being a worthy wife and mother as opposed to a half-hearted one; one who would much rather watch *Mad Men* or finish her book than play Junior Scrabble or cut the crusts off toast. If I can fill the house with the wafting, delicious smells of baking cookies and fresh bread then… God, I don't even have the ability to finish that thought.

I still don't know why I bought an oven.

I told John I wanted to roast vegetables. But then I looked at the chopping board and the pile of veg in the fridge and was like, *but damn, I have to peel them first. How tedious.*

I bought Alula a baking cupcake tray. But now I'm thinking, damn I have to buy an electric whisk 'cos, no joke, I'm not stirring that by hand.

But then it all became a moot point anyway. Because I got my $100 oven back home (spit-roast and all) and remembered that the last time someone plugged in a kettle they almost blew up our house.

I study the box. It has a lot of numbers and letters on it. I sigh to myself. Maybe I should have paid more attention in physics. Is this even physics? I don't know. I don't care. That's what dads are for. I fleetingly worry about what Alula will do when she finds herself in a similar situation in 20 years' time. John certainly won't have a clue. A generation of boys has grown up clueless of DIY and physics, and my daughter will suffer as a consequence. I'm supposed to think something feminist at this point about teaching her about wattage or amps and how to change a plug because why are we X-chromosome holders relying on the Y people? I could actually Google it myself right now and then teach her myself – that would be the ideal situation. Feminism in action.

I don't. I call my dad.

'Dad,' I say, across 14,000 kilometres. 'I have a problem.'

I switch the Skype camera on and turn the lens to face my oven.

My dad asks me, 'What ampage do you have in the house?'

'Huh?'

My dad sighs. I can't read minds but I know he's thinking: 'why on earth did I bother spending all those hours when she was 15 tutoring her through GCSE Physics? For what end?'

'Do you know what a fuse box looks like?' he eventually asks as a last resort.

'Yeah!' I answer rushing out to look. I'm just relieved he's asking me something I actually know the answer to. I return and tell him 240W.

'That's not an amp,' he says in his 'I'm speaking to someone of below average intelligence' voice. 'That's a watt.'

'What?'

Eventually we figure out that the 'interevertor' – this plastic box that Komang, our driver, bought me and that he assures me he uses to turn on his TV (no, not a remote) without blowing up his whole village – is actually an 'invertor' and that Chinese manufacturers from the 1970s just couldn't spell.

I plug the oven into the black box, plug the invertor into the wall and then, praying fervently, turn on the oven, while simultaneously shielding my face from any explosions that might occur.

Nothing explodes. The oven starts to heat up. I grimace to myself, wishing the house had actually exploded, because now I actually have to start cooking. Urgh.

TRICK OR HEALTHY TREAT

It's Halloween and because we are surrounded in Bali by expat Americans and Canadians this means having to suffer through trick-or-treat and Halloween hell. Being British, I'm faintly disturbed by the tradition, squirmy about the concept of fancy dress (the effort involved seems commensurate with axing the trees to light your own funeral pyre), cynical of the commercialisation of yet another pagan/Christian ceremony and also mightily stressed out by the email invite to trick or treat, which begins: *Come in costume, laugh and smile a lot!*

The British in me rears up like a fire-breathing dragon. Not only do they expect me to wear a costume (a costume, Goddammit!) but they also expect me to laugh and smile too? *Puh-lease*. Who are these people?

OK, I'm just a little envious. I've grown up in the land of sarcasm. I am not familiar with laughing and being happy *all* the time. I am more familiar with wry remarks while cocking a cynical eyebrow and complaining about the weather.

We're asked to bring healthy food for the pot luck and healthy snacks for the trick or treat, with a note in bold to be as environmental as possible.

I spend all week online, manically Googling healthy Halloween recipes. I have visions of extravagantly costumed parents handing out gluten-free, sugar-free, raw cupcakes with monster faces on them crafted out of cashew butter, cacao nibs and goji berries, while I lurk at the back in my jeans and T-shirt handing out Haribo and plastic-toy-filled Kinder Eggs.

Over on her website Annabel Karmel has made 'brain mush muffins'. Well whoopee-do, Annabel! Good for you.

Jamie Oliver has made fruit gums using real fruit. Congrats, Jamie!

I, however, can make nothing, because the oven has exploded. Our *new* oven, which cost us $100 and a lot of time working out wattage.

As you can probably guess, I'm secretly quite glad that the oven exploded. Just don't tell John. I'd promised to make him shepherd's pie.

Anyway, I wake up on Saturday morning, the day of the trick-or-treat thing, and decide that I am done with pretending. I know I've said this about ten times already, but this time I really am done with pretending that I am a yummy-mummy domestic goddess. I close down all those Google browsers, taunting me with images of vampire pizzas and googly-eyed fruit salads, and instead pull out my phone and ring the pizza place, ordering three pizzas and five packs of double chocolate cookies. I have never felt such a relief, let me tell you. I might be $80 poorer but I am $1m happier.

Then we get to the location of the trick or treating. I have to ask a passing Canadian woman what I am expected to do when the kids come knocking. She looks at me weirdly and tells me that I should compliment them on their costumes and hand out the cookies, then she walks off, shaking her head.

OK, I think to myself, I can manage that.

I hand out all the cookies, eating seven myself as I wait (it was stressful running over my lines).

Alula arrives, beaming with the shopping bag I'd given her already filled to the brim with goodies. We empty them out in the car. Every single treat is a plastic-wrapped, one-cent sweet from the local supermarket.

Even Haribo would have been an upgrade on this mound of sugary treats. I could have bought a bag of fizzy cola bottles along and they would have seemed like magnums of champagne by comparison.

The fire-breathing dragon in me really does rear up this time.

PRIMAL ME

'What is that?'

'It's rose quartz. It's to help clear my sacral chakra.'

'Oh.'

'I need to use it when I meditate.'

'OK.'

Now, I bet every penny in my bank account (which isn't very much, just in case you were thinking of taking me up on the bet) that you're reading that thinking *I'm* the one saying 'oh' and 'OK' while silently screaming, oh Jesus… I'm trapped talking to a freaky bliss-ninny, and glancing surreptitiously sideways for the exits.

Well, you're wrong! I'm the one holding the rose quartz.

I'll give you a few stunned seconds to absorb that.

For the last two weeks I've been embracing the esoteric in an effort to finally kick into submission the back pain caused by two herniated discs. I've had three sessions with an amazing energy worker, a watsu appointment, two Pilates classes, a chakra cleansing (yeah, you heard me right), a pedicure and I've meditated every day for three whole days.

The pedicure was done with a cheese grater and the pain it caused momentarily distracted me from the pain in my back. So, in that respect, it worked.

The three sessions with the energy worker were the equivalent of taking a hit on a bong the size of Denpasar (Bali's capital city). I was floaty-good for hours after. Needless to say, I think I've developed a dependency issue on the treatment he gives me, and I'm worried that my body subconsciously is refusing to heal because that will mean no more floaty-good. Kind of like how people get addicted to pain relief.

The watsu – let me explain this one. It's water plus shiatsu. You get into a kind of giant jacuzzi wearing only a bikini, and a man spins you around. You feel like a piece of lettuce in a salad spinner, or an old sock stuck on a warm-wash-delicate cycle.

If you were going all Ubud about it, you could describe it as a 'symbiotic relationship resonant of floating in the warmth and safety of the womb of the universe'. I kind of squirmed mentally at the idea of being in a womb when I read that on the leaflet, but I did like the idea of being in space. Until my imagination went all *Alien* on me.

It *was* a bit like floating in space though. If space were warm and didn't make your eyeballs explode, that is. (Or do they implode? See, it's Physics again. I need to call my dad to check.) It was strange and alarming and evocative, and at the end I felt seasick and collapsed, heaving, against the side of the pool, before sinking to the bottom and letting out a scream. Very primal of me.

The English in me was very embarrassed about the primal in me and apologised to the lovely man who'd been swirling me for an hour. He told me that some people went all-out and I was quite tame by comparison. I would love to know what 'all-out' means. Did they strip off their bikinis, beat their chests and urinate in the pool?

I really hope I never meet the watsu man in a social setting. That would be awkward. 'Hello, remember me? I screamed in your swimming pool and almost threw up on you. Remember?'

As for the Pilates, I've been doing it for a year now and I have to say I'm loving it. More for the endless gossiping I get to do than for the astonishing realisation that I have pelvic floor muscles and can squeeze them on demand – though put away your ping pong balls; I'm not that advanced yet.

And finally the chakra cleansing – which was part of a birthday present – also meant I could check off 'start meditating' from my list of things to do this year.

So I've been meditating every day now for – COUNT THEM

– three days. *Three* whole days – admittedly, not all day, but always while clutching my rose quartz stone and imagining I'm sitting in a ray of golden light. Ergo, this should mean I'm fully enlightened by now.

In the car earlier Alula turned to me and said, 'Mummy, why are you calling that man a wanker?'

Not quite so enlightened then. But Deepak Chopra does say it will take 21 days.

And as for the herniated discs. They're still herniated.

I AM SUCH A TEENAGER

'You always do this'

'Do what?'

'Act like this'

'Like what?' I ask – though in my head I know full well what John is talking about. He is suggesting I'm acting like a teenager. I shrug, huff and cross my arms over my chest. 'I'm coming, aren't I?' I ask, slamming the car door. I follow this with a silent yet dramatic: '*But don't ask me to be happy, because that was never part of the deal.*' Then I giggle to myself at the fact I'm now quoting lines from one of my books (ahh, the fuzzy lines where fiction and real life blur… Now, if they could just blur a bit more and land me with the skills of my protagonists to hurl car-shaped missiles at people's heads and decapitate demons with circular saw blades…)

Anyway, I digress. I'm huffing like a teenager not because I still am one but because John is dragging me up a bloody volcano at 7am. Last time I went up Mount Batur was a year ago and then I swore on someone's grave that it was the utter last time EVER – as in EVVVVVEEEEEERRRRR, full stop for all eternity, poke my eyes out and slap me around the face if I'm lying – that I was going anywhere near the place.

Mainly I swore like this because as soon as you get out of the car in the crater you're hit by a swarm of flies so thick you finally understand what a corpse might feel like if left for a month on a body farm. But here I am, having to go up the volcano again, because John has signed us up to a tree-planting expedition, which apparently, he claims, will be 'great fun'. Our ideas about what constitutes fun are clearly worlds apart and perhaps we should have talked further before getting married and having a child. Or rather, having a child and then getting married. But we didn't talk about the having-a-child part – she just sort of turned up by accident and the marriage part wasn't so much a discussion as me calling up John at work one day and telling him I'd gone ahead and booked the registry office.

John says something else about how important it is for us to take part in things like this. All I hear is: 'yada yada community yada green yada something' but all I'm thinking is, this sucks balls.

'It's to reforest the volcano.'

'But why?' I ask, frowning

John stares at me sideways and shakes his head in mute disgust.

'What?' I ask. 'I mean, seriously, Batur is still a live volcano so isn't it kind of pointless to plant trees, which in all likelihood are going to be directly in the path of the next lava flow?'

And indeed when we get to the place where everyone is meeting we discover that we're planting little saplings in lava rock. Lava rock left behind from the last time the volcano spewed out a little stream of molten fire. Just 40-odd years ago. I trudge in my flip-flops over the caustic rock, having borrowed a pair of sunglasses from one nice man and got a second to carry my trees for me.

'We don't have a shovel,' I say to John. 'How are we supposed to plant these things?'

John holds up an old tree branch. 'We'll dig with this.'

I want to hit him over the head with that branch. The other people laugh and take photos when I start scratching at the dirt to dig a hole. This is apparently as momentous an occasion as Will and Kate's wedding-day-balcony kiss.

John actually films me on my hands and knees. Someone cracks a joke about my nails. I think sadly of 12 hours earlier, when I was reclining on a day-bed by a pool overlooking the beach down south, drinking cocktails. I am *that* girl. I am not *this* girl.

However, I do plant all my trees. Then I take Alula's hand and march back down the volcano to the car, which is now filled with dead flies.

On the way back home John stops the car and buys a wooden table. Just saying. Now who's the bad guy?

I AM SO DONE WITH DRIVING IN THIS TOWN

There's a campaign in Ubud to stop the tourist coaches coming into town and clogging up the narrow streets. Of course, this being Bali, nothing changes fast, so the buses continue to belch their way into town to deposit their tourists outside the market so they can buy penis bottle openers and over-priced wooden Buddha statues.

There are virtually no rules to the road in Bali – other than two: never wear a helmet if you're on a bike, and if your side of the road is blocked by a car or another obstacle you have to give way to oncoming traffic until the road is clear to overtake.

If you like, you can drive on the left. I've never seen a moped pause at a stop sign and look both ways before pulling into traffic –

they always just pull straight out.

It's like they're born to play Russian roulette and have no care whatsoever that they might *die*. I can't figure it. As a driver you have to be totally on your toes. It's like playing Space Invaders. Three people a day die on the roads in Bali, apparently. *Three*.

So I'm driving up the hill into town. On the other side of the road is a long row of parked cars and bikes. By rights, anything at the top has to wait for me to pass before it can go. And then I see the fuck-off-sized coach at the top of the hill.

I narrow my eyes and think to myself, 'don't you dare', but does he telepathically hear me or does he just think, 'I'm going to crush you, sucker?'

Yeah, he thinks the latter. He comes speeding towards me, foot to the floor.

Seeing that there is no way in God's universe a coach – a fricking *coach* – can pass me without crushing the car whole, I slam on the brakes. I ram the car into reverse, checking my mirrors. A woman on a bike is behind me, sitting on my bumper, staring blankly into space. I beep at her, trying to get her to back up. She doesn't move. I honk again. She stays staring blankly as the coach descends on us. I reverse so I'm touching her wheel. She still doesn't move. And now there are about 50 bikes and three cars all up my arse, beeping me.

None of them seem to figure it out. 'BACK THE HELL UP!' I yell.

All the bikes start trying to overtake me instead. Of course they do. This is Bali. I sigh and put the handbrake on and let the coach meet me face to face. Now what, I think. I can't go back and he can't reverse either. I can't climb the curb as it's about a foot high. And he has parked cars and bikes on his side.

At just this point six men with whistles come flying down the hill, arms waving, cheeks puffing. I roll my eyes heavenward. I love these traffic guys whose job it is to help people park and direct traffic. I mean, how on earth would I know which way to turn the wheel without them to show me?

They're a swarm. All I can see is flaying arms and agitated faces. A man on a bicycle joins in. A western tourist starts taking photos. A motorbike tries to mount the curb to overtake me. Three men start banging my bonnet and telling me to turn the wheel – one this way, one that way, another man at the front telling me to back up. Yet another starts screaming at me to come forward. A fifth man tells me to stay put.

I wind the windows down. 'Can you all shut up?' I shout. 'You're all telling me different bloody things! YOU'RE NOT HELPING.'

This sets them to cursing out each other. It looks like fists might be about to fly.

I wind the window back up. And then the coach starts moving forward.

What the fuck, I think to myself. There is just no way that coach is getting past without taking off the side of the car. I watch it bear down thinking that this cannot be happening. I close my eyes. It squeezes by, leaving not a millimetre to spare. And then it gets stuck by my wheel arch.

Really? You don't say. That was *unexpected*.

The coach driver doesn't give a crap about my car though. He just cares about getting his coachload of tourists out of Ubud and back to Kuta. I want to get out the car, smash down the driver's door, grab hold of one of the wooden penis bottle openers no doubt on board and do serious damage to him with it, but unfortunately you can't even slide a piece of paper between my car and the coach. I am quite literally wedged inside.

Eventually, ignoring the gesticulating whistle blowers, I slam my car into first gear, smack my foot on the gas while wrenching the wheel and manage to jump the foot-high curb. It's a very *Mission-Impossible*-crossed-with-*Fast-&-Furious* move and I would be super proud of myself if the coach didn't then scrape itself along my wheel arch before thundering off.

Sodding, sodding coaches.

MUSINGS ON HOME

Home. What do we think of when we think of home?

For a while now I've been wanting a space that feels like home. Our house is very nice and everything, but it's not home. Even after two years here it doesn't feel like home.

Houses here aren't built with comfort in mind. I'm talking about the houses that the Balinese build to rent to foreigners because they themselves, almost without exception, live in family compounds. They're not built with anything in mind, I don't think, other than 'box, giant bathroom, tiny bedroom, outdoor kitchen… now let's ask for 200m rupiah a year (£10,000) and see if any *bule* (what the Balinese call us foreigners) is stupid enough to agree.'

When I close my eyes and picture my perfect home I see a place with a wooden veranda and swing chairs, creaky floors and sun-drenched windows, sandy soil and scrubby plants, a wild and rambling garden with roses trailing, somewhere so close to the ocean you can taste it and smell it in the air. It's hot, it's sunny, neighbours say hello and wave, there's an awesome café bookshop on our street, lots of independent stores and, of course, places to buy cake.

It's hippy and liberal and filled with awesome people all doing things they are passionate about.

I have a room in my dream house that is all mine and is where I write. It has paintings on the wall from all our travels, my usual plethora of Post-it notes, photographs and notes from Alula.

There are book cases floor-to-ceiling, and a sofa for lazing on. And here, in our dream home, there is massage on-demand, incredible sushi and daily frozen-yogurt delivery.

In all these visions of home, despite all the plus-points of living in Bali – coconuts on tap and the incredible friends we've made – I don't think of Ubud. Which is all to say that I, Sarah Alderson, vagabond, wanderer, consummate Sagittarius, am getting itchy feet.

I want that room of my own. And partly that might have to do with someone building a house right in front of ours, blocking our view and cancelling out the sounds of crickets and frogs with the sound of tile cutters and saws. The once-stunning town of Ubud is slowly becoming a sprawling urban mess as greedy developers (both Indonesian and foreign) build more hotels and villas, seemingly with very little thought as to the environmental impact. We are responsible for that too. Just by being here, by needing a home, we're using up valuable resources and encouraging the rampant development.

Or, is that a typically Western view of development? We want the unspoiled perfection of Bali, but that requires that the Bali and the Balinese stay stuck in poverty. It's a tough one. I just wish there was a way for Bali to develop but in such a way that what makes it special remains protected. It feels like Bali is going the way of the Costa del Sol. A concrete jungle could soon replace the actual jungle.

I sat in my swing chair this morning trying to avoid looking at the naked workmen (they were getting dressed – they don't work naked) and meditated on the concept of home. A voice in my head tried telling me that home is John and Alula; that home is a place inside you. A building is just a building, after all. But still, this image of our home sticks like one of my Post-it notes to my frontal lobe and won't be peeled off.

So now I just have to work on convincing John to uproot again to take part in *Can We Live Here? Part Two*. But what if the search is futile? What if this dream home doesn't exist and we spend the rest of our lives on the road, searching for it?

GREEN JUICE FAST

I am on the third day of a green-juice fast. And this is what it sounds like: *fuck juice. I hate Ubud. I hate the rain. I want coffee.*

I bet you that green-juicing fanatics would tell me that this anger and rage is normal and that my body is releasing emotions along with all the toxic waste in my colon and that eating just numbs us to these emotions that really need to be cleansed from the body or they'll make us sick and if I can make it through day three I'll feel like a light being filled with joy and bliss. Well… I WANT TO NUMB MY BODY WITH CAKE. I want sushi. I'll even blend it if necessary. I hate my life. I am bored. I'm never drinking anything green ever again unless it's absinthe. I'm tired. It's total crap what they say about green juice giving you everything you need because if it did, why do you lose weight? Why is your body chowing down on your fat reserves if the green juice is giving you everything you need? Oooh, I've lost two kilos. If I liquidise a hamburger and fries with wasabi mayonnaise does that count as green juice? Where's the number for the sushi place? I can't last until tonight. I'm not doing this again.

I AM A LOVE GODDESS

'I am a LOVE GODDESS.'

John and Till stare at me. Till is our housemate – he's like a German Larry David who's been cross-bred with Deepak Chopra, and in our affections he sits somewhere between Lily the dog and Alula.

'I am a love goddess,' I repeat, beaming at them.

Is that scepticism I see on their faces? I have been listening in the car to a Blissitation meditation thing. I know I'm not meant to meditate while driving because three seconds into it, the lady with the soporific voice tells me I should have my eyes shut and my hands open in my lap.

I wonder whether all the drivers in Bali are listening to this Blissitation tape while driving – it would explain a few things. Still, I decide I can skip the part about keeping my back straight, eyes shut and hands in my lap and just do the listening part. After all, if there's one place in the whole of Bali where I need to find the Zen, the love – the bliss inside me – it's in the car.

Recently we started car-pooling. What I hadn't factored into this equation was how much I swear at other people on the road – and with children who aren't mine in the car this has become a problem. I mean, it's one thing Alula learning how to say 'fricking moron' and quite another when a peace-loving hippy mum asks you where her daughter has learned to say 'arsehole'.

As I drive the lady intones in a calm, beatific way: 'I communicate with authenticity and integrity'. I repeat it.

A car cuts me up. 'Don't even think about cutting me up, you fricking eejit!' I yell as I put my foot down.

'I appreciate the awesome people in my life'.

'Get out of the damn way!'

'I do random acts of kindness for people'.

'No, I'm not letting you out in front of me. Think again, bozo!'

I pull into our drive. *'You are a LOVE GODDESS'.*

'I am a love goddess,' I repeat as I kill the engine.

'I am filled with love,' I tell John and Till. 'I have just been listening to a meditation tape in the car and now I am filled to overflowing with love.'

They keep staring at me, saying nothing. I think I see them exchange a quick glance. I walk upstairs and turn on my computer.

'Goddamn! The fucking internet's still not working!'

PLURAL MARRIAGE

I am so into this whole plural marriage thing. It totally makes sense. I don't know why it hasn't spread to the mainstream. I, for one, am *in*. Obviously, with a few tweaks… like the women should be the ones who get to marry multiple partners.

I feel I am something of an authority on this because:

a) I just read *The Red Tent* and that whole book is about plural marriage (and periods)

b) I'm currently experiencing something resembling a plural marriage myself. Well, kind of. I mean it's not consummated in any way whatsoever, but our housemate Till is, for all intents and purposes, like a second husband.

He's not gay (I need to put that in as a qualifier only because I think he'd like women to know he's available – and I can highly recommend him to any women looking for love with a German Larry David)… but he's basically like my gay husband because he's way more evolved than any other straight man I know. He's the husband that I go to to talk about horoscopes and to moan about feeling bloated or when John is too busy working to listen to me just talk. Till will always listen sympathetically without trying to solve my problems and then he'll offer to make me a banana coconut smoothie or to order food from Bali Buddha or he'll look up what's happening in the Mayan calendar to explain why I'm feeling angry/ sad/sick/tired (…and, weirdly, it's *always* a solar flare).

Also – he's brilliant at fixing my computer when it breaks. In multiple marriages you have different partners for different things (in *The Red Tent* the dude goes to one wife for advice on the goats, the other for her curries, the other for 'entertainment'), Till is my go-to husband for the girl stuff (he has long hair so we can even swap conditioner, whereas John shaves his head so he doesn't even know what conditioner is, and he knows all about astrology and PMT) and John is my go-to husband for, well… all the rest.

Imagine if you got to live with your best girlfriend *and* your husband. That's how cool it is. Witness this morning; John is working at the kitchen table. I'm preparing breakfast for Alula. Till is just hanging out. I start talking to John and Till about something. I want an answer to it. I want to be acknowledged. John ignores me but Till listens. And I realise that the beauty in this set-up is that with two men in the house the chances are that at any given time one of them will probably be listening. And that one will probably not be John. When it's just John in the house, chances are I will be talking into the void.

For this service that Till provides I think John feels insanely grateful. He doesn't need to tune in. Till's like his wingman. Then, feeling safe that I have a willing ear, I start talking about something else.

Till turns and walks out the door as I'm mid-sentence. 'This one's yours, John,' he calls over his shoulder.

They're tag-teaming me.

THE ONE WITH THE MERMAID AND THE EXTENUATING CIRCUMSTANCES

At midnight we land back in Bali, having just been to Singapore for the day on a visa run. I wake Alula. She's now so big that I can only carry her for about 0.4 seconds before I have to set her down again, so there's no way I'm carrying her off this plane. Plus, I have shopping bags laden down with Percy Pigs and a My Little Pony. Bless her though, she staggers sleepily to her feet and puts on her flip-flops and only starts to scream when we're half way down the aisle.

'I want water! I'm hungry! I'm hungry!'

I offer her a Percy Pig. She declines.

'I'm hungry. I want a mermaid.'

'You want a what?' I ask.

'A MERMAID!' she screams. 'A mer-MAID…'

'You're going to need to explain this one to me,' I say, glancing anxiously at all the tourists hemming us in.

'Remember, last time? We got a mermaid!'

I rack my brains trying to recall what Alula might be referring to. When, dear God, did we eat a mermaid?

'Was it a shop? Toys R Us?' I ask.

'NO!'

'This was in a restaurant?'

'They gave us food and a mermaid,' she insists.

It finally twigs. She's talking about McDonald's! She has only visited McDonald's once in five years of living. One too many times, I know. But there were extenuating circumstances (remember the time I got stuck with her in Singapore? McDonald's was the only place at Changi airport that had free Wi-Fi. I bought her a Happy Meal, which came with… you guessed it… a plastic mermaid toy.)

226

She still remembers this. Yet she does not remember the following: that I got up with her four times a night for the first eight months of her life and at least twice just last night; that she once washed elephants in a river in India; the name of her old childminder who babysat her for three years; that she took ballet classes for an entire year wearing ballet shoes that I spent several hours sewing elastic into; that I took her every week to Monkey Music when she was a year old; that she spent a year travelling around the *world* and went to school on the beach in Goa.

Alula doesn't remember a single damn thing we've done for her... But she remembers a Happy Meal eaten in a dingy airport basement a year ago.

Remind me again why we don't give birth to our children and just place them in cardboard boxes in empty rooms for the first ten years of their life, programming robots to deliver water and meals to them regularly?

But, to return to the moment, somehow Alula knows through some weird osmosis of knowledge, that McDonald's happens to be the only place open at Bali airport at midnight. We storm through immigration (she's still screaming about mermaids) and I hurry her to McDonald's. I tell myself that it's extenuating circumstances while wondering why, after five and a half years, I am still not one of those mums who remembers to pack bottles of water and snack packs and wet wipes.

'Do you have anything vegetarian?' I ask the servers as I eye up the menu.

It would appear from the photos, that's a *no*. The servers stare at me like I've asked them to chop off their own heads and drop them in the deep-fat fryer.

'I'll have a cheeseburger Happy Meal then,' I mumble, covering Alula's ears.

'A cheeseburger?' Alula screams. 'Does that have cow in it?' (Alula is now a committed vegetarian and has been for six months since she discovered that minced beef was actually minced cow.)

I hesitate. Here I have a dilemma. I could say yes but I know how that will play out. She will scream very, very loudly about being hungry. Possibly she will lie on the floor and have a full-on melt-down tantrum right here. I calculate also that there are no other food outlets anywhere that are open. I have an hour to go before we get home and the odds are she will scream the entire way. I just bought new headphones but they're not noise-cancelling ones.

So I do the only thing possible. I lie. 'No darling, there's no meat in it,' I say. And, technically, I think to myself, I'm pretty sure there isn't any actual meat in a cheeseburger. So I'm not really lying. I hand the burger to Alula and she tucks straight in. I do, admittedly, feel queasy watching her. But also a tiny bit jealous. Mmmmm, McDonald's burgers – I'm sure to some people it's the equivalent of eating testicles, but they taste so damn fine.

Alula stops mid-step. She puts her hand into her mouth and withdraws some burger patty – masticated and warm. She hands it to me. 'MUMMY, taste this! I think it's MEAT!'

'Really?' I say, my voice rich with bewilderment. I just want to get to the car. It's so late.

'Yes! This is meat!' she cries.

'Well, possibly,' I say. 'Maybe, it might have *some* meat in it.' (Again, not lying exactly).

Alula blinks at me, then she does this thing where she hunches over the pavement as people push past with their suitcases, and regurgitates the whole three mouthfuls like a mother bird feeding its young. A lump of burger plops onto the ground. She does all this while also letting out a loud, wailing siren noise. I'm sure if a Hoover had been present she would have tried to vacuum out her mouth. She is so hysterical that she won't walk. Seriously, you'd think I'd just told her she had eaten an actual mermaid.

Oh *God*, I think to myself. I just want to get home. So… 'When I said it might have meat in it, I meant vegetable meat,' I tell her.

Komang, the driver, stares at me. Alula blinks at me but stops wailing. 'Vegetable meat?' she asks.

'Yes,' I say, taking her hand and walking. 'Like tofu and broccoli.' 'Oh,' she says.

She finishes the whole thing before we make it to the car. I still feel really bad about this.

MY BAT-SHIT-CRAZY, MERCURY-RETROGRADING INSECT-MURDERING DAY

John went off to Singapore this morning at 4am. He never hears his alarm clock. Normally, I have to smack him around the head a few times with a pillow to get him to stir and then a few more times to turn it off, by which point I'm thoroughly awake. So I spend a couple of hours reading in bed before Alula jumps on me demanding her Weetabix and my help in colour-coordinating her knickers for the day.

I wander out onto the balcony and almost step directly into the pile of bat poo dropped there by the child-sized fruit bat that hangs out nightly upside-down from the roof beam. Groaning at the ickiness of that, I stagger blurry-eyed into the study and almost step on a *District 9*-sized cockroach. It is belly up, its spiky, tufted legs immobile.

Sighing, because John wasn't there to call on for cockroach duty, I man up and grab a wine glass still with the ashy dregs of Bali's finest coating the bottom. Using that and a dirty tissue I bend down to sweep said cockroach into the glass.

Turns out the cockroach is very much *alive*. It was just resting down there on the floor, belly up. Maybe it was some kind of cockroach joke, his mates laughing from behind the bin. *Scare the crap out of the human! Go on, it'll be funny.*

Once I zoom in on it with the tissue it bursts into activity, its antennae things waving drunkenly. I swear to God, I scream the entire village down. And yet I still manage, while screaming, to lurch toward the balcony and toss the thing across the roof. I do think, for an instant, of flushing it down the loo but I weigh up in a nanosecond whether I had the nerve to make it that far and decide not to risk it.

The day turns out to be one of those days where you meet people on the street and they say, 'Man, I wish Mercury would hurry the hell up and un-retrograde,' and you nod and say, 'Totally!', because this is Ubud and that's the UK equivalent of saying 'all right?', and you saying, 'Yeah, not bad.'

Finally, after a long day out, I get home and discover that the bat poo is now cemented to the floor, three days of washing-up sits forlornly in the sink and we've run out of bowls. I know this is lame but really, I'm busy trying to earn a living… and battling my way through the traffic in Ubud… and *oh shit*, I step closer to the floor cushion in the bedroom: it appears that it's moving.

I blink and focus on the half-eaten chicken carcass that Lily, our dog, has carried in and feasted on. She has left it here and it's now literally being carried off by an army of 3m ants. The pillow, once white, is now black and pulsating like some optical illusion.

Screaming, I pick up the chicken carcass between thumb and forefinger and run to the balcony, hurling it like a grenade into the bushes below. Too late, several hundred of the tiny things are swarming up my arm in a scene taken straight from *Indiana Jones*. I slap them away (screaming) and return to the cushion, which is now the scene of pure ant anarchy. Three million ants (minus the ones that got hurled with the cushion) are running this way and that in utter panic. Their chicken feast has vanished! What will come next? Earthquake? Fire? No… flood!

I fill a bucket with water, throw the pillow onto the roof and douse it. Ants are, however, stubborn little things. They cling to the cushion through several dousings until in the end the cushion goes the way of the chicken: tossed into the garden.

Only after I throw it do I think to shout a warning in case anyone is walking below.

Anyway, that was my day. How was yours?

THE BIRDS AND THE BEES

'But how are babies made?'

I admit I am not expecting this question while stuck in traffic on Ubud's main road. I'm caught, crunching through the gears, and for the first time probably ever I'm speechless. Given we've had six years to prepare for it, you'd think I'd have some sort of answer ready. But I don't.

'Well, you see…' I stammer, buying time. I'm half giggling and half trying to work out in my head what the right way of explaining this is. I mean, I *know* how babies are made but I'm not entirely sure what's appropriate for a five-year-old to know? I don't want to traumatise her.

Dual visions assault me. In the first, Alula runs into school and starts telling all her school friends in graphic detail about erections and penises and we receive angry phone calls from parents outraged at their child's loss of innocence, thanks to our daughter. In the second, I see Alula running into school and telling all her school friends that babies are grown in little pots of compost and watered regularly. I see her being socially shunned for 15 years of her life, at 17 still being teased for her lack of reproductive knowledge.

'What?' Alula interrupts my day-dreaming.

'Daddy sticks his willy inside Mummy and plants a seed' doesn't quite sound right, but it's also the first thing that pops into my head. I weigh it against the drier 'Daddy's penis inserts into Mummy's vagina.' This only makes me giggle some more.

I suddenly recall this book I had as a child. It was all about a boy called Thomas and a girl called Sarah, who were brother and sister. I thought this book was therefore written just for me, given that my own brother was called Thomas. Imagine my wonder! Thomas and Sarah's mum was having a baby and the book explained how babies were made and born in just the right amount of detail to satisfy my five-year-old self and also just enough to keep me poring over the pages, still intrigued. I cannot for the life of me, sitting in the car 28 years later, remember the exact wording of this book. Which is a great shame.

'But, Mummy, how?' Alula demands again.

I'm panicking, wishing John was there to add his thoughts to the fray. I try the clichéd route, laughing even as I say it: 'When a Mummy and a Daddy love each other very much...'

'Yes,' Alula interrupts impatiently, rolling her eyes. 'But *how* do they make a baby?'

'They make love,' I say, thinking how euphemistically lovely and vague this sounds and hoping it will satisfy her fairytale-rich imagination.

'What does that mean? *Making love*? What's that?'

'How about,' I say, 'we wait until we get home and then we call Daddy and get him to explain?'

I make a mental note not to warn him prior.

April 2013

BABI GULING AND VAGINAL ACUPRESSURE

Last night, John and I went to a party. It was brilliant. There was a *babi guling* feast. Vegetarians, look away now… It's an entire pig roasted on a stick over an open fire. It is then carved by the table, which isn't a table, but rather a ten-metre long mat made of banana leaves on which the food is beautifully laid out, pig skin and all.

We all sat around it and ate with our hands. It was so awesome that I looked at John and said, 'You know how yesterday I decided I was a vegetarian? Well, I lied.'

After the dancing girls had done their bit, and I had drunk at least a bottle of wine, and had a conversation in my head with the dead pig where I argued with it that it being dead meant that I wasn't doing anything wrong, I had this conversation with one of the other guests.

Me: 'Oh my God, vaginal releasing? Like, holy what-the-hell? Seriously?'

Her: 'Did you do it?'

Me: 'No! I took the card so I could photograph it and tweet about it. And it made the Twitterverse laugh their heads off. I was still getting responses about it 12 hours later.'

Her: 'I tried it.'

'No way!'

'Yes.'

'You did? What was it like?'

'Amazing!'

'Really? What does she do, exactly? With your vagina.'

'She massages you with coconut oil and then says, "I'm going inside, is that OK?"'

'And you said OK?'

'Yes.'

'And?'

'And it was incredible. Such a release. So different from an orgasm.'

I shoved some more *babi guling* in my mouth, wondering if I dared ask for details. How was it different, exactly? Wasn't it weird having a strange woman's fingers up your vagina in a non-sexual way? Did it not feel a little like having an ob-gyn appointment or a smear?

Later the conversation turned to products that are sold in a health store in town:

'And they have these vaginal sticks too.'

'Excuse me, what?' (That's me talking.)

'Vaginal sticks…'

At this point I must admit that I can't fully quote the conversation because my brain was doing too many loop-the-loops and I was laughing so hard I was spitting wine across the room. But I can tell you this: a vaginal stick is something made of clay that is smaller than a rampant rabbit vibrator yet larger than a finger.

It has crystals in it and is used for: 'rejuvenating, tightening and exfoliating', oh, and 'moisturising'.

Don't forget that crucial moisturising. Your insides really need it.

'Exfoliating?' I asked, wrinkling my nose. 'But why do you need to exfoliate a part of your body nobody ever sees?'

I was told something about dead smells or maybe dead cells. I can't remember because I was too busy *ewwww*-ing.

This is one of the many reasons I love Bali. Because you get *babi guling* and talk about vaginal sticks in one room.

You should know that while I was happy to undergo a colonic in order to entertain and inform, this is one finger too far.

AN INSANE FAST THING

My friend Liesel is doing this insane 21-day fast thing. When I say 'insane fast thing' I don't mean she's doing something really quickly, and I'm not talking about breatharianism either. (Remember the people who wanted to give up eating altogether and just live on light?)

This is even crazier than that. Here are the rules to this fast:

No criticising.

No complaining.

No gossiping.

No negative language.

No bitching.

And the rule is, if you slip up, you forgive yourself and start the 21-day fast over again. I look at my friend, my eyes as wide as the steering wheel I am clutching. 'But, but… what will you talk about? Isn't that tantamount to taking a vow of silence?'

'It lets positivity flow,' she answers. I think the words 'universe', 'manifestation' and 'creativity' were also in there somewhere.

Thing is, though my natural response is to piss-take, I'm also kind of intrigued by the idea of trying this 'fast', even though it would mean trying it for the rest of my *life* because I'd never last the requisite 21 days and would have to keep starting again. For all my piss-taking about Ubud, I'm actually being busted more and more by friends who narrow their eyes at me and shake their heads while saying incredulously: 'You're actually one of them, aren't you?'

They mean that I am slowly becoming an Ubudian. I use the words 'manifest', 'intention', 'positivity', 'universe' and 'raw' at least once a day. Sometimes when I speak I slam my mouth shut in shock that such things have fallen from my lips with no sense of irony whatsoever. What is happening to me? I draw the line at wearing fisherman pants however. And I only own one mandala.

Contemplating it more, though, I worry that if I try this fast it might limit my conversation. Wouldn't it make me kind of boring? Also, does 'don't fucking ride my ass!' (yelled at a really annoying driver the other day) count as negative language? Because I really do swear rather a lot… and I complain *all* the time (mainly about the drivers on the roads here), so quitting complaining might require me to quit driving.

No gossiping… I'm boggled by this one too. I'm sure everything that comes out my mouth could be constituted as gossip. As in, the exchange of information. But if it means not saying anything bad about anyone then that's fairly easy as I try not to do that anyway. unless it's someone truly evil, in which case fair game. Maybe I should try this fast after all!

On second thoughts, though it sounds like a noble intention (there I go again), I think I'd rather try breatharianism.

PROSTITUTION, THE HUMAN CONDITION AND THE GORGON STARE

'The first prostitute I ever visited was in Las Vegas. She told me that I was the youngest guy she'd ever slept with... and the best.'

I glance up from my sun lounger where I've been pretending to read my Kindle and stare (with my nostrils flaring) at the man speaking. He's about 60 and, up until then, I'd assumed gay. I am so grossed out by the fact he is talking about Vegas prostitutes at 10am by a hotel pool that I shoot him a stare that would make a Gorgon flinch. He doesn't seem to notice because he's far too busy telling the 50-year-old woman next to him that he'd love to wake up next to her and that her arse is perfect.

The woman preens a little and I think to myself, 'lady he just told you he sleeps with prostitutes... are you fricking deaf or something?' I don't know about you, but if a guy tried to pick me up by telling me that a prostitute in Vegas told him he was great in bed, and I happened to be standing by a pool at the time, I would push him in and then I'd probably stand on him until he drowned a bit.

OK, that's probably a little harsh, but you get me? I wouldn't preen. I wouldn't pout. I wouldn't giggle. I would find some way of expressing my disgust that would hopefully render him impotent for the rest of his life. I believe I have that in me.

'I'm celibate,' the woman answers, thrusting her cobalt bikini-clad breasts towards him like torpedoes. 'I swore off men three years ago,' she continues.

She doesn't act like someone who has sworn off men, I think to myself, eyeing her over my Kindle as she flicks her hair and bats her eyelashes. I glance around, wondering if I have in fact wandered onto the set of a really bad movie because these lines … these lines are beyond reality. Surely they've been scripted. But I see no lights, no camera. No one is yelling 'action'.

'I decided,' the lady continues, 'to go celibate after my fifth marriage ended in divorce.'

The man dives under the water at this point, resurfacing at the far end of the pool. I start to scribble down this epic dialogue for use at a later date in a blog post or a cheesy TV pilot or a comedy romance novel or a geriatric porn movie (you never know where my career might head, I have to keep my options open and maybe the universe put these people here in front of me so I could record these incredible lines and then use them in the future for something truly epic… Maybe I'll win an Oscar with it…)

Just then Alula comes skipping over to me and I decide it's too risky to stay to hear more. I don't want her asking me what a prostitute is. I grab our towels and my Kindle, ready to hustle her away from the skanky man talking about sex and the divorcee with the torpedo boobs. I head to the desk to pay for our drinks.

Suddenly, from behind me, I hear: 'Wow, what amazing eyes you have.'

I wheel around and see the man speaking to Alula, who thankfully has the same approach to dodgy old men in Speedos as I do. She stares at him and starts backing the hell off.

'So beautiful,' he continues, oblivious to her death stare. She gets it from me… I'm so proud.

My warrior-mama persona comes bursting forth. I'm about to go tearing over there like a lioness hunting down a lame gazelle. But

John is already there. And I'm waiting for my change.

'I draw eyes,' I hear the man tell John. 'I'd love to put her eyes in my painting.'

That man is not putting her eyes in his painting. I will push him in and drown him in the pool if he even thinks about putting her eyes in his painting.

'I think the eyes tell us everything about the human condition,' he adds, as though that might sway us into letting him paint Alula's eyes.

Push him in the pool, I yell silently to John. That'll teach him all he needs to know about the human condition.

I curse John for not having developed his psychic mind-reading abilities and myself for not having developed mind-control ones. How handy that would be right now. But John being John (i.e. being far nicer than me) and not having heard the prostitution conversation, just nods genially at the man and makes a non-committal sound followed by a polite goodbye.

IF YOU'RE GOING TO (PLAY)DATE YOU NEED TO WASH

After screaming blue murder for two hours last night because she didn't want to take a shower and thought her daddy and I were *evil* for even suggesting it, Alula fell asleep exhausted and tear-stained (the tears tracking pathways through the dirt we had failed to clean off).

She awoke this morning and promptly started screaming once more about how much she hated us/wanted new parents/couldn't believe we were insisting on a shower every day.

By the time 7.30am rolled around, I could not wait to hustle her out the door and collapse onto the bed in a catatonic ball of mother-guilt, idly wondering if it was too late to put her up for adoption. As she stomped off down the path I told her to check-in with her friends in the car pool as to whether they washed daily or not.

She came home quite sheepish, thank the Lord, and got in the shower without arguing. I mean, the kid goes to school in a jungle. A jungle with a farm attached to it. She goes on regular treks through said jungle and pretends to be an ant or a plant or whatever her Green Studies teacher (Pak Awesome, as he's called by the kids) is teaching them about that day. She comes home so encased in dirt we practically need chisels to prise her free.

That drama over with, Alula bounced on the bed and informed me that during Green Studies that day, while pretending to be a plant, she had shuffle-hopped over towards Jack, her *amour*, and whispered (in a plant-like voice, I assume…): 'Jack, do you want to go out to dinner with me?'

I suppressed the giggles for long enough to ask what he said in reply.

'He said yes, of course,' said Alula, tossing her curls. You gotta love her self-assurance. 'I'm going to wear my prettiest dress and take a flower from the garden.'

John, who happened to be there listening to this part, blanched. His eyes grew buggy. He stared at me as though I was to blame for our daughter's wanton ways. But secretly I'm delighted because it's about time she started having some boy playmates. I had an older brother and loved hanging about with boys as I grew up. It taught me a lot… like how to burp the alphabet.

'Mummy?' Alula asks as she lies there in a daze beside me (probably imagining the flower-decked unicorn she would ride to her dinner date), 'Why do all the boys love me?'

To be fair, this week two boys have declared their love for her so this isn't her being big-headed. She is naturally curious.

'Because you know how to read,' I told her. 'And you're super-smart.'

I am hoping that instead of picking out a dress to wear to her date, Alula will pick out a few books from her bookshelf to take along instead.

OFFERINGS FOR THE DEVIL

I'm in the car on the way down south. I would normally drive myself but I have work to do and it's easier to type (like I'm doing now) if I'm in the passenger seat. Though it wouldn't surprise me to see people on bikes here trying to drive and type at the same time... *That was a stop sign? Look at me! No hands! Why can't I talk on my mobile, drive one-handed, wearing no helmet and balancing two other family members and a small baby on my bike? What do you mean I have to be sixteen to ride a motorbike? I'm nine but I look twelve, that's plenty old enough.*

I, on the other hand, have a strong sense of self-preservation. And I really, really don't want to kill someone. Anyway, I digress... Our driver, Komang, (who deserves a sainthood for driving three screaming banshee girls every day to and from school... why'd you think I handed over car pool duties?) is bouncing me over the ruts. We almost bounce into a woman in a *kebaya* (the traditional blouse that women wear for ceremonies) and sarong, laying an offering in the middle of the road.

'Why is she laying the offering in the middle of the road?' I ask Komang. I mean, I'm used to the laying of offerings and I am a full believer in placating spirits (through several experiences we've all become full believers in the magic and spirits to be found in Bali) but I've never understood why sometimes the offerings are laid in the middle of the road.

'Oh,' Komang replies, swerving to avoid the beautiful coconut leaf tray of rice and flowers. 'It's for the devil.'

'The devil?' I ask, shooting nervous glances into the jungle on either side of us.

'Yes, if it's on the ground it's for the devil. We give offerings to the good spirits and to the devil,' he explains. 'At every junction,' Komang goes on, 'the Balinese make statue and temple because there were so many collisions and people dying before.'

'Oh,' I say. 'So they built the statues to help slow people down?'

I'm thinking of this giant statue that sits on a really dangerous intersection near our house. It's almost impossible to see what's coming because it blocks the view, so you have to creep slowly forwards and lean over the steering wheel to get enough of the road visible to know if it's safe to pull out. The Balinese normally fly straight out without so much as a pause. They do this at every junction – the attitude being, I believe, that it's the responsibility of the person behind to brake. Maybe notions of karma and a different approach to mortality help. But every day on Facebook it feels as if there's another story of someone dying in a bike accident. We already know of several people – friends of friends, teachers at the school, even one of my closest friend's ex-husband – who have been killed in bike accidents.

Back to the statue. I'm thinking that's actually some wise and clever urban planning right there, plonking giant statues at intersections to try to slow people down and force them to stop and look first before pulling out but...

'No,' Komang replies. 'They're for the offerings.'

Of course they are.

Though, judging from the number of deaths on the road here each day, perhaps some traffic lights might also be in order?

I AM BUT A PLAYTHING TO THE GODS

Fuckity fuckity fuck, fuck, fuck. Today is the kind of day that makes me just want to curl up in bed and close my eyes and tune out until tomorrow comes. Except if I did that, today would find a way to fuck me over while I slept. An earthquake would hit and the ceiling would collapse on the bed, or, I don't know... something would inevitably happen just so that today could prove to me that all I am is a plaything of the gods...

It's funny because last night I went to this inspirational talk by someone who once upon a time died and lost an arm in a car crash and now gives motivational speeches about counting our blessings. He even had the whole room on their feet as he strummed a guitar with his bionic hand, singing a song that went: 'I am blessed... I am blessed' (very 'Kumbayah'). And I went home thinking, 'yeah I am blessed' and singing it into my pillow.

It's like the gods wanted to *laugh* in my face at my naïveté (or maybe they didn't like my singing) so they connived all night to make this next day suck to teach me a lesson. First off, I wake up and realise that I have work to do. Now, I'm not a work-shirker. I work my ass off and I don't complain because I love my job (my author job, that is). But lately I've been having to put my blog and my book-writing on hold to do copywriting so I can pay the bills. Because – NEWSFLASH for all you deluded folk out there who think authors make money – we *don't* (so if you are one of the many who download my books illegally I really, really hope that karma comes and bites you on the ass one day).

The long and the short of it is that I'm stuck writing copy about man-boobs and retro bikinis and liposuction and, honest to God, about Hulk Hogan in neon Spandex. Google that. Most likely, I wrote it. Seriously. I'm having to earn money for food by selling my soul and writing copy about celebs in Speedos. Some days, I actually contemplate just not eating ever again and keeping my integrity intact, but then I get a reminder about the school fees.

John and I sip our coffee and discuss the perennial problem we have: namely money and earning enough to stay in Bali. Green School fees don't come cheap, rents have almost doubled in the last three years, the cost of living is rising rapidly thanks to inflation. (*Shhhh*, I don't want to hear it about the pedicure obsession. I've cut back. Honest.)

Anyway, 'boohoo,' I hear you say, 'you live in paradise.' And you're right. I should quit complaining. I don't have a bionic arm. Kumbayah. But I keep wondering when the time will come that I can make a good living from doing the things I love (i.e. not sourcing images of David Hasselhoff showing off his floatation device). Is that day ever going to come?

Our biggest risk – quitting our jobs in London – was rewarded almost instantly. It made us think we were invincible. Now we contemplate a second jump off the precipice. Should we start saying no to work we don't love, trusting the universe will leap in and fill the gap? I want to believe, I do. But, judging by the day I've just had, I think the universe right now wants me to do that so it can laugh in my face when I slice myself open on the jagged rocks below.

Evidence 1: John bought me a lovely new nail polish: Chanel

Rouge Noir, gorgeous. The exact shade of arterial blood. I am carrying it downstairs and drop it. It plunges 10 metres and smashes on the kitchen floor below. There are crime scenes with less splatter. And blood hoses off. Nail varnish doesn't. I do acknowledge that by sitting on the kitchen floor dipping the brush in the splatter and painting my nails in order to at least get some worth from it, I didn't help matters when it came to clearing it up. Goddamn it. Glass splinters in my knees, ruined nails and my entire bottle of nail polish remover used up trying to scrub off pink streaks from the tiles and kitchen cabinets.

Evidence 2: I've spent about 50 hours editing a book using my Kindle. I switch on my Kindle this morning and every single edit note has vanished. What? Mercury isn't even retrograde. I hate you, Kindle.

You see where I'm going with this? Yes. That's right. To the cupboard that contains the gin.

PS. I know, I know… I really don't have anything to complain about. I'm just having a whinge. Humour me.

ON CREATIVITY AND A RETURN TO THE UK

Last night was the first time in three and a half years I've cried because I missed home. I had a craving for fields. Yes, fields. And woods. And the smell of bonfires. And strawberries. Summer and autumn sights and smells.

But, most of all, I was crying for my family and friends. An email from my brother triggered it. Talk of my nieces and nephews. An email from my best friend too, with the butterfly heart-beating possibility that she might be coming to visit in March.

The hope of that being tempered by the possibility she may

not, just squeezed my emotions in such a way I burst into tears. OK, there was also the fact of a tax bill I have no idea how I'm going to pay. It had been a hard week. Hard in that, after three and a half years, John and I are still finding our feet here financially. We walked out of well-paid jobs into a life of instability but outrageous potential. To pick yourself up from nothing and get back to a state of feeling comfortable takes a lot of hard work or a lottery win. Though maybe that's the point. Maybe 'comfortable' is not a place I subconsciously want to reside in. Being uncomfortable makes me work hard, push boundaries, try new things, keep trying new things when the first ones fail, keep throwing stuff at the wall in the hopes that one day something will stick. Would 'comfortable' equal 'lazy and complacent'? It's a possibility.

My mum asked in an email: *Why not come home?* Even through my tears (some now of guilt) I shuddered. Because, even though I miss fields and strawberries (Bali strawberries have nothing on English ones) and bonfires and family and friends, I don't think I could ever move back there.

It's hard to explain to people who haven't been here. I have days when I hate Bali (the days when I'm told that, no, your hard drive still hasn't arrived from Singapore because it's been diverted via Surabaya and now they're holding it back until you pay a bribe. The days when the internet fails for no reason and it takes a week before anyone can fix it. The days when I'm told I have a black magic curse on me, for sure. But 99 per cent of the time I love it here. And that's not just because I don't have to do the dishes.

I love who Alula is here. I love the world she gets to grow up in – this magical, TV-free, advertising-free place where she is so, so happy. Never has a six-and-a-half-year-old child been so innocent.

She's growing into a conscious, kind, generous, empathetic and wildly imaginative child, as at-home in a developing Asian world as in a first-world city, able to flit between an American and English accent before ordering a juice in Indonesian.

Yesterday she said to us, 'I love living in Bali,' before skipping off to play among the butterflies.

I love that, just as Alula gets to be creative and explore her imagination 100 per cent of the time, so do I. I love that John's creativity has soared and he's poured it into two incredible new businesses to inspire others' creativity and connections, including Hubud, a collaborative workspace for global nomads and locals alike.

I love the friends we have made here – all passionate, creative and entrepreneurial. The word I keep coming back to is 'creativity'. And the more I reflect on it the more I realise that, for me, creativity has become a central component of living. It's one of the main things that now gives my life meaning. Not always happiness, that's for sure, but definitely meaning. I see it give meaning to John and to Alula every single day as well. This is how we live now. We can't ever go back from that. It's inconceivable. Which isn't to say you can't be creative in the UK. But I think for me it would be a hell of a lot harder to be creative there. It would be something we squeezed in between going to work, doing the dishes and prising Alula away from CBBC.

This place is where we get to explore outrageous possibilities, unfettered and unhindered, supported by the energy and people around us. So no, we're not moving back to the UK, we've decided. While so much potential has been fulfilled there's still so much ahead of us.

SNAKE!

It's 10pm. The lights are off. I'm sitting on the bed watching *Mad Men* on my laptop. Beside me, Alula splays in sleep, indifferent to the charms of Don Draper. All of a sudden the soft sound of Jenga blocks tumbling over startles me.

I hit the pause button on my laptop. It was probably a mouse, I think to myself. Maybe a big cockroach. Four years ago this would have roused me to action or screams but now I'm seasoned to the tropics. And besides, Don Draper is on the telly. I hit play. But then it comes again – more blocks tumble. Alula has been building Jenga block houses in our bedroom. Something is knocking them over. Would a cockroach even have the muscle mass to do that?

Tentatively I creep from the bed and reach for the light switch. I'm expecting to see a mouse. What I am not expecting to see is a two-metre long snake.

I always imagined I'd be fearless – like Katniss or Buffy – in the face of danger. When I imagine the zombie apocalypse or myself in the lead role of any TV show from *Falling Skies* to *The Walking Dead* to *The 100*, I am always the kick-ass girl who can hit a moving alien-vampire target at 500 paces, who can stitch an arterial bleed one-handed, while simultaneously making ironic yet brilliantly self-deprecating quips and flirting with the hot-but-haunted hero with the cheekbones you could grate cheese on. All while looking suitably hot in skinny jeans and a leather jacket, my hair glossy yet artfully mussed (oh my God, I have spent way too much time in my head and writing young adult fiction). Anyway… the reality is, I freeze. I cannot move. I am paralysed. It is a snake. An actual snake. And it is slithering over Alula's Jenga house – has crushed her Jenga house into oblivion – and is now sliding behind the book case.

Hyperventilating, still unable to move a muscle, I manage to scream John's name. He ambles into the bedroom rolling his eyes. He knows this pitch of scream. It is my 'John there is a cockroach, can you come and kill it' pitch. He looks at me, irritated. I have brain freeze. I still can't move. My hand is still resting on the light switch. All I can do is lift my other arm and point, shakily.

Ha! John's look of mild irritation gives way to total 'Holy shitballs' shock. 'Take that!' I think, 'I am not crying wolf.' (For once!) John springs immediately into action in a manner that would make Bear Grylls jealous.

'Move Alula!' he barks at me.

Huh?

'Move Alula!' he tells me again.

I blink at him. Oh shit. Not only are my wilderness skills utterly appalling but my mothering skills are clearly under-par also. I'm happily standing on the far side of the room. Between me and the snake lies the bed. The bed with our daughter on it. A fact I've only just realised.

John has to repeat himself another six times before I leap into action. I rush to the bed and pick the still-sleeping Alula up and carry her through to the other room.

'Find the number for the snake guy,' John orders me next.

Snake guy. Snake guy. Right. The Snake guy. With shaking hands I turn off Don Draper and Google the snake guy who lives in Bali. It takes him an hour to arrive. A whole hour in which John and I don't take our eyes off the snake that is half hidden behind the book case in case it decides to slither somewhere, like inside our mattress. Or, you know, into the other room to eat Alula.

The snake guy has barely walked in the house before he starts admonishing us over the state of our garden – a veritable snake utopia. He tells us he is surprised that deadly pit vipers and venomous kraits aren't leaping out at us on a nightly basis. Are we insane? Why have we let our foliage grow so thick? There is no anti-venom, he warns. We would be dead in minutes.

'OK, but can you just please catch the snake?' I ask him, feebly.

He whips out a stick and a sack and within seconds he is wrestling, literally tussling, with a very angry snake that is taller than he is. I scream. I admit it. I scream and leap onto the bed, heart thumping. He manages to get a grip on the snake's head and calmly shows us the rows and rows of fangs. The deadly poisonous fangs. It's like the basilisk from *Harry Potter*. Maybe a bit thinner. But every bit as scary, I promise.

Heart attack. I'm having a heart attack. The snake craps all over the floor.

'It's stressed,' the snake man tells us, staring in awe at the fangs.

IT is stressed? I think to myself. It's a miracle *I've* not crapped all over the floor.

He drops it into a sack.

'What will you do with it now?' I ask him.

'I'll release it into the wild.'

My eyes widen. Aren't you supposed to drive the sword of Gryffindor through its skull or something? I realise in time that this isn't a movie and I should not suggest this out loud. I should be showing some compassion. I mean, the poor snake didn't mean to wander in here in its search for food. It just got hungry. 'Into the wild, far, far from here?' I ask.

'Yes,' the man says. Then he glances at Alula, sleeping next door.

'I have a dozen baby cobras at home; do you think she might like one as a pet?'

BEACHWALK, KUTA: HELL DISCOVERED ON EARTH!

'I am never, as long as I live, stepping foot in Kuta ever again. *Ever!*' I tell John after a day at Kuta's new and glitziest mall, Beachwalk, which should have the tagline 'Check your soul at the door.'

I should have known to be suspicious when I took Alula to the loos – brand spanking new and already the locks were falling off; the floor was some weird fake-brick linoleum and there were signs warning people not to squat on the toilet seats. (Actually, Alula does need reminding because once a colonic therapist told her she should squat to poo, so she does. Every time.*)

But you know what I'm saying. The place was filled with crazed holiday-makers. Who goes on holiday to shop in a mall that has all the same brands as you can get in your home town, at more expensive prices? Who does that? Who, in fact, goes on holiday to Kuta? WHO? My brain demanded an answer to this seemingly unfathomable question. If you holiday in Kuta, please for the love of God email me and tell me why.

Back to the mall. There was this tinny elevator music that pierced my brain like blunt fork tines. Repeatedly. Violently. Until I wanted to smack a real fork repeatedly into my eardrums to make it stop.

Every single shop assistant had been replaced with manic robots programmed to bounce up to you at the door, grin and then follow you, standing over your shoulder as you tried to browse. And, most

*I feel the need to make clear that I did not take Alula for a colonic. Our friend, the colonic therapist, told Alula the correct way to poo was by squatting. (I'm sure she's going to really appreciate this being in print when she's an adult. Sorry, darling.)

annoyingly, none of them had been programmed to understand that the subtle subtext of 'I'm good, thanks,' is actually 'fuck the fuck off.'

I was not feeling the Christmas cheer. I was feeling like I wanted to hurl myself into the seven-centimetre-deep pond and drown myself. And then the choir started up and I almost did. Alula, of course, wanted to play in the Hellzone. Sorry, Kidzone, where a water feature had been set up with one stinking toilet and changing room beside it.

John and I stood frozen in mutual horror at the chlorinated, HazLight-lit area, ringed on all sides by scored Plexiglas. The shudder rode up my spine.

'Why is this so grim?' I shouted to John over the screaming, competing Guantanamo soundtracks of techno pop and arcade-game background-noise.

'Because it smells like a UK swimming pool.'

'Oh yeah.'

Alula was undeterred and went careering in. There weren't even any seats for parents to watch. So I did what I normally do in times like these: I grabbed my Kindle and immersed myself in a book, thanking God for authors for creating worlds I can escape into, even worlds involving murder and psychotic drug-fuelled crime sprees, because those worlds are still infinitely nicer than Beachwalk.

Alula then needed a wee. I hustled her into the *only* ladies' for the entire ground floor food court. And guess what? There were only three cubicles. The queue was out the door and round the block.

'This is because a stupid man designed this stupid hellhole,' I hissed to Alula while people started edging away from me in the

252

line. 'Only a man would think to design a mall with only three toilets for women. A stupid man or a woman-hating, stupid man. Either way, said stupid man should be forced to lie down while all the women in this place who need a pee squat on his head.'

People started to edge away from me.

I left that mall loathing, in no particular order, Christmas, shopping, consumerism, elevator music, Topshop and the whole world. 'Tis the season to be merry. Good will to all men. Bah humbug. And screw you, Beachwalk.

THE POWER OF NO

I'm sobbing on the bathroom floor, feeling the cold tiles beneath me, clutching my towel to my face. Then I sit bolt upright, stunned by a realisation. I stagger to my feet and rush to my laptop. Before I can give myself a chance to rethink my epiphany, I dash out an email with the subject header: QUITTING.

I don't like to think of myself as a quitter. No one does. But what if we have that wrong. What if quitting is the answer?

Four years ago, John and I both quit our jobs in London. Handing in that resignation letter was one of the scariest things I've ever done. I remember the shakes, the adrenaline coursing through my body as though I'd just gone cold turkey. The feeling of elation followed by abject, mind-bending terror. The 'what the hell have we just done?' feeling that made my throat close up and my heart pound violently. It was like jumping out of a plane. That nano-second after you pull the cord and don't know if the chute is going to open. That moment was our life. Permanently. That still is our life, in many respects.

In the months after we resigned from our jobs in London and

packed up our belongings, we went through spiraling rollercoasters of emotion. Fear, panic, joy. Did I mention panic? In its most pure, unadulterated form? Or, at least, I suffered from all these things. John, as ever, stayed calmed under pressure. I had never been unemployed before. John is a designer, and was used to the freelance lifestyle.

Bali is full of expat bliss-ninnies. Some call them sparkle ponies, soul-seekers, Elizabeth Gilbert-types (she of *Eat, Pray, Love* the book and the film, starring Julia Roberts) here to find themselves. We live next door to a girl who professes to be a 'priestess of the goddess Gaia'. She holds regular sound-healing sessions where dozens of people primal scream en masse. I will never be one of those people. In fact, I'm the one yelling out of my window at them to shut the hell up and pounding Eminem on full volume right back at them. I even admit to having launched some wrinkly *jicama* at their house. (*Jicama* is a vegetable-like a potato. I was never going to eat them; just peeling them seemed like way too much effort.)

But living here has opened my mind up to the possibility of magic, to the idea that if you are following your passion and doing something you love, if you are bold and brave and dare to follow your dream, you're rewarded. I am the poster child for this, surely?

But the fact is, authors earn diddly-squat. And Bali ain't cheap. In the first two years I pounded out books at a rate of knots hoping I'd hit the jackpot and make enough money to not have to worry any more. And worry I did. I lived in a constant state of fear about being broke and not being able to pay the bills. All the pressure was on John, who was commuting to Singapore and working his butt off and then busy setting up a business in Ubud. I wanted to make sure I was contributing equally. Then, one day, through a friend, I got freelance work writing copy for a content company in Australia.

It was boring, soulless work, but it was money. Easy money. I felt relaxed once more. My bank balance was once again in the black. Then the work became more and more search engine optimisation-focused. 'Please could you use the phrase 'health and fitness' 14 times in the first 200 words, a further 27 times in the remaining 600 words' – that sort of thing. I'd sit there, tearing my hair out, screaming at the stupidity of clients, frustrated at having to write about cosmetic surgery and male breast reduction when I wanted to be writing about girls with mind powers, evil government military units, car chases, hot boys and kissing.

Until yesterday, that is, when I found myself sobbing on the bathroom floor. The day before I'd been chairing a session at the Ubud Writers' Festival. I was mobbed afterwards by a group of girls who wanted me to sign copies of my books. I'd had a great chat the same day with Japanese film-maker and expert in happiness, Eiji Han Shimizu, about how, if you want to take your career to the next level, you have to learn to say no. We spoke about the author Neil Gaiman's college commencement speech where he talks about always moving towards the mountain, keeping it in your sights and not getting distracted by jobs that take you off your path.

It felt like the universe conspired to test me on that very thing. The next morning, a difficult, exceedingly bitchy editor pushed me over the edge. I'd had enough. I was sick of saying yes out of fear and accepting work that I hated. I'd had enough of feeling like I had no choice. I wasn't going to be made to feel bad by some girl who hated her own job so much she was taking it out on me.

So I wrote an email telling them I was done with copywriting. That from that moment I was quitting to focus on what I loved doing. I hit send on the email, then collapsed on the floor wondering how I'd tell John. Eventually, I emailed him. He sent me this response:

Yes, do it. I'm here and I can see the mountain, it's next to my hillock. Love you always, especially when you say Fuck It.

I'm still shaking. Hoping what I did was courageous and not stupid. Praying that the universe takes note of my bold leap and pops the chute.

But in the meantime I'll just keep moving towards the mountain. I said that our life was full of uncertainty. But I would never choose to go back. I would always choose to leap into the great unknown.

NB: A year on from this and I can say that, though the first six months were exceedingly bumpy, it has paid off. I'm now earning more than I have ever earned, just from writing books and screenplays, and the future is looking even brighter.

2014

TOO MUCH INFORMATION

I go next door to buy tomatoes. As I'm queuing to pay I see someone I know vaguely and ask how he is.

He says, 'Yeah, not so good. I just had a vasectomy.'

I blink. And clutch my tomatoes tighter. I feel a little uncomfortable. I expected a 'fine'. I smile and nod in what I hope is a sympathetic way.

Then he tells me that he's telling all his guy friends not to do it because: 'it throws the body out.'

At which point I can't help but interject with a remark about the Pill. I mean, what does he think happens to all the billions of women who are stuffing their bodies with fake oestrogen each month? Frankly, it's about time men took some responsibility for birth control, you know what I'm saying?

Then he starts telling me – completely out of nowhere 'cos, believe me, I was trying to shut that conversation *down* – 'I used to use the rhythm method.'

'Oh,' I say. Now all I can do is picture him having sex. And you know, that would be OK if it was Ryan Gosling telling me he uses the rhythm method but it isn't. I'm starting to wish I hadn't gone to buy tomatoes.

Then he tells me that he had to get the vasectomy as the rhythm method stopped working and he kept ejaculating by accident (does that make it premature? I don't know, but I'm going with that.) I can't even process this right now. I'm too traumatised. This is too much fucking information. Literally.

Also – dude. Don't ever tell stories like this to someone who writes for a living.

WHY IT'S TIME TO LEAVE BALI

I'm heartbroken to admit that I've fallen slightly out of love with Bali.

Bali is the lover you cling on to longer than you probably should because the memories are just so good and you keep hoping that things will get better, but you know in your heart of hearts you can't be together long-term. So it's with sadness that I write this. Bali has been good to us. It's given me a new beginning – allowed me to explore my passions and develop those into a successful career. It's granted me the space to dream bigger and bolder and realise my strengths. Five years ago I never dreamed so big, nor had such self-belief. Now I feel like we can achieve anything. No obstacle seems insurmountable. I feel like an adventurer who's climbed a mountain and who can now climb any other peak that gets in my way.

Even two months ago, if someone had told me we'd be leaving Bali I would have laughed in your face. The idea was unthinkable. We'd talked about staying another year or two… but then John got a great job offer in London and things started to take off with my books and screenwriting and suddenly we were in a situation where *Can We Live Here? Part Two* might be on the cards. As you know, I've always claimed I'd never move back to England, and here I am really contemplating it. Gulp.

Alula has flourished in Bali – it's a magical place to raise young children. She's full of delight at the world, knows nothing of Justin Bieber and has an innocence, yet knowledge, of the world, of poverty, of religion and people, that I think will stand her in good stead the rest of her life.

I just got back from a seven-week trip to the UK and US, and stepping off the plane in Bali, for the first time my spirits didn't lift like they always used to. Instead, as we drove through miles and miles of traffic-clogged streets, past rivers of trash, I felt my heart sink lower and lower. Arriving home we were greeted not by the sound of crickets and frogs – the sounds we once fell in love with – but by the incessant sound of next door's tile cutter, now so normal to my ears it's like white noise. The noise of construction never ends. The rice paddies outside our house once stretched to the horizon. Now houses spring up like mushrooms every week. I have to wear noise-cancelling headphones all day in order to work, in order to stay sane. I'm saddened by Westerners who have bought rice-paddy land from poor and financially ill-educated Balinese who, enticed by earning more money than they've ever seen in their lives, hand over the deeds to their land for 35 years or more, often resulting in further abject poverty when they no longer have any sustainable income (the money they receive from the deal often being spent immediately on cars, ceremonies, family needs).

I'm saddened that Westerners think this is OK. That it's OK to send your children to Green School and spout a green agenda while building a concrete McMansion on rice fields with an Olympic-sized swimming pool, possibly thrusting a Balinese family into poverty in the process. No. That's not OK. In what world is that OK?

It feels as if greed has become the underlying sentiment on the island. I'm mad at the Indonesian government for not putting in place legislation to better protect the beauty of this island and local communities. Because the fact is, I'm now warning off friends from coming here.

I sat next to two honeymooners on the flight over and felt awful for them that they were flying 20 hours to come to Bali. The beaches are filthy. The rivers are basically open sewers. The rice paddies are vanishing beneath concrete. I was here 20 years ago, when Bali truly was a paradise. Now, I have to say, it more and more resembles hell. I no longer dare head into town – aware that the streets are so jammed that Ubud could contend with Mumbai or LA for worst traffic congestion.

I'm also aware that I'm one of the people making the situation worse by adding yet one more car to the equation. It simply feels wrong being here, contributing to the destruction of an island so magical and beautiful. Watching its decline before my eyes is too much. I feel too sad and too angry at myself for not doing anything to stop it. The only thing I feel I can do is leave, be one less person using up the valuable water table, be one less person consuming, abusing and polluting. And in the last day I've spoken to three other people who are also leaving because they can't bear to see the devastation either. Is this the turning point? Is this now the moment when Bali sees its tourist economy crash and burn?

What happens when Lombok opens its international airport and that becomes the new hot destination – Bali as it was 25 years ago? What happens to Bali and to the Balinese then? Who will stay around to fix the problems? There are so many lessons we will take from Bali, the biggest of which is about consumption. We came to Bali with nothing. And we'll take nothing to wherever we move next. Except, perhaps, a Ganesha statue and some palm sugar.

I've learned we don't need anything – not even a second bedroom. We just need each other. We live big lives in a small home. We love it. We have let go of all the Western nonsense about belongings and a huge home and shiny appliances equalling success and happiness (John never had these ideas). I've learned that struggling is part of living and that we are stronger than we thought. We've had five blissful years of re-learning what community really is about. I've made the best friends of my life. I've learned from the Balinese to believe in magic. I've learned to take things slower and to be more present. It's time to see if I can put those lessons into practice back in the West.

HOW A BEIGE TOILET DID IT FOR ME

A beige toilet. That's really the reason I'm moving from Bali. It isn't the trash or the pollution or the death metal band that's been screeching for 12 hours across the rice paddies, drowning out the sound of the tile cutter. It's not even the fact John has a great job in London and my screenwriting career has taken off. It's the beige toilet.

It all started like this (and now I think about it, actually I'm wondering if this wasn't orchestrated by the universe). The toilet won't flush. I lift off the cistern lid, place it on the toilet seat and prod at the plastic parts inside the cistern like I have a clue what they actually do. After a few minutes of sighing and prodding I lose patience, turn to yell for John and knock the lid to the floor. It smashes into a gazillion pieces and cuts my foot in the process.

This being Bali, you can't just head to Homebase and buy a new cistern lid. No. You're screwed. You have to buy a whole new *toilet*. So I go to buy a new toilet. I select one – white, normal, whatever – and head to the desk and ask for the price. They can't find it. They spend 15 minutes calling various people to find out the cost of the toilet. They still don't know. After 20 minutes of this I tell them I'll come back later. I don't go back later because I'm busy. I have a book to finish and three other books to promote and I'm spending 15 hours a day working. (Being an author is *really hard work*. Why did no one tell me?)

And days pass and I know we need to get a new loo… but when? Then the time comes that I wake up one morning at my normal time of 5.30am. It's dark. Needing a wee, I grab my iPad to check my email en route. I prop the iPad on the cistern lid… but *wait* – there is no cistern lid. And my $80, bomb-proof, splash-proof, nuclear-proof iPad case ain't all it claims to be. It's not cistern-proof, at least.

So we really need a new toilet before we drop any more expensive tech items into it, but, both of us being busy, we decide to ask Komang, our handyman and sometime driver, to buy it for us.

We send him off with clear instructions as to what to buy (or, as it turns out, maybe not so clear). Nothing happens. This is Bali, after all. Nothing happens for a week. And then I come home and find this beige monstrosity installed in our bathroom.

It looks like a toilet. It could be worse. It could be a hole over an open sewer. But the thing is, I never knew that toilets could be uncomfortable until I tried this one. It's like sitting on a ring of thorns. I'm sure there are spikes that are more comfortable than this toilet seat.

I look at John and tell him that, after five years, it turns out to be a beige toilet that will make me leave Bali.

THE SEARCH FOR UTOPIA

The sky is so blue today and the greens so green and the tile cutter so silent (though my ears are pricked and my shoulders hunched, just waiting for it to start up again) and for a moment as I sit in the garden watching the butterflies I actually wonder what the hell I am thinking. Leave Bali? *Am I insane?*

This year, I lasted approximately three days in the UK before I broke down and screamed 'I hate England!' at my dad. And that was in the middle of summer. I'm going to be heading back in the dead of winter. And I only own a pair of flip-flops. To be fair, it was 13°C and hailing in the UK when I screamed these words and I had just been told by Waterstones Chester that they didn't want me to go and sign any books there because… they didn't have any of my books in stock to sign.

But my point is, I'm not sure I know where I want to live, and this endless striving for somewhere 'other', somewhere 'else' – where does it lead? Not to utopia, that's for sure. I know that doesn't exist.

But I can't help looking. The traffic and pollution and construction in Bali is out of hand. I think it's easier to break up with someone if you start noticing and listing their bad points, which is what I'm doing to make the break up with Bali less painful when the inevitable comes.

And the truth is we are leaving for more reasons than the construction and the beige toilet. We're leaving because our careers are beckoning us to new places.

I want to launch myself again into the stratosphere. Last time, the universe caught us and rewarded us hugely, and I'm hoping the same will happen again. We have no home to go to, no real plan, no concrete work in the pipeline. But this time I'm not so worried. I think the hardest part is done. The hardest part is making the decision then announcing it to the world. The rest is relatively easy because from that moment you're in the flow (oooh I sound so hippy). I feel that it's the most important thing we've learned being here: that big decisions are only really scary up until the point you make them and then the fear gives way to excitement and the adventure of 'what if?'

THE PRIESTESS AND THE DEATH PENALTY

About a year ago our Western neighbours started running these 'tantric sound-healing workshops' (I use inverted commas because I think they would be better described as 'fleece the naive soul-seekers workshops') from out of their house – a house, I hasten to add, that has no walls.

Aside from the fact they had no work permit and were charging money for these workshops, the noise was insane. The screams would start up at around ten in the morning and continue until about eight in the evening. I'd see the fisherman-pant-wearing crew start arriving en masse and stick my headphones in, though not even cranking up my music to the max would drown out the noise. Imagine what hell would look like if created by the *Game of Thrones* writer, George R. R. Martin. Now imagine the noise of a million Theon Greyjoys being tortured. That was my life for three months.

I tried everything. I went around there and politely asked them if they wouldn't mind keeping the volume down. They acted all wide-eyed as if they couldn't understand why I would have a problem. There was no apology. The noise continued. I yelled out the window at them to shut up. I blasted Eminem at them at top volume. I threw wrinkly *jicama* from the balcony at their roof. Condemn me if you will for my immature behaviour, but know this: if I had owned a missile-firing bazooka I would have used it.

Taking a deep breath, I sent an email to the girl and asked in the most polite way possible if she wouldn't mind being more mindful of the fact she lived in a community and telling her that I couldn't even hear my daughter speak when she was sixty millimetres from me in bed because the noise was so great.

She wrote me back the most hilarious email I've ever had the fortune to receive. She told me she was a 'priestess of the goddess Gaia' and that I wouldn't 'dare to ask a Balinese priest to stop his praying' so why would I dare ask her to stop? She went on to tell me that she was on the planet to 'serve the community'.

It was basically a long *f– you*, but dressed up in Ubud gratitude-speak. Gobsmacked, not just by her total insanity but by the irony of someone claiming to be spiritual, and community-minded while acting in such a selfish way, I wrote back to her without bothering to dress up my long *f– you*. John solved the issue at the end of the day (my hero). Being nice, unlike me, he went and talked to them and told them they needed to cease and desist immediately. And just like that, they did. I'm still not sure how he managed to get them to stop when my *jicama* throwing/Eminem blasting/pointed emails didn't.

Anyway, I have since found out that these same people just sent out a public Facebook post inviting dozens of people in Ubud to a 'sacred ceremony' to drink *ayahuasca*… a drug that carries the death penalty in Bali. Smart, huh? Advertise on Facebook the time, date and venue of the place where you are going to be taking drugs and then invite all your friends to indicate if they're coming or not… in a country, I repeat, with a *death penalty* for taking drugs. I wonder at the IQ of some people. Though not these people. I already knew they weren't the brightest elves in the forest. It was nice to be given further proof, though.

FACING MY DEMONS

Perhaps it's because I've finally started venturing out of the house after a bout of dengue or perhaps it's just because living in a small town you are eventually, by the laws of probability, bound to have run-ins with the people you have blogged about or been in conflict with, but this week has been all about facing my demons, quite literally.

Witness: last Friday at school, picking up Alula, I ran into the man who had told me all about his vasectomy in great detail while I was queuing to buy tomatoes. This would have been embarrassing enough, because now every time I see him I just see testes split open like pomegranates (I know that's not how they do it but I have

265

a writerly imagination), but I had then written a blog post all about it. What if he had read it?

With burning cheeks, I ran and tried to hide behind my sunglasses. Epic fail. I can't keep writing blog posts, I told myself sternly, and assuming people won't read them. Not after the last post about leaving Bali went viral and was read by 20,000 people or thereabouts. I haven't been able to go anywhere since then without people saying, 'Oh are you the person who wrote that blog post about leaving Bali?'

I keep forgetting that people actually read my blog. I am so used to thinking of my writing as being a bit like a NASA broadcast into deep space. I must learn to censor before hitting publish... but maybe not quite yet.

Witness yesterday, pulling into our drive, blissed-out from the beach, I see this girl (a girlfriend of an acquaintance we let stay in our house while they were between places) and slam on the brakes. This girl had some kind of psychotic meltdown in our house about six months ago, smashed all our belongings, including my favourite hand-blown vase, called me a whore, screamed and bellowed like a cow in labour for hours, terrifying Alula, and then told John via email to 'fuck off and die looser' [sic] when he suggested politely that it was time for her to leave.

I tried to be compassionate. Clearly, she's messed up. Call me what you like (I've heard way worse), but spell loser 'looser' and I've got an issue with you. And let's not even talk about the vase. I loved that vase.

She turned and saw me getting out the car and gave me this evil glare. It took a lot of willpower (OK, and a stern talking-to from John) to walk into the house without saying a word. I reminded myself that people like her are a gift from the writing gods and that one day I will use her and the 'looser' anecdote in a book (oh look, hello!). I will probably kill her off too (I'll need to put her in one of my fiction books to do that, darn). That made me feel better. But I did also have this strange compunction to draw chalk markings outside the house to ward off evil.

So where was I? Oh yes, Becky, my writer friend, and I were sitting in our favourite writing spot (which, handily, has waiters to bring you coffee and cake) trying to work, and were constantly being interrupted by the booming voices of girls in yoga outfits talking about:

a) how much cocaine they snorted last night (hello, *death penalty*, you idiots. Also, um, doesn't snorting cocaine undo the effects of all those downward dogs?)

b) how they are, like, totally healing their auras

c) how Moringa powder is the answer to, like, everything.

I turned around in the cafe and realised that the priestess of the goddess Gaia (self-professed) was sitting beside me. The same lady who told me she wouldn't turn the volume down as she was 'serving the community'. The same lady whose house I threw *jicama* at in a fit of frustration.

I looked back at Becky. 'It's her!' I hissed. 'The priestess who I threw jicama at!' Out of reflex I glanced across the table for something that I could throw, in case she started up with the chanting.

After a few minutes she got up and scampered out. I like to think it was because she knew I was there and was embarrassed and didn't want to get hit in the head with some flying cutlery, and not because she'd finished her kombucha.

It is becoming clearer and clearer to me, however, that this town is way too small for someone with a mouth so big.

THE PSYCHIC HAS SPOKEN...

John left Bali yesterday. For good. He's gone back to start his job in London, and Alula and I are joining him in three months' time. I still haven't wrapped my head around it. Our housekeeper Kadek cried all day when John left. I stood, looking at all the junk he'd left for me to clear up, and scowled.

When I first heard that John had been offered a job in London my first thought was, well at least there's Skype. It was funny, though, because about three months before he received the job offer I had a conversation with a psychic that went like this:

Psychic: 'I see you going back to London.'

Me: 'Hahahahahahahaha.'

Honestly, I laughed, while simultaneously thinking this woman is clearly the worst psychic *ever*. There's more chance of me moving to live in a hermit cave in the Urals with Russell Brand.

Then she added: 'You'll move before Christmas this year.'

At this point, I rolled my eyes and considered asking for my money back. It seems, however, that the psychic is actually psychic. Quite unexpected.

Once we had decided that John absolutely had to take the job, the next question was: do I come too with Alula or do we live apart until next July when John's contract's up? Or, to pose it another way: do I give up sunshine, a great life, great friends, Alula's place at Green School and lots of home help to move back to London in the dead of winter to live with my mother-in-law, do all the washing up and send Alula to a local school where the only thing green is the uniform? Are you freaking kidding me? That's not a question. That's the punchline to a joke. In which case, I guess the joke is on me. Because today I made the decision to leave Bali at the end of

November and not stick out the school year at Green School, thus ending five wonderful years here.

I'm trying to look at it in the spirit of adventure. It's just for eight months. After that, the dream is to head to pastures new. A second round of *Can We Live Here?* is in the pipeline. And yet, just as happened the first time, when we quit our jobs in London and stepped off the ledge, I'm terrified. I'm waking in cold sweats. I feel almost permanently nauseous.

I try telling myself that we've done it once before, that we can do it again. I remind myself of the crazy, swinging pendulum of feelings that hit me in the run-up to quitting our lives five years ago, how I managed then and will manage now (by drinking lots of wine and saying *Fuck It*).

I've made myself a list of 'the worst that can happen', which includes:

falling out with my mother-in-law over the washing up

driving the car into an oncoming truck thanks to my newly acquired Bali driving skills

getting obesely fat because of all the chocolate and wine I will have to consume to get me through a UK winter

getting depressed because I won't see the sun for months

spending all the money we are meant to be saving on thermal underwear.

I have countered this list with a list of all the things I'm looking forward to. It took a very long time to compile. Here it is:

John

friends and family

smoked mackerel pate

museums
racks of lamb
Curzon cinemas
Konditor and Cook's Curly Whirly cake
bookshops
M&S knickers and Percy Pigs
cheap wine

It's funny that having done it once before doesn't make it much easier. Stepping out of the known into the unknown is never going to be without risk. And taking risks requires courage (or just plain naïveté).

Dealing with uncertainty requires nerves of steel. I don't have those. But John does. Luckily for me. So, the journey continues. And the psychic tells me that we'll be out of the UK by the summer. Too right we will.

I'm booking those tickets before I even book the flight back.

IF I CAN'T STAY WHERE I AM

My heart is hurting. It's aching in my chest. I feel a state of panic. Adrenaline coming in fits and starts. How can I leave this? How is it possible? What am I thinking? The days are all like this at the moment. I make a decision to go. The next day I change my mind. I think in my heart I know I'm leaving, but I'm finding it hard to let go, to sever the ties.

The sun is rising red over the palm trees and the rice paddies. We're on our way to the airport for a visa run. 'Look!' I say to Alula. 'Look at the sun!'

'Oh, it's so pretty,' she says in awe. 'It would be even prettier if there weren't a million ugly houses in the way.'

It's true, this whole area of land was once all rice paddies and is now built over with concrete villas. Yet still, how to leave this? How? There are the small things: the light, the chirp of the crickets at night, the brightness of the bougainvillea, the neon green of the rice, the sleeping with the windows wide open beneath the haze of a mosquito net. Then there are the big things: nine to ten hours a day working, solid, uninterrupted time pouring words onto a page. It's perhaps too much. But right now also necessary (three books and a script to write by January).

In the UK I might manage five hours if I'm lucky – the hours when Alula will be at school. How will I manage?

Stupidly, I've been re-reading old blog posts. The ones I wrote before we left London. The ones that dreamed of a life lived somewhere hot, the ones where I railed about doing the laundry and mainly about the cold, and dreamed of another type of life. I read those now and I literally weep. How can I leave? It feels as if we're turning our back on outrageous potential. It's just a step along the way, I remind myself. I've ordered a deluxe double electric under-blanket for the bed (five heat settings! A timer!) and some thermal tights from M&S. Can you order Prozac off the internet these days too?

Then I read these words by Jeannette Winterson and it gives me some measure of comfort:

'If I can't stay where I am, and I can't, then I shall put all that I can into the going.'

HOW DO YOU MEASURE A JOURNEY?

John and I are Instant Messaging each other about the offer I've just had from a publisher to turn my blog into a book. In the light of the offer, I've been reading back over the blog posts from when I first started blogging – almost five years ago to the day, now. I've been laughing over some, cringing over others, frowning at who I was at some moments in time, wondering whether it would in any way make a good book. Then weighing that against the advance and all the bills we have stacking up.

John asked me how I felt about the old me who wrote the earlier posts. It was an interesting question. This is what I typed in response: *I feel much less judgemental now. More centred. Much more aware of my privilege. More open. More full of gratitude. I feel older, I guess. Less crazy. Also very grateful that Alula is no longer a toddler. Man. Those were dark, dark days.*

The reality is that I'm probably still way too judgemental, probably not that centred at all (I definitely wasn't this morning when I stood on the balcony and screamed at the tile cutter). I'm definitely more full of gratitude though. I'm not even sure five years ago I even paused to consider the meaning of the word, but here it's become a daily practice, as close to meditation as I'll probably get. Even Alula, just the other night, pulled John and me into bed for a sandwich (a hug) and when she started crying and we asked her what was the matter, she said; 'I'm just so grateful that you're my parents.'

I'm definitely older and sun damage has probably aged me way beyond my years but I don't care. I love those lines around my eyes. They'll always remind me of the magical time we spent here. I'm so much calmer and less crazy now we don't have a possessed toddler on our hands. Reading those old posts, I almost didn't recognise that toddler Alula from who she is today: a beautiful joy who lights up our lives.

I wonder if I would feel the same if I'd stayed in England; if I would be the same person; if Alula would be the same child she is today. No way to tell, of course, but I think not. This has been a journey in so many ways.

I DON'T KNOW IF I'M COMING OR GOING

The psychic says, 'Yes, go, once you do, new doors will open.'

One of my best friends says, 'No, stay'. The other has a baby and I feel I must be there for her as she was there for me when I had Alula.

My dad says, 'Come home.'

John says, 'Do what you need to do. I don't want you to be unhappy.'

Alula says, 'Yes but not if I have to go to school in England.'

My gut says... I don't know what it says. I can't hear it. Or maybe I can and I'm just ignoring it.

I throw the question out to the Twitterverse. All but two people ignore it. The two who reply tell me that Christmas is only Christmas in England and for that reason I must return. Oh dear, they don't know me well. They obviously don't know how allergic to Christmas I am.

The Twitterverse failing me, I ask for a sign from the universe that leaving Bali is the right thing to do. I open my eyes. There's a dead cat in my path. Honest to God. A dead cat. Its eyes milky and opaque, staring up at me. Great. What does that mean? I ask again as I come in the house, whispering the question to Ganesha, the stone god who guards our entrance.

I sit down on the step. The wind blows the inflatable globe belonging to Alula out from under the bench where it had been discarded, and across the lawn. It comes to a rest. It's showing me North America, the world.

I stare at it, and laugh. My gut says go. OK, OK, I hear you!

AN INVINCIBLE SUMMER

I'm sitting in my swingy chair on the balcony wearing a light cotton slip, listening to the soothing afternoon chirrup of the crickets, looking out over the sweltering blue sky and sipping an iced coffee. This is my world and I love it. Then someone I know sends me an article about Britain being set to endure the 'coldest winter for a century' (along with a smiling-faced emoticon, for which I will never forgive them).

I'm already teetering close to tears most days about the thought of leaving Bali. Now I just want to curl into a ball and sob for hours on end. I know you think I'm being a wimp. And hell yes, you would be right. But the cold and I are not friends. In fact, if the cold were a person, I would be throwing *jicama* at its head.

Last night in Bali it was probably 26 C and I was wearing jeans and a jumper. I slept under two blankets. I don't do cold. I can't. That's not to do with being spoiled – OK, maybe it is a bit – but it's also to do with the weird fact that my basal temperature rests a good degree lower than what's considered 'normal' (just like the rest of me). Various reasons for this temperature anomaly have been put forward:

a) the thermometer is broken

b) I'm a vampire

c) I'm a cold-hearted bitch with ice for blood (this one not to my face, but I know there are people out there who would suggest this as a reason (ex boyfriends, for example) so I'm getting in there first)

d) I have a thyroid problem.

Let's go with the second or the fourth options. My point, though, is I really, *really* feel the cold. And this isn't even cold. This is

Arctic. This is polar-bear weather. OK. Now I actually am crying. At least, I tell myself, forcing some optimism, I work from my bed. And, though it won't be a mosquito net-draped bed and there will be no view of palm trees swaying in the distance, it will have a luxury electric blanket on it with *five* heat settings. (Can I set all five at once?)

I picture my M&S delivery of thermal tights. No. I'm still crying. I look up quotes on winter for some inspiration and find that most are offering some variation (usually flowery and poetic) on the alleged fact that winter is awesome as it allows us to enjoy the sun and the blooms of spring that much more.*

Well, sorry, I don't need an Arctic front to remind me how awesome the sun and warmth is, in the same way that I don't need to swallow a mouthful of vinegar in order to appreciate how good ice cream tastes.

A LITTLE SELF-IMPROVEMENT

'I'm planning on being a nicer person when I'm back in England.'

'You are a nice person already,' I tell Alula.

'I think I could be nicer. I'm already practising,' Alula informs me.

I feel humbled into silence by my eight-year-old daughter's level of emotional intelligence and self-awareness. Feeling I need to up my own game, I nod and say, 'I think I could be a nicer person too. I need to be less grouchy and more patient. My patience is a little thin these days because I have a lot on, three books to write, an entire house to pack up, you to look after and no daddy around to help out.'

Alula cocks an eyebrow at me. 'Mummy, your patience is always

---

*I would quote directly but this one particular author wants an obscene amount of money in exchange for letting me include his dozen flowery and poetic words, and that ain't happening.

a little thin.' Hmmmmm. 'I think you could swear less too.'

OK, now I feel wretched, as ashamed as if I'm standing at the pearly gates in front of Archangel Michael himself (is it him at the gates or am I getting my archangels confused?), listening as he reads off a list of all my wrongdoings. We could be here until the Second Coming, I think to myself.

It appears as if Alula is just getting into her stride. She's ticking things off on her fingers now. 'You could also perhaps be a little kinder,' she says. 'You know, for example when children ask for something and don't say please, instead of saying, "you're not getting anything until you remember your manners," you could say, "what's the magic word?" instead.' She pauses. 'And smile when you say it.'

I wrinkle my nose at her. This is how I imagine a North Korean criticism session or a Scientology auditing session might feel (though, admittedly, with a lot less terror and no Tom Cruise). My amazement at her maturity is being eroded by the ten-year-old inside my head who feels like stamping her foot and storming off to her bedroom, slamming every door in the house on the way. How dare she criticise me? What does she mean, smile? Oh God, she's right! The penny drops. The shame!

'I'm working on sharing my Lego,' she tells me, 'letting other people come up with ideas for games to play, and also being less bossy. I'm finding that last one a little difficult,' she admits.

'Yeah. I hear you,' I say.

We make a pact that I'm going to work on patience and my swearing and generally 'being nicer'. (Secretly, I'm thinking that this all might be as impossible as unravelling a DNA strand using a pair of knitting needles.) If only I had started working on improving myself when I was eight.

'Who is this child?', I think in awe. When we left, she was three and we thought it possible she was Pol Pot reincarnated.

She's now much more Dalai Lama. Well, they do say your children are your best teachers.

THERMAL ONESIES AND AVOIDANCE STRATEGIES

I'm busy ordering feather pillows and silk thermals online for our return to England.

Let's put that into perspective. We don't yet have a house to live in. I think my feather pillows might be a little premature unless I plan to use them to make the pavement more comfy. I have a feeling psychologists might call the fact that I am shopping for comfort items rather than shopping for a place to *live* an 'avoidance strategy'.

In which case, bring it on. I'm spending hours trying to find a sexy silk thermal onesie when I should probably be searching for two-bedroom flats in zone two, and the only thing I've discovered is that Google fries its own synapses when you try to search for 'sexy silk thermal onesies'. Nothing comes up. I seem to remember reflecting, way back when we left the UK, that possibly what we were doing was a giant avoidance strategy, one I put in place subconsciously to avoid having to deal with our thousand-year-old neighbours and the buddleia pruning.

In between searching for sexy silk thermal onesies I am also single-parenting and working full-time. (The psychic was right again – doors did open! Since deciding to move back to the UK I've received three new offers from publishers. Though now I'm contracted to write three different books in four months. I've also been hired on two big screenwriting jobs – the most exciting of all being an adaptation of my first book, which looks like it might be going into production soon.) All of this on top of packing up a house to move continents.

I am on a mission to leave Bali with just the 23kg suitcase I am allowed and will ship only one box of books that I cannot bear to be parted from (OK, and a little Ganesha statue to remind me of the giant one by our front gate).

I want lightness. I don't want baggage. I am giving away most of my books and all of my clothes, the latter of which I won't be needing, as I fully intend to just spend the winter wearing my sexy silk thermal onesie.

WHAT SHE'S LEARNED

'It's time to leave Bali, Mummy,' Alula declares as we walk out of Green School gates for the last time ever.

She doesn't mean literally. We're not going for another three days but, in her infinite wisdom, Alula's hit the nail on the head. It is time to leave. Though the feeling is vague and nagging, it is there in all of us. It's a gut feeling, I guess, driven by a multitude of emotions and thoughts and hopes and dreams.

'There are some things that I will miss,' Alula muses, 'and some things will not be as good in England. But there are some things that will be better.'

Indeed. 'We are going on a new adventure,' I say. 'And it will be hard at times but it will also be really exciting because who knows what great things could come from it.'

Alula nods and I realise that this is the greatest gift of all; forget everything else she's gained from living here. At eight years old, she is learning the power of her own agency – that if a situation doesn't serve her any more, she can bid it farewell. She's learning that taking a step into the vast territory of the unknown can be terrifying and that it requires courage and boldness. And, at eight years old, she's already discovered those qualities within herself.

I repeat: she's eight. Not many adults have figured that one out.

And if at eight years old she can summon the bravery to overcome her fears and worries, and if she can happily embrace uncertainty because she knows that within it lies the possibility of achieving outrageous potential, and that that pursuit – the pursuit of your highest dreams and purpose – gives colour and wonder to life, then I can't wait to see what she's like in 20 years' time.

DEAR ALULA

Yesterday you cried. You were inconsolable.

You want to leave now, you sobbed. You don't want to make friends in England, you said, because you'll just end up leaving them, so what's the point? You're really bad at Maths, you cried. And you call braids 'braids', not plaits. Who calls them 'plaits' anyway? We laugh at the 'splat' sound of plait. Braids is much prettier, we agree.

You are foreign. This is the subtext. You will be a stranger in the place you're meant to call home.

I'm sorry. I know it's hard. As a mother, it's hideous to watch your child so torn up and to know that you are the cause. Everyone says to me, 'Oh but children are resilient' but I don't think that's as true as we like to believe. I think you're deeply sensitive and that change is hard on you. You crave structure and stability, and the universe has cursed you with a Sagittarius for a mother who craves instability and adventure, and who constantly questions the word 'home'. At least, on the upside, you have a father who is much more grounded.

I wonder what the hell we are doing. I worry about how this impacts you. It isn't the perfect solution, I know that. We are only going to be in the UK for nine months or so before we take another leap into the unknown, heading off who-knows-where. It's terrifying for me. I can't imagine how it must be for you.

I found myself speaking today to an old friend I bumped into at Green School, who happens to also be the school guidance counsellor. We talked about the challenge of raising third-culture kids (children growing up outside of their parents' culture) and the difficulty inherent in moving them around the world.

Do the pros outweigh the cons? How can a child be made to see the advantages when all they care about is the moment and the friends they've lost, and are dealing with the fear of starting a new school? Should we just stay put, I wonder; settle down in one place? Give her the stability she craves? Are we selfish beyond belief?

All these questions rush around my head while you cry and I hug you. I tell you I understand how hard it must be. I talk to you about the whys and the wherefores and the what-fors but I know that, with your mind so much in the present, it's difficult for you to see beyond the hard, narrow ledge of the horizon.

It might be difficult now, Alula, is what I want to say, but what *we* see over that horizon is a you aged 18, ready to take your first unaccompanied steps into the world. What we see is how comfortable you are in that world – East or West, developing or developed, among cultures different from your own. What we see is a you unrestricted by a narrow world-view but able, hopefully, to see the bigger picture and your place within it.

You will know the value and the joy of following dreams, and of working hard, and of the beauty of creating, because you have been surrounded by this every single day with your daddy and me and the community around us.

You will know that the highest and best kind of satisfaction can come from those things – from following dreams and working hard and creating.

You will have friends in every corner of the world ready to open their arms and welcome you home.

You will know and inherently understand the biggest fallacy of all: that there is no certainty in the world, only uncertainty, and you will, I hope, be able to use that knowledge to your advantage, embracing it rather than reaching for the security blanket of a nine-to-five job that might not fulfill you and all the accoutrements that we grasp at to help fix our identity and place in the world. You will know that none of that matters.

So, while you cry, and it hurts my heart to see it, I have to believe that in the end it will all be OK, more than OK; that you won't look back with resentment but with gratitude. But, just in case, we'll start saving up for therapy now.

LEAVING BALI

I don't feel much in the run-up to leaving. I think I am in denial. It's easier to just keep moving forward and not think about what we are leaving behind, but then, in the last minutes, I wobble. Watching Alula say goodbye to her best friend is one of the most heartbreaking things I've ever seen, but it's also a lesson in how to say goodbye. They giggle and laugh for 45 minutes then do a spit-swear that they'll see each other again and then make up a special handshake. Surely that's the way to do it?

In the car on the way to the airport I feel like I am in a particularly vivid dream/nightmare, my brain struggling to compute, throwing out an increasingly panicked litany of thoughts: *this is the last time you'll drive this road. This is the last time you'll see Mount Agung. This is your last Balinese sunset. This is the last time you'll play car kamikaze with Komang.*

It won't be the last time, I tell myself sternly. I will come back, even if just for a holiday.

'I won't miss the drivers. Or the potholes,' Alula announces from the back seat. Ever the pragmatist, she seems to be dealing with leaving a whole lot better than me.

It won't be until you're on the plane that you'll cry, everyone told me.

I get on the plane. I sit in my seat, heart pounding thanks to the litres of adrenaline that have been flooding my system for the last four days, as the future started to collide with increasing velocity into the present.

And the plane takes off. I close my eyes and I expect to cry, but I don't. Instead the only thought in my head, clear as a clanging bell, is, 'Yes. This is absolutely the right thing to do.'

And in the deepest part of my belly I feel a flutter of excitement because I know we've just thrown open the door to the next adventure.

THE AFTER PART

EPILOGUE

Wanting to put off my arrival in the UK for as long as I could, I negotiated with John a week in Goa on my own. To be clear, this was not a holiday, I explained to him, and more a 'I have 45,000 words to write in eight days and I want to write them on the beach and not wearing a silk, thermal onesie in bed, even if the bed does have an electric blanket on it with five heat settings'.

Goa is where it all began. Ironically, in a place called Home, a guesthouse on the beach. I'm back in the exact place where we started this journey five years ago. Remember when we lived in a pink sauna and Alula went to that free-play nursery and I caught a fever and lung infection, and dreamed of a bedside table with drawers and cursed my imagination for not fantasising a life-size Alexander Skarsgård? That's where I am again.

I am walking around with a stupid grin on my face, taking it all in.

The place is much the same; the chai shop on the corner, our little pink house (albeit faded to a poached-salmon colour now), the same tuk-tuk drivers hustling for business, the same grizzled Brits with skin like burnt biltong, hollering at waiters to bring them one more Kingfisher beer, the same south-west London mummies with kids called Xavvy and Skye discussing in loud, cigarette-hazed voices how they've been coming here every year for the season since Jade (Jagger) invited them as teens in the nineties.

I sit in the exact same place I wrote my second book, *Losing Lila*, this time finishing my tenth book, and I ponder the circle that's brought me back here; finishing one journey and starting a new one, just as I was back then.

Goa was our jumping-off point, the place where possibilities were born, where I finished a book and signed with my agent, and where we started to envisage a life where we both worked remotely and pursued our dreams. It's where I decided that being a writer was what I wanted to be.

And five years almost to the day, I sit in the same seat, staring at the same sea at another jumping-off point in my life, marvelling at how much I've experienced and grown and learned in those five years, and how not even our wildest dreams ended up matching the reality.

But, despite all the changes in ourselves, one thing remains the same: we were homeless then and we're homeless now. We were living out of rucksacks then. We are living out of suitcases now. But whereas five years ago we were desperately searching for home, we're not any more. We've discovered – revelation of revelations – we don't need a home. As Alula said when I asked her if she wished we had a home, a place to call her own and where she felt settled:

'No. If you have a home then it's harder to leave and then you don't get to have so many adventures.' Wise girl.

Someone said to me that Bali was never meant to be a final destination; it was only ever meant to be a pit stop along the way – which got me to thinking about what and where the final destination is. But, after some pondering on the matter, I wonder if there is in fact a destination at all. What if, by always searching for a destination – a place to call home – we miss out on the most vital part – the journey?

As Ursula Le Guin once wrote: 'It is good to have an end to journey toward; but it is the journey that matters in the end.'

'Where's home?' a curious person asks me as I sit drinking chai on the beach.

'Nowhere,' I answer quickly.

I pause and think back to our house in Bali, ostensibly a home, and the first memory that springs to mind is of Alula's hand slipping into mine as we walk down the garden path and out the gate, John walking just ahead of us.

ACKNOWLEDGEMENTS

John and Alula – forget the book, forget the blog, there would have been no journey and no story to tell without you both. What I've learned is that you two are home. I love being on this great, wild adventure through life with you. John, your belief in outrageous potential kept us going through every down point, through every moment I doubted our ability to keep going. Alula, your gratitude, openness and wisdom has taught us so much about how to see and enjoy the world.

I'm so grateful to all my blog readers over the years who've followed our journey and supported us (not the ones who sent me black magic poems though – you guys suck).

My parents, who seeded a love of travel and encouraged my independence from a young age, and who didn't once complain that we were moving to the other side of the world.

Venetia, my first editor, who took a risk on a debut author and who is also responsible for my Mila Gray success and in large part for this book too. Thank you a million (again).

Amanda, my lovely agent, who is always full of wisdom, insight and humour and who has guided me through about a dozen books in five years. Can't stay thank you enough.

Emily at Blink, for thinking my blog was worth turning into a book and being so fun and easy to work with.

Lizzie Dorney-Kingdom for all her support and hard work around the PR, Oliver Holden-Rea for his eagle eyes, Justinia at Head Design for the cover, Nick Otway for typesetting and Jenny Jacoby for copy-editing.

Liz and Becky Wicks for being my first readers and pointing out valuable things like 'maybe you need to add dates'.

But, above all, I need to thank the people whose words, stories, friendships, wisdom and antics gave me such rich material. So: Pooja, Richard, Tara, Aaron the manny, Jay, Natasha, Dumpy, Eggy, Megan, Becki, Matt, Elfie, Suki, Till, Eiji, Asa, Becky, Kathy, Liesel, Claude, Vic, Nichola, Andrew, Leila, Claude, Komang, Kadek, Ibu Made – and the many others I may have forgotten not to mention: thank you so much for your friendships. I would mention, too, the names of the crazy people who smashed up the house and performed Tantric sound healing next door and almost drove me to homicide, but I don't want to get sued.